MAN, MYTH, AND MAGIC

MAN, MYTH,
AND MAGIC

Beliefs, Rituals, and Symbols of the Modern World

Cavendish
Square

New York

MAN, MYTH, AND MAGIC

Published in 2015 by Cavendish Square Publishing, LLC
243 5th Avenue, Suite 136, New York, NY 10016

Website: cavendishsq.com

This publication represents the opinions and views of the author based on his or her personal experience, knowledge, and research. The information in this book serves as a general guide only. The author and publisher have used their best efforts in preparing this book and disclaim liability rising directly or indirectly from the use and application of this book.

CPSIA Compliance Information: Batch #WS14CSQ

All websites were available and accurate when this book was sent to press.

Library of Congress Cataloging-in-Publication Data
Sanders, Malcolm.
Beliefs, rituals, and symbols of the modern world / by Malcolm Sanders, et. al.
p. cm. — (Man, myth, and magic)
Includes index.
ISBN 978-1-62712-684-7 (hardcover) ISBN 978-1-62712-686-1 (ebook)
1. Faith — Juvenile literature. 2. Symbolism — Juvenile literature. 3. Rites and ceremonies — Juvenile literature. I. Sanders, Malcolm. II. Title.
CB475.S26 2015
302.2—d23

Editorial Director: Dean Miller
Editor: Amy Hayes
Art Director: Jeffrey Talbot
Designer: Jessica Moon
Photo Researcher: J8 Media
Production Manager: Jennifer Ryder-Talbot
Production Editor: David McNamara

Photo credits: Cover photos by: SuperStock, cybrain/Shutterstock, File:Franz Marc - Der Traum - Google Art Project/Franz Marc/Wikimedia Commons; Burgruine Werfenstein/Pfeifferfranz/Wikimedia Commons, 1; DEA PICTURE LIBRARY/De Agostini/Getty Images, 2-3; File:Rembrandt-Belsazar.jpg/Rembrandt/Wikimedia Commons, 5t; Silver Screen Collection/Hulton Archive/Getty Images, 5m; Ann Ronan Pictures/Print Collector/Getty Images, 5b; Luis Davilla/Cover/Getty Images, 7; Mark Wragg/Getty Images, 8; File:Bahai's shrine of bab.jpg/israeltourism/Flickr/Wikimedia Commons, 10-11; Leemage/UIG/Getty Images, 13; Buyenlarge/Getty Images, 15; Hermitage Scene, possibly from a Devi Mahatmya series, from the Punjab Hills (opaque w/c on paper), Nainsukh (c.1710-78) (attr. to)/Museum of Fine Arts, Boston, Massachusetts, USA/Ross-Coomaraswamy Collection/The Bridgeman Art Library, 16–17; The British Library/Robana/Getty Images, 19; Olivier CHOUCHANA/Gamma-Rapho via Getty Images, 21; PM Images/The Image Bank/Getty Images, 24; File:Zenerkarten c/John Henne/Wikimedia Commons, 27; George Doyle/ThinkStock/Getty Images, 28; Albert L. Ortega/Getty Images, 33; COLUMBIA PICTURES/Album/SuperStock, 34–35; Silver Screen Collection/Hulton Archive/Getty Images, 37; Sundance/WireImage/Getty Images, 38; Silver Screen Collection/Getty Images, 41; Melkor3D/Shutterstock, 42; DEA PICTURE LIBRARY/De Agostini/Getty Images, 46; Mary Evans/Ian Evans Collection, 49; Keystone/Getty Images, 52; Library of Congress Prints and Photographs Division, 55; National Pr. & Eng. Co./Getty Images, 58; File:Isaac Newton, English School, 1715-20.jpg/English School/Wikimedia Commons, 60; PLEASE INSERT CREDIT FOR P 62; Pecold/Shutterstock, 66–67; Lange, Dorothea/Library of Congress, 69; U.S. Army photograph/Library of Congress, 70; tankist276/Shutterstock, 73; Topical Press Agency/Getty Images, 77; TIM ROBERTS/AFP/Getty Images, 78; File:Elektrolokomotive E 19 12 DB Museum NÝrnberg 002.JPG/Janericloebe/Wikimedia Commons, 82; JOHN MACDOUGALL/AFP/Getty Images, 86-87; Hugo Jaeger/Timepix/Time Life Pictures/Getty Images, 90; File:Kapucyni Lomza fc05/Fczarnowski/Wikimedia Commons, 93; Hulton Archive/Getty Images, 94; meshaphoto/Getty Images, 96; File:Psychokinesis refer for definition and research on Stan Lee's Superhumans - Mind Force - History Channel - RTL2 Germany 31.07.2013/Miroslaw Magola/Wikimedia Commons, 101; Blend Images/Jon Feingersh/Getty Images, 102; Watt, Chris Mirrorpix/Newscom, 105; gosphotodesign/Shutterstock, 106; File:File William Young Ottley - Prospero Summoning Ariel - Google Art Project/William Young Ottley/Wikimedia Commons, 111; Transcendental Graphics/Getty Images, 113; New Line/WireImage/Getty Images, 114; Mondadori Portfolio/Getty Images, 116; Carlos Osorio/Toronto Star/Getty Images, 117; SSPL/Getty Images, 122; Roxana Gonzalez/Shutterstock, 125; File:Rembrandt-Belsazar/Rembrandt/Wikimedia Commons, 126–127; Culture Club/Getty Images, 128; Ann Ronan Pictures/Print Collector/Getty Images, 131; File:Franz Marc - Der Traum - Google Art Project/Franz Marc/Wikimedia Commons, 132–133; File:JFK limousine/Walt Cisco, Dallas Morning News/Wikimedia Commons, 134; Paul Popper/Popperfoto/Getty Images, 138; Imagno/Hulton Archive/Getty Images, 139; SuperStock, 140–141; Bringing in the plum pudding (colour litho), English School/Private Collection/The Bridgeman Art Library, 142; Prisma/UIG/Getty Images, 144; File:Mâquina do Tempo (5388447241) (2)/Leandro Ciuffo/Flickr/Wikimedia Commons, 147; File:FrankinSt Johnstown/Casey.B.Bassett/Wikimedia Commons, 148–149; cybrain/Shutterstock, 150; Maharishi Mahesh Yogi during a 1979 visit to MUM/Keithbob/Wikimedia Commons, 151; Buyenlarge/Getty Images, 153.

Cavendish Square would like to acknowledge the outstanding work, research, writing, and professionalism of Man, Myth, and Magic's original Editor-in-Chief Richard Cavendish, Executive Editor Brian Innes, Editorial Advisory Board Members and Consultants C.A. Burland, Glyn Daniel, E.R Dodds, Mircea Eliade, William Sargent, John Symonds, RJ. Zwi Werblowsky, and R.C. Zaechner, as well as the numerous authors, consultants, and contributors that shaped the original Man, Myth, and Magic that served as the basis and model for these new books.

Printed in the United States of America

Contents

A Reader's Guide to *Man, Myth, and Magic: Beliefs, Rituals, and Symbols of the Modern World*

Humans have made incredible advancements in the areas of science and technology, but this knowledge has done nothing to sate our thirst for more information about the supernatural, the unexplained, and the mystic. In fact, our increased knowledge has led to further quests about the outer edges of understanding of the universe, consciousness, and so much more. New faiths and areas of study have cropped up over the past century, as people look to take religion and mythology in new directions.

Man, Myth, and Magic: Beliefs, Rituals, and Symbols of the Modern World is a volume devoted to the bizarre and unexplained of the past century or so, with in-depth articles on such topics as ESP, messianic movements, modern art forms such as films, crop circles, men in black, time travel, and more. Strange occurrences such as spontaneous combustion, psychokinesis, ghost hunting, and the collective unconscious are covered as well, and leading psychological pioneers like Jung and Freud, who examined the strangest universe of all, the inner recesses of our minds, are discussed too.

Then he remarked that Dr. Hopkins had two coins in his pocket—which was indeed the case—and asked him for one. He held it in his hand, and it vanished.

Objectives of *Man, Myth, and Magic*

Each volume of the *Man, Myth and Magic* series approaches individual topics from an unbiased position. In *Beliefs, Rituals, and Symbols of the Modern World*, presenting how goals and objectives of Hare Krishna without editorializing commentary allows readers to best comprehend the topic and develop their own position on the sect. The comprehensive coverage of Bermuda Triangle, as well as crop circles, Neo-Pagan German Cults, and Psychotronics, for example, can aid students researching these controversial topics, and understand why many followers so passionately believe in them.

The Text

An impressive lineup of expert contributors have created articles arranged alphabetically, and the depth of coverage varies from short entries defining a singular subject through multipage contributions providing far-ranging discussion of complex issues. From Bahá'ís to UFOs, key movements, figures, concepts, and new-age topics are profiled, with articles focusing on how the past mythology and religion have morphed into modern thought.

The work is highly illustrated, with colorful images of sects and cults as well as informative pictures of leading figures and science fiction and fantasy topics. Subjects of major interest are provided with individual bibliographies of further reading on the subject at the end of each article, making *Man Myth and Magic* an important resource for any avid researcher.

For the past few decades, there's been an explosion in the popularity of mythology and history in the realms of both popular culture and scholarly study. The revival of scholarly interest has shaped the modern study of comparative religion, and modern anthropology with its investigation of so-called indigenous or first peoples and their beliefs and rituals (which have been found far more complex that originally believed). At the same time there has been a flourishing revival of popular interest in ancient civilizations, mythology, magic and alternative paths to truth. This interest has shown no sign of diminishing this century; on the contrary, it has grown stronger and has explored new pathways. Scholarly investigation of these subjects has continued and has thrown much new light on some of our topics. The present edition of *Man, Myth, and Magic: Prophets and Prophecy* takes account of both these developments. Articles have been updated to cover fresh discoveries and new theories since they first appeared.

With all this, *Man, Myth and Magic: Beliefs, Rituals, and Symbols of the Modern World* is not intended to convert you, to or from any belief or set of beliefs and attitudes. The purpose of the articles is not to persuade or justify, but to describe what people have believed and trace the consequences of those beliefs in action. The editorial attitude is one

Rappel, a clairvoyant working in his office using Tarot cards to divine the future

of sympathetic neutrality. It is for the reader to decide where truth and value may lie. We hope that there is as much interest, pleasure and satisfaction in reading these pages as all those involved took in creating them.

Illustrations

Since much of what we know about myth, folklore and religion has been passed down over the centuries by word of mouth, and recorded only comparatively recently, visual images are often the most powerful and vivid links we have with the past. The wealth of illustration in *Man, Myth, and Magic: Beliefs, Rituals, and Symbols of the Modern World* is invaluable, not only because of the diversity of sources, but also because of the superb quality of color reproduction. Rituals, myths, sacred paintings and modern rites are all recorded here in infinite variety. Examples of artwork from all over the world are represented.

Index

The A-Z index provides immediate access to any specific item sought by the reader. The reference distinguishes the nature of the entry in terms of a main entry, supplementary subject entries, and illustrations.

Skill Development for Students

The books of the *Man, Myth and Magic* series can be consulted as the basic text for a subject or as a source of enrichment for students. It can act as a reference for a simple reading or writing assignment, or as the inspiration for a major research or term paper. The additional reading at the end of many entries is an invaluable resource for students looking to further their studies on a specific topic. *Man, Myth and Magic* offers an opportunity for students that is extremely valuable; twenty volumes that are both multi-disciplinary and inter-disciplinary; a wealth of fine illustrations; a research source well-suited to a variety of age levels that will provoke interest and encourage speculation in both teachers and students.

Scope

As well as being a major asset to social studies teaching, the book provides students from a wide range of disciplines with a stimulating, accessible and beautifully illustrated reference work.

The *Man, Myth and Magic* series lends itself very easily to a multi-disciplinary approach to study. In *Beliefs, Rituals, and Customs of the Modern World*, literature students will be interested in the articles on HP Lovecraft, Science Fiction and Fantasy, and the various excerpts from other texts. Math and science students will be fascinated to read about Time and the Fourth Dimension as well as the statistical anomalies associated with Spontaneous Psi Experiences, while students of art, sculpture, carving, pottery and other crafts will find the marvelous illustrations and special articles on the subjects particularly helpful. Readers interested in sociology and history will gravitate to the discussion of

A fortune teller using her crystal ball to predict the future

Messianic Movements and the strange mysticism described in Nazism. Students of psychology will gravitate quickly toward the articles on Freud, Jung, and Synchronicity.

As well as its relevance to study areas already mentioned, the book will provide strong background reference in anthropology, philosophy and comparative religion.

Conceptual Themes

As students become involved in the work, they will gradually become sensitive to the major concepts emerging from research. Students can begin to understand the role of the modern belief systems and superstitions and how they contribute to current social structure.

Ancient Astronauts

The idea that Earth had been visited by extra-terrestrial beings at an earlier time in human history and that these beings were responsible for the creation of ancient civilizations was brought to a wide public by the work of a Swiss hotel manager. In 1968, Erich von Däniken (b. 1935) published his first book, translated into English as *Chariot of the Gods?* The book provides the theory that the achievements of ancient peoples would have been impossible given the technical limitations of the time without knowledge and input from alien visitors to Earth, who were then adopted as gods in the cosmologies of these civilizations. He cited examples such as the pyramids in Egypt, the great circle of Stonehenge in southern England, and the Nazca lines in Peru, all of which had intrigued generations of archaeologists and historians who had long sought to understand both not only how, but also why, they were created.

Von Däniken's book was a huge publishing success but it attracted criticism from academics and educationalists on the grounds that his theories were not supported by any scientific or historical evidence, and merely fed what the headmaster of one of Britain's leading schools described as the 'extreme gullibility' of the young.

However, the book excited the popular imagination. It appeared a few years after Pauwels' and Bergier's controversial book, *The Morning of the Magicians*, at a time of growing interest in alternative culture and ideas. There were precursors to von Däniken including the Russian-born Immanuel Velikovsky (1895–1979) who propounded the view in his book, *Worlds in Collision*, that the orbit of the earth had been altered by the passage of a comet, causing a series of catastrophes that can be discerned in the mythology and belief systems of earlier civilizations. The Irish peer, Brinsley Le Poer Trench (1911–95), one-time editor of the *Flying Saucer Review* and founder of an organization dedicated to collecting data about unidentified flying objects, was a believer in the existence of ancient astronauts.

The French writer, Robert Charroux (1909–78), published several books on the same topic, the first one appearing some five years before von Däniken's.

ELIZABETH LOVING

The Bahá'í Faith

On May 23, 1844, Mirza Ali Mohammed, son of a Persian merchant and a resident of Shiraz in the southwest of Persia, declared himself to be a manifestation of God on Earth. He as-

> *The principal writings of the faith have been translated into more than 400 languages and dialects, evidence of the appeal that it has exerted.*

sumed the title *Bab* (Arabic for 'Gate') and predicted that an even greater manifestation was soon to appear, one who would usher in the dawn of a new age. Assisted by eighteen 'Letters of the Living,' or disciples, the Bab hoped to pave the way for the coming of this divine messenger, who was to be known as Baha-Ullah, or Splendor of God.

Baha-Ullah duly appeared, after the death of the Bab, and the Bahá'í faith, as it is known today, takes its name from him. Bahá'ís are those who accept Baha-Ullah as the manifestation of God for our age.

Today, more than 150 years later, the Bahá'í faith has emerged from the obscurity of its beginnings in Persia and is now represented in countries and communities all over the world. The principal writings of the faith have been translated into more than 400 languages and dialects, evidence of the appeal that it has exerted. India is believed to be the numerically largest of the Bahá'í communities worldwide.

Execution of the Bab

Belief in a 'second Coming,' when God will return to earth to establish peace and justice, is a theme common to many of the world's religions. In Islam the members of the Shi'ite sect expect the coming of the Mahdi ('guided one'), or Qaim ('he who shall arise'). The Shia believe that Mohammed, at his death, handed on his authority to Ali, his son-in-law, who in turn passed it on to twelve successive Imams or leaders, who were to act as spiritual messengers and guides. The last of the Imams disappeared mysteriously in AD 874 but his followers believed that they kept in contact with him through a succession of intermediaries or Babs.

When the Bab made his declaration in 1844, many flocked to his cause, calling themselves *Babis*. His descent from the Prophet Mohammed on both his father's and his mother's side, gave impetus to the Bab's cause.

The Babis were not without enemies, for both the Persian government and the orthodox Muslim divines viewed the ever-increasing popularity of the new movement as a threat to their existence. The 'revolutionaries' were hounded from city to city, suffering many indignities. In Persia people were incited to whip the Babis and to humiliate their women. In one case a Babi was pierced through the nose and dragged by a cord through the streets.

The movement continued to flourish in spite of adverse conditions. The Bab spent the greater part of this

period of his life being moved from one prison to another, and many of his followers were brutally massacred. However, even from his prison cell at Mah-Ku, the Bab continued to exert considerable influence. Mah-Ku lies in a remote part of northwest Persia, inhabited by the Kurds, a Muslim community of the Sunni sect, extremely hostile to the Shia. After a few months internment in this region the authorities were forced to remove the Bab, for he had so gained the confidence of the people and his warden that the term 'imprisonment' no longer applied. It was here that the Bab compiled the work known as the *Bayan*, in which he constantly refers to the 'greater one to come,' to 'him whom God would make manifest.'

The Persian authorities hoped to stem the spread of the Babi religion by taking the Bab, then aged thirty, to Tabriz for execution by shooting. The extraordinary events that took place on the day of the Bab's execution, July 9, 1850, are described by a contemporary follower of the Bab named Nabil in his book *The Dawnbreakers*. The city was in a state of turmoil. The Governor had washed his hands of the affair and it was left to the brother of the chief minister of the Shah to carry out the orders.

As the hour approached, a disheveled youth threw himself at the master's feet and asked to be allowed to accompany him in death. His wish was granted and both the Bab and the youth were suspended by ropes from a nail in the prison yard, in such a way that the head of the youth rested on the breast of the master. When the clouds of smoke from the 750 rifles had cleared, only the youth was to be seen, alive, and unharmed.

The shrine of Bab on Mount Carmel near Haifa, Israel

It was then discovered that the shots had only severed the ropes holding the prisoners, and the Bab was later found in his room, in conversation with his secretary. The officer in charge of the firing squad refused to repeat the order, when the Bab declared himself ready. A subordinate finally gave the order. Nabil says that as soon as the fatal shots had been fired, an severe gale of dust shrouded the city in darkness for the rest of the day.

Fifty years later the Bab's remains were enshrined on Mount Carmel, near Haifa in Israel, and the site has become a centre of the Bahá'í faith.

The Bahá'í movement is based on the belief in Baha-Ullah as the messenger of God for our time. The Bahá'ís believe that God himself is unknowable but that he communicates with men through manifestations, who reveal themselves from time to time on Earth. These manifestations, who all derive from the same God, are the founders of the great religions of the world. When Baha-Ullah, in 1863, declared himself to be 'him whom God should make manifest,' he not only fulfilled the prediction of the Bab that a greater one was to come but also claimed to be the most recent in a line of manifestations which has included Jesus, Mohammed, Zoroaster, and Buddha. Each fulfilled God's purposes for *his* age but Jesus said, 'I have yet many things to say to you, but you cannot bear them now. When the Spirit of truth comes, he will guide you into all the truth' (John, chapter 16). Bahá'ís believe that with the revelation of Baha-Ullah, that time has come.

The Coming of Baha-Ullah
Mirza Hussain Ali, who declared himself to be the expected Baha-Ullah, was born in 1817 at Tehran. He was of noble descent and spent much of his early life in ministerial circles. He became an ardent follower of the Babi doctrine. After the Bab's execution, the movement split into two groups, those who followed Mirza Yahya, nominated

> *Bahá'ís believe that there is one God for all mankind and therefore only one true religion.*

by the Bab as his successor, and those who gathered around Mirza Hussain Ali. The first group dwindled in numbers and eventually disappeared.

The Babi faith suffered a serious setback in 1853 when two Babis attempted unsuccessfully to assassinate the Shah of Persia. There resulted a purge of the Babis, in which all the leaders were killed except the future Baha-Ullah who was thrown into prison. It was here that he became aware of his mission on Earth.

On release he was exiled to Baghdad, outside Persian jurisdiction, and from there he continued to attract followers to the Babi faith. The Turkish authorities viewed the dissemination of his ideas with distaste and when in 1863 he retired for twelve days to a garden outside Baghdad and proclaimed himself to be the 'Promised One,' as foretold by the Bab, they intervened and sent him first to Constantinople and then to Adrianople.

The scene of the declaration, which was the birth-moment of the Bahá'í faith proper, has been named the 'Garden of Ridvan.' The twelve days are celebrated annually by Bahá'ís and known as the Ridvan Festival, from April 21 to May 2.

The hostile pressures on Baha-Ullah, increased by the bitter dissension between himself and his half-brother, Mirza Yahya, culminated in several attempts by Mirza Yahya to murder Baha-Ullah. As a result Mirza Yahya and his associates were banished to Famagusta in Cyprus and Baha-Ullah was sent to the prison city of Acre where he died on May 29, 1892.

In spite of these confinements and harassments the Bahá'í faith began to make widespread gains, even during the lifetime of Baha-Ullah. Baha-Ullah committed many of his teachings to so-called 'Tablets,' which were passed on to his followers. While in Adrianople, he wrote to many of the political and religious leaders of the world, appealing to them to pay heed to his doctrines and in Acre he completed the *Kitabi Aqdas* (The Most Holy Book), which contains the essence of his beliefs.

The Oneness of Mankind
Bahá'ís believe that there is just one God for all mankind and therefore only one true religion. Although in the past God has manifested himself in different forms to suit the requirements of different ages, he nevertheless expounded through all his manifestations the same basic truths. Differences between religious movements have arisen, the Bahá'ís claim, because the original teachings were misinterpreted. The coming of Baha-Ullah is a sign that man has reached a stage of maturity in which social and religious unity may at last be realized. Bahá'ís devote themselves to this end.

Baha-Ullah himself, in his wrtings, gave much attention to the reorganization of social administration. However, the task of putting his ideas into practice was left to Abdul-Baha (1844–1921), the eldest son of Baha-Ullah and 'Exemplar' and 'Interpreter' of his teachings.

To achieve world unity, Baha-Ullah advocated certain goals at which Bahá'ís were to aim. They must seek to abolish all forms of prejudice with regard to colour, race, class, and creed, thus breaking down national boundaries in preparation for an administrative body that will unite the whole world. A commonwealth of the world will be established. Men will be thought of no longer in terms of black or white, Christian or Buddhist, Russian or British, but as members of a united world community.

In this new order men and women will have equal status and all children will be given equal opportunities of education. An international system of currency will be introduced and an auxiliary world language (either newly invented or an already existing language) will be taught in schools.

In the meantime, by exemplary personal conduct Bahá'ís can show the world the virtues of belief in their cause. They are forbidden to gamble and are discouraged from taking intoxicants and drugs. Fasting continues to be an important element in Bahá'í practice with the nineteen-day period before the Bahá'í New Year being observed as a fast between dawn and dusk. The intention is focus on the concerns of the spirit rather than the body. A commitment to social and economic development is an important aspect of Bahá'í belief: projects carried out in consultation and partnership with the groups for which they are designed so that resultant material improvements are integrated with increased social cooperation.

An Absence of Ritual

One outstanding feature of the Bahá'í faith is its lack of clergy and religious ritual. Bahá'ís meet in a spirit of prayer more akin to a social gathering than a religious ceremony. Small Bahá'í communities, by grouping themselves into local and national 'spiritual

Le Petit Journal

ADMINISTRATION
61, RUE LAFAYETTE, 61
Les manuscrits ne sont pas rendus
On s'abonne sans frais
dans tous les bureaux de poste

5 CENT. SUPPLÉMENT ILLUSTRÉ 5 CENT.

24me Année — 44 — Numéro 1.172

DIMANCHE 4 MAI 1913

ABONNEMENTS
SIX MOIS UN AN
SEINE et SEINE-ET-OISE.. 2 fr. 3 fr. 50
DÉPARTEMENTS......... 2 fr. 4 fr. »
ÉTRANGER .... 2 50 5 fr. »

LE NOUVEAU PROPHÈTE DE L'ISLAM
Abdul-Baha prêchant l'apaisement et la fraternité dans une mosquée à Constantinople

Abdul Baha preaching in Constantinople, Turkey, as shown on the front page of French newspaper *Le Petit Journal*, May 4, 1913

assemblies,' prepare themselves for the 'World Order of Baha-Ullah,' the day when mankind shall become one. A spiritual assembly is formed wherever nine or more Bahá'ís over the age of twenty-one congregate. These are subordinate to the supreme administrative body, the 'Universal House of Justice' that came into existence in 1963, 100 years after Baha-Ullah's declaration of his mission. Its seat is at Mount Carmel, at the shrine of the Bab, while the

shrine of Baha-Ullah lies to the North, a few miles outside Acre.

When Abdul-Baha was released from prison in 1908, Bahá'í communities had already been established in Chicago and nearby Kenosha. He traveled extensively in Western Europe and the United States, although nearly seventy years old.

Today numbers of Bahá'ís worldwide total approximately six million. The significant exception is the birth-place of the faith—Persia (modern-day Iran). Here the faith has suffered persecution since the overthrow of the Shah in 1979. The hostility has become systemic with individuals routinely denied access to education and employment, as well as being the subject of violent attacks on person and property. By January 2014, all seven leaders of the Bahá'í community in Iran were serving prison sentences on the grounds that they presented a threat to national security. The plight of the community has been highlighted in a 2013 United Nations report.

MALCOLM SAUNDERS

FURTHER READING: J. Ferraby. All Things Made New. (Bahá'í Publishing Trust, 1960); J. E. Esslemont. Baha-Ullah and the New Era, 4th rev. edition. (Bahá'í Publishing Trust, 1980); R. Meyer. Bahá'í: Follower of the Light. (Bahá'í Publishing Trust, 1979).

Bermuda Triangle

The myth of the Bermuda Triangle may be said to have begun when five US Navy Grumman TBM Avenger light bombers left Fort Lauderdale, Florida, on a navigational training exercise on the afternoon of December 5, 1945. In rapidly deteriorating weather the bombers lost track of their course, and the flight leader reported by radio that his compasses did not seem to be working. Sighting the Great Sale Cay to the north of the Bahamas—the point at which the flight was planned to turn westward on the return to Fort Lauderdale—he identified it as the Florida Keys, some 200 miles to the southwest. As darkness fell and the wind rose, he led his flight in one direction after another, until at some time after 7 p.m. they ran out of fuel and were forced to ditch. No sign of them was ever found.

Two years later the British Tudor IV airliner *Star Tiger* was nearing the end of a scheduled flight from the Azores to Bermuda. Strong headwinds had forced her down to a height of only 2,000 feet and she was low on fuel; somewhere short of Bermuda, she vanished without trace.

Writer Vincent Gaddis (1913–97) was one of the first to seize on these events in his book *Invisible Horizons* (1965); Charles Berlitz (1914–2003), in two books, *The Bermuda Triangle* and *Without a Trace*, added to the story, quoting a wide variety of marine and aerial disappearances within the triangle of sea bounded by Bermuda, Puerto Rico, the Bahamas, and Florida; and other books, novels, films, and television documentaries have further developed the dramatic theme of the 'Devil's Triangle.'

It is claimed that an unprecedented number of vessels have disappeared in the area, almost always in calm weather; that aircraft instruments fail; and that even a weather satellite has regularly malfunctioned while passing over the region.

Seeking an Explanation

The explanations put forward for the phenomenon have been many. John Wallace Spencer, in *Limbo of the Lost*, proposes that ships and aircraft 'are actually being taken away from our planet' by UFOs. On the other hand Ivan T. Sanderson (1911–73), in *Invisible Residents*, suggested that an intelligent civilization existed on the seabed and that the 'abducted' ships and crews were taken periodically for an examination of mankind.

Other explanations have seized on magnetic anomalies that appear to affect navigational instruments; small 'black holes;' or possibly openings to other dimensions where time runs at a different rate.

Unfortunately for these theorists, their arguments appear to be based

upon a misinterpretation of the facts. The Bermuda Triangle is one of the busiest traffic areas in the world: shipping and aircraft lanes converge from Europe and the South Atlantic, and coasters, fishing boats, and pleasure craft are also present in large numbers. In addition, the area is close to the tracks of many hurricanes, and violent storms are frequent—even Shakespeare referred to 'the still-vex'd Bermoothes.' More than 150,000 vessels pass through the area in the course of a year: of these fewer than 100 are lost, and only some twenty or thirty without trace.

Lawrence Kusche (b. 1940), a librarian at Arizona State University, and subsequently the Englishman Paul Begg, have investigated a number of the more outstanding cases cited by the proponents of the Bermuda Triangle 'theory.' They have shown that frequently, when it had been claimed that the disappearances took place in calm weather and under clear skies, the conditions were in fact violently stormy—and that a number had occurred many hundred miles away.

Typical of the distortion of fact on which the fantastic theories are based is the case of the freighter *Sandra*. She is said to have been 355 feet in length, to have carried a crew of twenty eight, and to have disappeared inexplicably in calm seas, and under blue skies, in June 1950. In fact, the *Sandra* had a length of only 185 feet, carried a crew of eleven, and vanished in hurricane-force winds in April 1950.

In another case, a Douglas DC-3 disappeared on December 28, 1948. It is claimed that the pilot radioed that he could see the lights of Miami, and was standing by for landing instructions; the aircraft then vanished and,

Opposite page:
Poster for the classic mystery film
***The Bermuda Triangle* (1979)**

Time Warp in the Triangle

One of the strangest reported experiences in the Bermuda Triangle was that of a young pilot, Bruce Gernon Jr, who, with his father as copilot, was flying his Beechcraft Bonanza from Andros Island in the Bahamas to Palm Beach, Florida, on December 4, 1970.

Some time after takeoff, Gernon found himself approaching 'a strange, cigar-shaped cloud.' He increased speed to fly above it, but it seemed to rise to meet him, and then surrounded the aircraft. Seeing a tunnel through the cloud, with blue sky at the end of it, he dived toward it—but the cloud seemed to be something very out of the ordinary. 'The walls were glowing white,' Gernon later reported, 'with small white clouds rotating clockwise round the interior.' The aircraft seemed to move faster and faster, and Gernon and his father felt a sensation of weightlessness for some seconds.

When the plane emerged from the cloud tunnel, it entered a greenish haze, quite unlike the expected blue sky. As he tried to work out his position, Gernon was alarmed to see that his compass was rotating counter-clockwise; his instruments were not functioning, and he could not contact any radio tower.

Then he caught sight of land ahead, and from his estimated flight time he took it to be Bimini Keys, a little over halfway between Andros and Palm Beach. A minute or two later, as he came closer, he was surprised to recognize Miami.

Landing at Palm Beach, Gernon again checked his instruments. According to his account, a flight that normally took over an hour had lasted only 45 minutes, and he had used 12 gallons fewer of fuel.

A similar phenomenon is reported to have been experienced by the passengers and crew of an Eastern Airlines plane that disappeared from the Miami radar screens for a full ten minutes. Emergency procedures were immediately put into operation, but the aircraft suddenly reappeared, and landed safely—but with every clock and watch on board, it is said, ten minutes slow.

However, subsequent investigations of both these incidents were unable to uncover any flight plan or incident report to substantiate the allegations.

although the sea below the approach was only 20 feet deep, no trace of the aircraft was ever found. The facts are that the plane had a defective radio, that the last message received reported its distance as 50 miles from Miami, and that, although much of the sea bottom is only 20 feet below the surface, it plunges in some places as deep as 5,000 feet.

As for the weather satellite that allegedly malfunctioned over the Bermuda Triangle, the explanation was simple. The job of the satellite was to collect data on cloud formations and movement and transmit this back to Earth. Part of the data was stored on tape aboard the satellite, and then transmitted in a burst, after which the tape had to be rewound for further recording, so that temporarily there was no transmission—and this was at a time when the satellite's orbit brought it over the 'Triangle.'

The Persistent Myth

The legend of the Bermuda Triangle is a contemporary example of a phenomenon that is characteristic of the way in which myths have developed throughout history: the need to distort available facts in order to support a previously-formulated system of belief. Nevertheless, there are still those who believe, as Alan Landsberg (b. 1933) wrote in *Secrets of the Bermuda Triangle*, that 'something strange is unquestionably happening.'

Collective Unconscious

The theory of the collective unconscious was C. G. Jung's response to the fact that the same patterns, themes, and images tend to appear and reappear in human ways of thinking all over the world and all through the past and present notably in myths,

legends, folk tales, and religious and artistic symbolism. They are drawn from the fundamental well of ideas which, he at first believed, was created by the experiences of the human race since far back in its earliest days, housing patterns of behaviour and ideas inherited from all past generations.

Jung first put forward the idea of the collective unconscious, though not the term itself, in a book published in

1911 (now in English as *Symbols of Transformation*). He had been impressed by the recurrence of the same motifs and patterns, the 'universal parallelism' as he described it, in human ways of thinking generally and in the dreams and fantasies of his patients. Deep in our make-up, he deduced, are ingrained propensities or dispositions that govern the contents of the conscious mind, but are not peculiar to any one person's psyche. They are manifest in everyone and predispose us to approach life, interpret it, and organize it in certain ways.

Jung called these 'primordial images,' but he was not happy with the phrase. He also tried 'inherited pathways' or 'deposits' to get nearer what he meant, but he decided that the images were not inherited, generation by generation, but were responses to the basic human experience of life and its fundamental rhythms, which remain the same everywhere, throughout history.

In 1919 Jung used the word 'archetype' for the first time (in *The Structure and Dynamics of the Psyche*). From Greek and literally meaning 'first mould,' the archetype is the original document from which copies are made, or the producer behind the scenes of a stage show. Jung's archetypes cannot be examined directly, for by definition they lie in the realm of

Hermitage Scene, **possibly from a Devi Mahatmya series, from the Punjab Hills by Nainsukh (c. 1710–78), shows a Jungian archetype of a Wise Old Man**

the unconscious, but can be apprehended only as they manifest themselves in the conscious mind. They include for instance the Wise Old Man, the powerful and benevolent father figure who appears in religions as the chief of the gods, and the corresponding female figure of the Great Mother, in everyday life the ideal mother of the family.

Others are the Hero and the Trickster, the Anima and the Animus, which are respectively the feminine and masculine components in the psychological make-up of the opposite sex, and which Jung equated with the soul. The Anima, which often appears in mythology as a helpful female figure, a guide or inspirer, is closely connected with a man's relationship with his mother and influences masculine responses to and relationships with women. The Animus, correspondingly connected with a woman's relationship with her father, is the latent masculinity that Jung believed exists in all women.

The Shadow Side

There is the Persona, the self that we display to other people and that is influenced in its composition in youth by the expectations of parents, teachers, and friends. Opposed to it is the ominous, sinister Shadow, which represents the unacknowledged aspects of the self and the individual's potential for evil. Jung diagnosed the emergence of the Nazi Party in 1930s Germany as a collective manifestation of the Shadow.

In *Psychology and Alchemy* Jung wrote: 'It must be admitted that the archetypal contents of the collective unconscious can often assume grotesque and horrible forms in dreams and fantasies, so that even the most hard-boiled rationalist is not immune from shattering nightmares and haunting fears. The psychological elucidation of these images leads logically into the depths of religious phenomenology. The history of religion in its widest sense (including therefore mythology, folklore, and primitive psychology) is a treasure-house of archetypal forms from which the doctor can draw helpful parallels and enlightening comparisons for the purpose of calming and clarifying a consciousness that is all at sea.'

> *There is the Persona, the self that we display to other people . . . influenced in its composition in youth by the expectations of parents, teachers, and friends.*

It was Jung's realization that the archetypes exist across culture frontiers that led him to the idea of the collective unconscious, and he came to think that the archetypes lie behind not only religion and mythology, but also behind science, philosophy, and all human ideas and behaviour. Each human being contains from the beginning the fundamental unconscious patterns of human functioning, and the psychotherapist's task is to help them realize fully the potential within.

FURTHER READING: A. Stevens. On Jung. (NY: Routledge, Chapman and Hall, New York, 1990).

Crop Circles

The first incidence of the widespread interest that was to develop in the phenomena that have come to be known as 'crop circles' can be traced to a report in the English local newspaper *Wiltshire Times* on August 15, 1980. Three inexplicable circular areas had appeared in fields of oats near the town of Westbury: the oats were almost completely flattened in a clockwise swirling pattern, with a diameter of some 60 feet, but continued to ripen, apparently little damaged.

The area near Westbury had for some years attracted the attention of groups interested in 'flying saucers,' and one of those who noticed the newspaper report was Ian Mrzyglod, editor of a small (now defunct) magazine, *The PROBE Report*. He made measured drawings of the 'circles,' pointing out that they were in fact slightly elliptical—rather than truly circular—in shape, and that one had a small excrescence to one side.

Another interested visitor to the site was Dr. Terence Meaden, editor of the *Journal of Meteorology*, and a senior member of the Tornado and Storm Research Organization (torro). He soon established by enquiry that the three 'circles' had been formed on three widely separated dates between May and late July, and opined that summer whirlwinds were the most probable explanation. Nevertheless, he found it difficult to explain how these whirlwinds could have been apparently stationary.

Other explanations were also put forward. The fields of Wiltshire overlie the remains of many prehistoric earthworks and burial mounds, and it had been known for a long time that crops developed differently in the soil above these circular traces: aerial photographs frequently reveal the presence of these remains as patterns in the ripening crops. The UFO enthusiasts, on the other hand, were happy to identify the circles as places at which space vehicles had temporarily landed.

The next report came on August 19, 1981, when three circles were discovered in a large field of grain occupying a bowl-shaped formation lying below Cheesefoot Head in the county of Hampshire not far from the city of Winchester. They were similar to the Westbury circles, but lay in a line pattern, the large middle one being about 60 feet in diameter, flanked by two smaller circles, each about 25 feet; and they all appeared to have been made at about the same time.

Dr. Meaden now elaborated his meteorological theories, relating the formation of whirlwind vortices to 'steep grass-covered hillsides having a kind of punchbowl or concave shape to them.' Eventually, following extensive discussion in the pages of *The Journal of Meteorology and Weather*, he developed a theory that involved 'the descent of an energetic vortex from the atmosphere, a vortex of air which is ionised to the point at which it is better regarded as a species of low-density cool plasma producing a high-energy electromagnetic field.'

'Not only does the assembled evidence point to a plasma source of electromagnetic radiation, with direct consequences for radio-communications interference, radar ghost-images, and ionizing effects on vehicle performance and animal and human behaviour, but the work explains thousands of reports of previously unidentified luminous phenomena seen spinning close to the ground or high in the air. Although a few percent of these may have been incorrectly categorized as "ball lightning" in the past, a great many have been compartmentalized as "unidentified flying objects."'

In 1983 a more complex pattern of circles occurred in four separate locations: in the same field below Cheesefoot Head; at two sites in Wiltshire, and just below the Ridgeway (a prehistoric trackway crossing a wide tract of southern England) near Wantage in Oxfordshire. These comprised a central circle some 40 feet in diameter, with four smaller circles, each some 13 feet, set at 90–degree intervals on a radius of 70–80 feet around it.

Dr. Meaden was hard put to explain these events in terms of his vortex theory, and the whole enquiry was set back when a local hoaxer, who had been encouraged by the *Daily Express* newspaper, cheerfully admitted to producing a fifth set of circles.

From this time on, however, the phenomena began to proliferate, and in the summer of 1986, the patterns became more complex, some circles even being surrounded by an outer ring. They continued to occur on the downlands of Hampshire and Wiltshire, no less than thirteen circles appearing in a field near Silbury Hill (the largest manmade hill in Europe, and the location of many ancient legends) in the last two weeks of July 1988.

Explanations, too, began to proliferate almost as widely as the circles themselves. Some theorists suggested that the majority of circles lay along a southeast-to-northwest 'corridor,' with obvious implications for those interested in UFOs. Others, confusingly, drew attention to the prevalence of place names beginning with the letter W: Wessex, Wiltshire, Wantage, Warminster, Winchester. Large tracts

Account of how a crop appeared to have been mowed by the devil as an early example of a crop circle, from *The Mowing-Devil: or, strange news out of Hartfordshire* (1678)

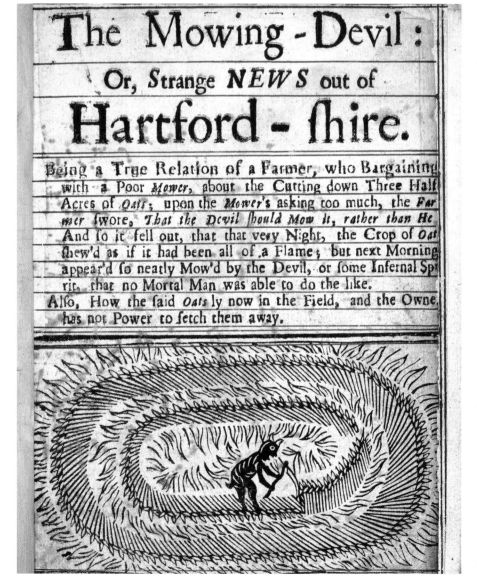

of Wiltshire are taken over by the British Army for training purposes, and those of a more mundane turn of mind pointed out the regular presence of low-flying helicopters, which might have produced flattened circles in crops with their downdraught.

Press reports of the phenomena appeared all over the world, and soon news came from other countries: from Australia in December 1989 and from the United States in 1990. Crop circles were found in France and Italy.

And then came a development that caused a sensation, not only among those who were deeply involved with the matter, but also among the public in general. From May 1990 onward, the patterns found among the growing crops of Wiltshire and neighbouringing counties were no longer merely circular: they began to appear as giant 'pictograms' involving long axial avenues joining a succession of circles, arcs, rectangular areas, and strange finger-like excrescences. The precision of the patterns was striking, and vaguely reminiscent of some of the pictograms to be found on the plains of Nazca in Peru. Certainly no plasma-vortex theory could explain them.

For months controversy raged over these pictograms, some enthusiasts finding similarities to the formal patterns of Celtic art, others relating them to more ancient, prehistoric, symbols. Then two local residents claimed that they, and they alone, were responsible for some 80 percent of all 'crop circles,' which they had created with the aid of a garden lawn-roller; and an exercise, mounted with the help of many teams of volunteers, showed that all kinds of intricate patterns could be produced in fields of crops, in total darkness, using no more than a ball of string and some boards to bend the ripening stalks.

Few remained unconvinced that a great deal of energy had been devoted to constructing a mysterious phenomenon from a simple hoax. It seems that circles have often appeared in growing corn—particularly where the mineral content of the subsoil was changed by the presence of circular earthworks and burial mounds—over many centuries; and that the excitement

> *Abraham Lincoln's dream too, in which he is said to have seen himself in the coffin in which he lay some days later, also has to be viewed against the background of literary license.*

engendered by the sudden interest taken in them, principally by towns-people who were unfamiliar with the phenomenon, encouraged the hoaxers to elaborate them.

Dr. Meaden's theories should not be entirely discounted, however. He published a report of the formation of a crop circle in Scotland, witnessed by a Mr. Sandy Reid. 'For half a minute as he watched, at a distance of 15 metres [50 feet], the wind was violently rustling the corn over a circular area, all the time making a strange noise, but where he stood there was no wind at all. Then suddenly a "force" shot downward and a circle appeared almost instantaneously.'

Eckankar

Eckankar was founded by Paul Twitchell (1909(?)–71) in 1965 in Las Vegas, Nevada. His aim was to gather previously scattered esoteric or secret teachings and publish them through books, lectures, and courses disseminated under the banner of Eckankar, a synthesis of practices like astral projection, allied to a theory of successively reincarnating 'Eck masters.' Thus

systematized, these teachings were designed to lead to self-, and eventually God-, realization.

Twitchell claimed that the teachings of Eckankar emanated from a school of Eck masters, some of whom were known historical personages and some disembodied. At any one time there would be a living Eck master, and Twitchell claimed to be the 971st in a long line of incarnations. Upon his death in 1971, Darwin Gross (1928–2008), followed by Harold Klemp (b. 1942), took on the mantle of the living Eck master.

Twitchell wrote more than twenty books on the teachings of the Eck masters. In one, *Anitya*, he describes Eckankar as 'the science of soul travel or the ability to lift one's consciousness to higher dimensions or planes where one may realize the divine consciousness of his soul.' Eckankar states that man has five bodies, the physical, astral, causal, mental, and soul bodies. The practice of soul travel is similar to astral projection and the rising on the planes of traditional Western magical practice, but undertaken with a more 'subtle' body. The Eckankar spiritual exercises help to train the individual in soul travel, leading eventually to meetings with disembodied Eck masters. The concept of spiritual liberation or 'total awareness' within this lifetime is central to the system and reminiscent of Buddhist teachings.

'Eck' is defined as 'the God force' or holy spirit, and 'Eckankar' means, according to its originator, 'co-worker with God.' Eckankar at its peak claimed members in more than 100 countries, provided study programs, produced cassette tapes, and organized seminars, conferences, and workshops. The movement also published the monthly magazine *The Mystic Word* and an annual—*Eck Mata Journal.*

Medium City in Cassadaga, United States, in April, 2004. The image shows the hands of the students of mediums Donald and Jeanette Zanghi during a table turning session.

Esalen Institute

Founded in 1962 in Big Sur, California, as residential centre for 'humanistic' psychology promulgated by anti-Freudian Abraham Maslow and Gestalt therapy developed by Fritz Perls (1893–1970); also active in pioneering 'encounter' groups.

Extra-Sensory Perception

The reception of information by a person through other means than the senses is known as extra-sensory perception or ESP. It is thus one aspect of a two-way exchange with the environment that is not mediated by the senses and muscles. This more inclusive 'extra-sensorimotor' interaction is the area of study of the science known as parapsychology, and it is now conveniently identified by the use of the Greek letter psi. Extra-sensory perception is therefore one kind of psi communication, the other or 'extra-motor' part of the exchange being called psychokinesis (the manipulating of matter by mind alone) or PK.

Three types of ESP have been recognized. They were known long before the term extra-sensory perception was first used in 1934. Clairvoyance is the ESP of objects or events, precognition the knowledge of future events, and telepathy the experience of another person's mental state.

The types of human experience represented by these three ESP classifications are not only very old but also broadly distributed through the cultures of mankind, and one recognizes the similarity of experience.

For example, premonitory dreams of personal tragedies, which are among the most commonly reported psi experiences in our own time, can also be found among the records of ancient times. The dream credited to King Croesus, in which he foresaw the murder of his son, differed from the type today chiefly in that it was the guard the King appointed as a consequence of his dream who turned out to be the murderer. This circular feature, which rarely appears in modern premonitory dreams, could well have been invented by a clever storyteller, as indeed the whole story itself may have been.

Abraham Lincoln's dream too, in which he is said to have seen himself in the coffin in which he lay some days later, also has to be viewed against the background of literary license. However, the point is that this type of ESP, precognition, in which information of a future event is seemingly acquired, is typical of a vast amount of reported human experience. The dream is one of the vehicles of extrasensory communication; future events definitely appear to be conveyed in some way, even against the stream of time; and this has been going on for a long, long time all around the world.

The Person 'Just Knows'

In the waking state, however, while ESP can be found in the daydreams that sometimes intrude, the device that most often brings ESP to the conscious experience of the individual is intuition, a form of knowledge that hides the means by which it is accomplished. The person 'just knows,' and while they may know of something yet to happen or may intuitively know the thought of a distant friend or loved one, somewhat more commonly they know of an objective event. In most of these cases of ESP in everyday life, there is no sharp boundary and no one can tell for certain that a case is pure clairvoyance or half telepathy. The woman who knew there was something wrong at home, and who insisted on being driven home by her host in the midst of a dinner party, seemed to have only a dim half-awareness of the tragic situation; but this and the house afire, and her invalid husband asleep, at least suggest clairvoyance.

However, the mother who, in the midst of a bridge game, telephoned her home to ask what was the matter with the baby may have been telepathically experiencing the baby's painful predicament at the moment rather than 'seeing' the objective picture by clairvoyance. What emerges is the strong probability that in a few rare cases it is thought alone that is conveyed. In other cases it seems as clearly to be the objective situation that is conveyed. Such experiences have provoked the scientist to ask the question: 'Is it possible for one mind to convey a message directly to another without

using sensory channels? Is it possible for an objective crisis to be picked up in some way by a person far beyond sensory range?' The experiences as they accumulated and fell into types threaded themselves on a common hypothesis long before experiments were undertaken to verify it.

In the waking state there are other ways of getting information to a person's mind by ESP besides intuition. One of these is hallucination, which is a comparatively rare experience, but among those that do occur, telepathy is a common ingredient. The recipient usually sees or hears the person from whom they seem to be getting a message. Voices are more common than visual apparitions. A person experiencing the mental state of the 'sender' may undergo the specific state and even the suffering actually felt by the sender. This can involve going through the birth pains of the other, or the agonies of a heart attack, or even falling to the ground like the victim.

There will be no doubt in anyone's mind about the importance of these puzzling human experiences if they are what they seem. It was the fact, however, that it was impossible to be sure about them that delayed the investigation of the questions they raised. They were also not as easy to investigate as the phenomena of the more objective physical and biological sciences.

These case reports of mysterious happenings represent a class by themselves. If reported, as most of them are, by sane and respectable people, they cannot be lumped with the pathological and they definitely do not fit in easily with any other branch of the sciences. If they have any sound basis of fact, it would be something new for the scientific world—something very different.

As a result of this sharp difference, the tendency developed among the earlier sciences to regard these claims as not amenable to serious scientific

treatment. They were looked down on as something that could not be explained, as most scientific findings could, by the known and familiar principles of Nature. This meant they would have to be classified as supernatural, which amounted to putting them on the shelf so far as scientific investigation went, which greatly delayed their investigation.

It can be said with unreserved confidence that the belief in ESP (and the related ability, psychokinesis) has had a long and a powerful impact on humankind and its institutions. Quite probably no other single belief has exerted so large an influence on humanity. But this is much harder to see now that over much of the world belief in ESP is at a low ebb in comparison with ancient times. Consider first what such belief did for the individual who could impress his or her fellows with superior powers of knowing of events to come, of distant happenings, of matters on all sides that the senses could not reach. Such a person, other things being equal, could assume leadership and power.

Wise Men and Soothsayers

Governing systems long clung to the counsel of the 'wise men,' the prophets, the soothsayers, the oracles. Most of the magic that was such an important part of all cultures, the farther back from modern technology we look, depended heavily upon belief in extra-sensorial cognitive powers. Even such magic as lingers in our Western cultures still usually carries an element of belief in ESP, obscured as a rule under other formulations. The dowser may hold to a theory of terrestrial magnetism, while essentially assuming an ability more properly recognizable as clairvoyance.

The popular concept of luck in games of chance comes close to qualifying as magic; casino games so far approximate to loose tests of psi ability as to provide important elements for testing techniques for ESP and PK.

It is in religion, however, that psi has played by far its greatest role in human life, and here it is important to stress that it is belief in psi that is under discussion. How much genuine capacity has underlain this belief would be difficult to estimate. However, it can be said that it is the belief in the powers of psi that has given the religions of mankind their main principles of communication between man and the divine. There is of course a great deal more to religion than the mere basis of exchange, the modes of interaction. What has come to be called the supernatural (the miraculous and the transcendent) in religion is much the same as the types of capacity that are now the subject of study in parapsychology.

The parallel is rather impressive. All the types of psi are present in the theological system: precognition as prophecy, clairvoyance as revelation, telepathy in prayer, and the answer to prayer through physical miracles as psychokinesis. It would be hard to conceive of religion without psi principles of communication. In a word, the religious follower is bound to believe in psi. This is obvious regardless of the validity of psi or religious doctrine.

The change from thinking of divine agency as the reason behind such puzzling phenomena as psi, to thinking of psi as a natural principle of communication, called for some explanatory idea that made sense. The mere thought of a natural principle of that kind had to wait until men were at the cultural stage when they began to grasp at general laws that could explain natural phenomena. By the eighteenth century, however, the emergence of the science of physics had brought forth theories of universal fluids and interplanetary forces. Franz

Mesmer's theory of a universal animal magnetism encouraged rational thinking as to how people could influence each other without sensory contact, and how communication with the spirit world might occur. Emanuel Swedenborg (1688–1772) was believed by his followers to have

Telepathy turned out to be much more difficult to work with than most of the other mental abilities being tested in those days.

demonstrated that it actually did so. The nineteenth century concept of a universal ether and of wavelike communication in this medium favoured the search for a natural explanation for what had been hitherto regarded as miraculous. It brought within the bounds of the more venturesome speculation of the day the claim of survival after death of spiritual or ethereal bodies, as well as possible communication with the dead on telepathic lines.

The Spiritualist movement based on communication with the dead through mediums was a natural result of these and other favouring systems of thought. The somnambulism that developed from later mesmeric practices contributed an important device for the practice of mediumship. By the 1880s enough evidence from mediumship had accumulated to impress a number of scholarly people and to bring the methods of science to bear on the claims made. The Society for Psychical Research, founded in 1882 in London to investigate 'mesmeric psychical and spiritualistic claims,' set an example that was followed by similar societies in a number of other countries in succeeding years. This movement was capably led, especially

in Britain, and made considerable progress in drawing the problems connected with mediumship into better focus, but it did not succeed in bringing the major issue, that of spirit communication, to a scientific conclusion. Rather there was a growing realization over the next forty years that the problem was indeed more difficult than the Spiritualist demonstrations had suggested.

Nevertheless the attack on the problem of survival after death did direct attention to the claim of thought transference. It was obvious from the start that a medium would have to be gifted with telepathy to intermediate between two worlds; but at the same time; if they were gifted with telepathy they might in this way be able to get the information for her messages from living sources rather than nonmaterial. Telepathy became almost as important an issue as the survival issue itself. It led to experimental work not only under the sponsorship of the Society for Psychical Research but also, during the first quarter of the last century, within university departments of psychology. The US universities of Harvard and Stanford and the University of Groningen, in Holland, were especially active at this time.

The experiments at these three universities, judged by the standards of the day, fully justified continuance but in no case did this happen. Telepathy turned out to be much more difficult to work with than most of the other mental abilities being tested in those days, and ease of demonstration had much to do with the eligibility of a subject for a typical university research program. Psychology itself was still on trial. Psychical research could add nothing to its respectability, and it could not offer scientists a successful career. The effort was premature.

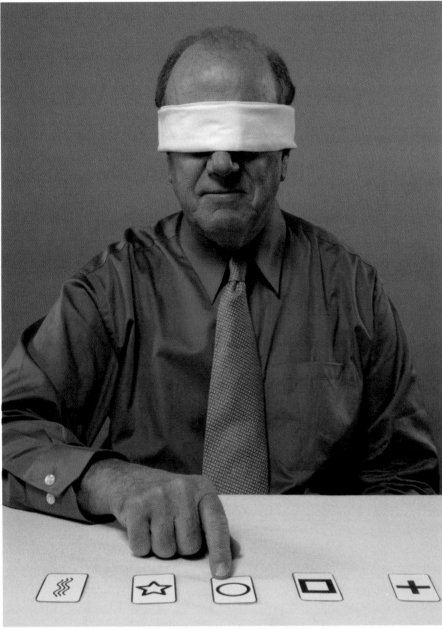

Blindfolded man carries out a test for ESP using a set of Zener cards

While J.B. Rhine established the scientific study of ESP in the laboratory, L.E. Rhine observed how ESP manifested in everyday life, gathering large numbers of spontaneous reports of ESP experiences in order to look for patterns that might give some clue as to the nature of psi phenomena.

Different methods are used to study ESP 'in life and lab.' Together, they can give a more complete understanding of extra-sensory perception. Researchers may have different aims that can affect how they gather and interpret data. The most common distinction made is between proof-oriented and process-oriented research.

Looking for Proof

Proof-oriented research attempts to show whether or not extra-sensory perception exists. To achieve this aim, it is necessary to rule out other 'normal' explanations for the 'psychic' event. The proof-oriented investigator has to ensure that the experiment could not have gained the information through any known channels.

Evidently, it is easier in the laboratory than in real life to rule out information exchange using the known senses because the laboratory provides a controlled environment that is much simpler (at the same time more artificial) than complex everyday life. For this reason, most—if not all—proof-oriented research is carried out in the laboratory. However, in parapsychology as in the other sciences, no experiment is perfect, and it would be wrong to think that one could prove or disprove the existence of ESP with a single 'conclusive' experiment. Scientific progress comes only from the gradual accumulation of results from many experiments conducted by many different researchers.

Discovering How it Works

A number of parapsychologists consider that the process-oriented approach

However, something was established that was important. First, a number of psychologists had obtained significant results in telepathy tests; beginnings had been made. Second, in some of these tests the subjects were unselected volunteers. The way had certainly been made easier for the work that was initiated at Duke University in North Carolina in 1927.

With the sponsoring interest of the professor of psychology, William McDougall (1871–1938), and a new and liberal university administration, a more favourable setting was provided for psychical research at Duke University than had existed anywhere before. In addition the two biologists, J. B. Rhine (1895–1980) and his wife, Louisa E. Rhine, who went to Duke to work under McDougall, had undertaken the exploration after some years of independent and critical study of the claims and evidence for ESP.

J. B. RHINE

Modern Psi Research

Both J. B. Rhine and L. E. Rhine made significant and complementary contributions to parapsychology.

is more productive and informative. In this case, the aim is not simply to prove that ESP exists, but rather to find out how it works. For example, does it make a significant difference if the sender and the receiver in an ESP experiment are friends rather than total strangers? Are ESP results as positive when the sender and receiver are 5,000 miles away from each other, as when they are 50 feet apart? What are the personality characteristics of individuals who report having psychic experiences in everyday life, and what sorts of people do well in laboratory ESP tests?

Evidently, if consistent and meaningful patterns can be found in process-oriented studies, these trends indirectly provide proof for the existence of ESP. Let us now look at how the problems are studied, in life and in the lab.

Surveys of beliefs about psi in Western cultures have shown that psychic experiences are relatively common. In 1979, for example, questionnaires were sent to a random sample of 300 students at the University of Virginia and 700 other adult local residents. Eighty-nine percent of the students replied, as did 51 percent of the locals. Over half of those who responded said that they had experienced some form of psi. For example, almost 40 percent of respondents reported having at least one waking ESP experience, and the information tended to be received in an intuitive form rather than in the form of a visual hallucination.

How do we know if these were 'genuine' ESP experiences rather than simple misunderstandings or misattributions by the experiments? With such surveys we can never be certain. Studies of the reliability and accuracy of the memory of eyewitnesses to crimes and accidents have shown how memory may fade or distort dramatically with the passage of time, so it is always a good idea to note down a detailed description of one's impressions, and to tell others, as soon as possible after one has had a possibly psychic experience. In the case of the survey, more than one-quarter of those reporting an extra-sensory experience had told another person about it before learning of the event through normal means, and the confirming event usually occurred within 24 hours of the experience itself. This means that the experiences were less likely to be misremembered because independent witnesses could confirm the reported details, and because events were still fresh in the memory of those involved.

The 1979 questionnaire survey found that ESP dreams were just as frequent as waking experiences, and two-thirds of respondents reported that their ESP dreams seemed more vivid than ordinary dreams. Similar patterns have been found in other surveys, though one must bear in mind that a person who has had an extra-sensory experience is probably more likely to fill out and return a questionnaire on ESP than someone who has had no such experience. While people's everyday experiences might still be mistakenly interpreted as ESP experiences, surveys such as these show that there is little doubt that a considerable number of people believe that they have telepathic, clairvoyant, and precognitive experiences.

The SPR Investigates

Perhaps the most progress in understanding extra-sensory perception in everyday life has come from the study of collections of spontaneous cases. This is the area in which L.E. Rhine made her greatest contribution to parapsychology, although she was not the first to gather together large numbers of cases. Soon after its founding in 1882, the Society for Psychical Research called for the public to send in reports of spontaneous experiences. As a result, 702 cases were investigated, classified, organized, and finally published in two massive volumes.

The investigators adopted a proof-oriented approach, and consequently took great pains to describe the cases as fully as possible, and to gather supporting testimony from witnesses who were regarded as reliable and responsible. For its time, this case collection provided some of the most impressive evidence available for the existence of psi phenomena. However, many less well-documented cases were discarded so, while the investigators took tremendous efforts to document rigorously the cases they included, they ran the risk of missing some important information that might have been gained from the weaker cases.

More recently, L. E. Rhine took the alternative process-oriented approach to the study of spontaneous cases. Working from the assumption that spontaneous cases, by their very nature, could never provide good evidence for psi, she set about gathering large numbers of cases to see if they might contain patterns that would suggest hypotheses to be tested more rigorously under laboratory conditions. Over decades, she analyzed more than 15,000 cases that were sent in to the Duke Parapsychology Laboratory. Unlike the nineteenth century SPR researchers, she did not attempt to document each case thoroughly; of course she was aware that many cases could be badly flawed, containing inconsistent and sporadic features, but she assumed that most of these flaws would be canceled out with large numbers of cases, so that only truly consistent trends would remain.

Such patterns could be due to the characteristics of psi functioning, or to normal factors, or to a combination of the two. For example, there is a tendency for more women to report psychic experiences than men. This could be for at least two reasons: women have more 'psychic sensitivity' than men; or women have the same number of experiences as men but feel less inhibited about reporting them. Whatever their basic cause, such patterns could suggest hypotheses that could then be subjected to more stringent laboratory testing.

Looking for Patterns

So what kind of patterns emerged from this huge and mostly unselected group of cases? The first thing that was found was that the ESP experiences could indeed be categorized into three basic types as conceptualized in experimental parapsychology: clairvoyance, telepathy, and precognition. There were also a number of cases involving physical effects that could be classified as possible spontaneous PK cases.

Restricting attention to the nature of the ESP experiences, however, it was found that these experiences came into the percipient's consciousness in one of three basic forms: as dreams, as intuitions or, in a relatively small number of cases, as hallucinations. In fact about half of the experiences came in the form of dreams, but there was no tendency for any of the three forms of ESP experiences to occur more often in clairvoyance, telepathy, or precognition cases.

Attention was next focused on the so-called crisis telepathy cases, where one individual, usually regarded as the agent, is experiencing some form of trauma at the same time a second individual, the percipient, has the impression that the agent is in trouble. In some of these cases, the agent was actively thinking of and 'calling' to the percipient; yet in others the agent was entirely unaware of the percipient, and in some cases did not even know them. This finding suggests that, although it may be appealing to think of telepathy in terms of a communication model where information is

'sent' from the active agent to the relatively passive percipient, in reality the percipient can play a more important role, just as in clairvoyance and precognition cases, where there appears to be no agent at all.

These cases were not only informative in themselves, but they also stimulated the development of experimental research methods. For example, the finding that in everyday life psi experiences seemed to occur most often in dreams stimulated the development of experimental studies where the

Parapsychologists must therefore always keep on their toes, alert for possible methodological weaknesses that could produce spurious results . . .

subjects were put into altered states of consciousness while responding to ESP information. This line of research has evolved into one of the most powerful and successful experimental techniques for studying psi in the laboratory.

Both L. E. and J. B. Rhine accepted the limitations of spontaneous case research, and saw the value of being able to control and systematically manipulate possibly important variables under laboratory conditions, where the experimenter could at first hand observe and record results. For its time, the work done between 1930 and about 1960 at Duke University was innovative and pioneering, and certainly represented the best effort yet made to study psi systematically. Since then, there has been considerable evolution in experimental methods, and few researchers now use exactly the same techniques as were pioneered by J. B. Rhine at Duke. Nevertheless, before considering modern parapsychological techniques,

it is important to review the earlier experimental methods, which were to lay the foundation for later generations of researchers.

Experimental Principles

The basic principles of the early research still hold today. In most experiments there is a 'target' that the experimental subject, the 'percipient,' is trying to identify. The experimenter is careful to set up 'barriers' around the target so that the percipient cannot use any known senses or inferential techniques to gain information about the nature of the target. For instance, the target could be a card in a sealed envelope that is housed in a separate room from the percipient. There must be no normal way that the percipient could gain any information about the target, and this includes making sure that the experimenter (and anyone else whom the percipient might have contact with before, during, and after the experimental session until the target choice has been recorded) also is 'blind' to the target's identity, because the experimenter might unconsciously or deliberately give out subtle cues that could make the percipient more likely to identify the target correctly.

The percipient selects what they think was the genuine ESP target from a known number of alternatives or 'foils,' making up the 'target pool.' If there is an agent involved, perhaps holding the target picture and trying to 'send' it to the percipient, it is important that the percipient does not have access to the target held by the agent, in case subtle sensory cues may have been left on it—but not on the foils—that could guide them to choose it. This is known as the 'greasy fingers' hypothesis, but it is easily circumvented by using duplicate target pools.

Most experimenters conduct many 'trials,' in which a number of different percipients respond to a target on a number of different occasions. Once the actual targets become known, it is possible to calculate the 'hit rate—' that is, the number of times that the correct target is chosen in preference to one of the foils. Simple statistical techniques are then used to evaluate the probability that ESP has occurred. The hit rate that would be expected by chance alone is compared to that which is actually found (for instance, with four target possibilities, one would expect to find a 25 percent hit rate by chance alone).

However, it must always be remembered that there could be other explanations for extra-chance hit rates than just ESP. High hit rates could be produced as a result of as yet undetected methodological flaws that have enabled the percipient to gain information about the target through more straightforward, though perhaps subtle, means. Parapsychologists must therefore always keep on their toes, alert for possible methodological weaknesses that could produce spurious results, and ready to develop improved research methods in response to the suggestions of their peers and other informed critics.

Moving on to consider ESP research as a whole, the two main research techniques remain unchanged: those using forced-choice methods, and those using free-response methods. The forced-choice methods were pioneered by J. B. Rhine and his associates at Duke University, and at the time they represented the most common experimental approach. More recently, the popularity of forced-choice methods has waned and free-response techniques have come to the fore.

Also known as restricted-choice, forced-choice, as the name suggests, requires the percipient to select the target from a known set of alternatives. J. B. Rhine specially commissioned the design of a set of cards that presented the percipient with a set of neutral symbols. These became the standard ESP, or 'Zener,' cards, which were used for the next forty years.

They consisted of twenty-five cards showing five sets of five symbols: circle, cross, star, wavy lines, and square. The percipient therefore had a restricted choice of target possibilities—the target would always be one of those five symbols—and there was a one-in-five probability of guessing the target correctly by chance alone.

J. B. Rhine tended to prefer clairvoyance techniques. In a typical forced-choice clairvoyance test at Duke, the experimenter and the percipient would be in the same room, the cards would be shuffled either by hand or in some cases mechanically, and the percipient would be asked to guess the identity of one card at a time. Without looking at the actual card order, the experimenter would record the percipient's calls, and once all cards had been guessed, the experimenter would turn over the pile of cards to find the sequence of the target symbols and the number of hits would be calculated.

J. B. Rhine claimed fairly consistent extra-chance scoring for these tests, but a number of methodological flaws meant that there was controversy over the interpretation of his findings. Often there were insufficient precautions against sensory cues between experimenter and percipient (though this criticism did not apply to those experiments where the two were in

separate rooms), and hand-shuffling might have resulted in cards being inadequately randomized. Also there was a possibility of errors in recording the target and call sequences. As a result of this controversy, refined testing methods were developed.

The Decline Effect

An important feature of the forced-choice ESP results, at Duke and elsewhere, was a tendency for scores to be high to begin with, and then to decline with time. This tendency became so widespread that it was named the 'decline effect.' J. B. Rhine felt that the excitement and novelty that surrounded the early experiments at Duke gradually wore off, so that the decline effect was due to the changing motivations of percipients and experimenters. It would certainly be understandable for the percipient to become gradually bored with a procedure where he or she repeatedly guessed one of five neutral symbols, dozens or even hundreds of times. The kinds of unique dramatic events that can often occur in real-life psi experiences are a long way from the repeated guessing of five neutral symbols, in terms of the psychological involvement and motivation of the percipient.

Critics said that experimental conditions were lax to begin with and that the ESP scores declined as methodological improvements were made. Whatever the reason for the decline effect, parapsychologists began to explore alternative testing methods, notably free-response techniques.

Set of Zener cards

The main characteristic of free-response techniques is that, although the number of target alternatives may be known, the possible content of the target pool is not. In other words, the targets are generally richer, more complex, and conceivably more interesting than forced-choice targets. For instance, free-response targets could be line drawings, magazine photographs, postcard-sized art prints, View-Master slide reels, video clips, three dimensional objects, even geographical or architectural sites. Rather than simply guessing from a known number of alternatives, the percipient in a free-response study reports any impressions that come to mind.

These impressions, known as 'mentations,' can be in the form of mental imagery, feelings, thoughts, even emotions, and sensations of smell and movement. Such varied impressions more closely resemble the ways in which psi impressions seem to appear in consciousness in everyday ESP experiences.

Given the potentially infinite range of target and mentation possibilities, how do we know if the target has been correctly identified? In forced-choice methods a 'hit' is unambiguous—the percipient calls 'star' and the target is (or is not) a star. In free-response methods it is necessary for the percipient or another individual to judge the similarity between the mentation and the items in the target pool.

It is extremely rare for the percipient to give a complete and accurate description of a free-response target, because the mentation contains target-irrelevant thoughts and impressions of the sort that typically float round our heads when we are allowing our thoughts to wander, and because psi impressions are generally faint and subject to distortion and misinterpretation. The hope is that more of the mentation will relate to the target than to the other members of the pool.

While forced-choice methods enable the rapid generation of a large number of responses to simple targets, free-response methods are relatively time-consuming. On the other hand, free-response techniques have the advantage of enabling much richer ESP impressions to emerge into consciousness, and the qualitative correspondences between mentation and target can allow greater insight into the psi process than the forced-choice method.

Altered States of Consciousness

Bearing in mind L. E. Rhine's finding that a large percentage of spontaneous cases involve dreams,

A young woman holding her temples with eyes closed in an ESP experiment

several researchers began to explore the use of altered states of consciousness (ASC) in conjunction with free-response techniques. This has become a very productive line of research. In many free-response experiments, a mild altered state of consciousness might be induced in the percipient in order to facilitate the emergence of psi information. Extreme ASC, such as that induced by psychedelic drugs, is not thought to be helpful because the percipient is inclined to become somewhat disoriented. Generally, the percipient should remain relatively alert so that he or she can respond to the ESP task, while at the same time allowing less structured and nonanalytic thought processes to occur.

The assumption that lies behind the use of ASC in psi research is called the 'noise reduction model.' This model, introduced by Charles Honorton (1946–1992, holds that ESP is a weak signal that must compete with other sources of external and internal stimulation, or 'noise;' the purpose of the ASC is to reduce potentially target-irrelevant noise.

Various techniques are used to induce ASC. Hypnosis was popular some time ago, but it was not generally found to be associated with particularly strong ESP performance. There was also considerable interest in dream research, where the percipient slept in the laboratory, his or her eye movements were monitored and a target was repeatedly sent to the sleeper during dreaming periods. Some impressive results were obtained in these dreaming-ESP studies, but in practical terms the methodology was time consuming and difficult, so researchers began to opt for more simple techniques, such as meditation, relaxation, and the 'ganzfeld.'

Although meditation can have religious associations for some practi-tioners, the majority of those who use meditation in ESP experiments do so in order to focus the mind on the task at hand, and to remove other distracting thoughts. Meditation can consist of mentally focusing on a simple object, a sound, a thought, or even on nothingness, in the attempt to clear the mind completely.

Forms of relaxation range from taking a few deep breaths to following a procedure that focuses on different parts of the body, alternately tensing and releasing muscle groups until the body becomes very relaxed. Mental relaxation may be achieved with the

> *. . . the most important outcome of Honorton and Hyman's ganzfeld debate was that they published a paper giving detailed guidelines for methodological improvements that should be adopted . . .*

use of simple imagery techniques, for instance imagining oneself sitting in a beautiful garden full of wonderful smells, sights, and sounds, where one is completely safe and happy.

The Ganzfeld

Braud and Honorton introduced the ganzfeld technique into parapsychology, and Honorton is credited with developing the technique to the stage where it has become one of the most important lines of ESP research. Ganzfeld is from the German meaning 'whole field,' and the aim is to provide the percipient with uniform or unpatterned sensory stimulation so that the attention becomes focused on internal thoughts and images.

This is usually achieved by seating the percipient in a comfortable reclining chair. Headphones play 'white noise' (something like radio static) to the ears, goggles are placed over the eyes, and a red light is shone on the percipient so that, with their eyes open, they see a pleasant pink light through the goggles. In the absence of any meaningful external stimulation, internally-produced imagery usually becomes more prolific, and the percipient reports aloud any thoughts, feelings or images (the mentation) that occur during the 20 to 45 minutes that they are in the ganzfeld. At the same time (in telepathy studies), an ESP target is being viewed by a sender and it is hoped that the mentation will contain elements that are related to the target.

By 1986 forty-seven authors had published reports detailing the results of forty-two ganzfeld experiments. Honorton claimed that the successful ESP results of many of these studies were extremely unlikely to be due to chance, but a debate opened in the *Journal of Parapsychology* between him and a critic, Ray Hyman (b. 1928), over the possibility of flaws in the original studies, and flaws in Honorton's statistical analysis. In the same journal, Robert Rosenthal (b. 1933), an independent statistician expert in the techniques used to analyze groups of studies like this, reported his own analysis of these studies, and stated that (in the sub-group of twenty-eight studies that gave enough information for this analysis to be conducted) the likelihood of the ESP hit rate being due to chance alone was 0.0000000000337—in other words, very small indeed.

One question that has to be asked when evaluating results is the number of unsuccessful studies that have not been published and are languishing in various researchers' file drawers—the 'file drawer problem.' If a significant number of unsuccessful studies has been conducted but not published, then the published studies will give an exaggerated impression of the success of a particular technique.

It is possible to calculate the number of studies that would be required in order to 'cancel out' such strong effects. Rosenthal calculated that there would have to be 423 unreported studies to negate the significant effect from twenty-eight ganzfeld studies. Given the relatively small number of parapsychologists, and given the fact that parapsychology journals usually publish results whether or not they are statistically significant (if the study is well-designed), it seems extremely unlikely that the significant results of the early ganzfeld studies are due to the file drawer problem.

Results from the Autoganzfeld

Perhaps the most important outcome of Honorton and Hyman's ganzfeld debate was that they published a joint paper giving detailed guidelines for methodological improvements that should be adopted by future ganzfeld researchers in order to strengthen the quality of their studies. Honorton and his colleagues then proceeded to incorporate these guidelines in developing a new ganzfeld methodology, the 'autoganzfeld.' Between 1983 and 1989, eleven experimental series were conducted by eight different researchers using the autoganzfeld. The main feature of the autoganzfeld was that the targets were stored on video tape, the sender and the receiver were sequestered in separate acoustically-isolated and electrically-shielded rooms, and a computer randomly selected and displayed the target to the sender while keeping the experimenter and any others involved blind as to the target identity.

Half of the targets were 'dynamic,' consisting of clips from movies, documentaries, and cartoons, and half were 'static,' consisting of photographs, art prints, and advertisements. A target

pool consisted of either four static or dynamic targets. In some of the experiments the receivers were novices, while in others they were experienced receivers. Sometimes the sender was a friend of the receiver, at other times a member of laboratory staff acted as sender. There were no unreported trials in the period discussed, so there is no file-drawer problem.

Perhaps more than any other body of ESP studies, those involving the ganzfeld have forced many scientists to sit up and take notice.

An analysis of the results of the autoganzfeld studies confirmed the findings of the earlier group of studies. The effects did not appear to depend on who was the experimenter. Experienced receivers had higher ESP scores than novice receivers. The autoganzfeld series also replicated patterns found in the original ganzfeld database: ESP scores were higher when senders were receivers' friends than when lab staff acted as senders; scoring was far higher for the dynamic targets than for the static targets; and extraverted receivers scored more highly than receivers who were introverted.

It is sometimes difficult to gain an impression, from bald statistics, of the qualitative nature of the correspondences that can occur between mentation and target. Of course, striking correspondences can and do occur by chance alone, and to select an impressive example of a hit could give an exaggerated impression of the quality of the hits in the ganzfeld database as a whole. Bearing in mind these caveats, however, the following excerpt from a 1990 paper by Honorton and his colleagues gives some flavour of the dreamlike quality of the

receiver's mentation. The target was a reproduction of a painting by Salvador Dali (1904–89) in the Metropolitan Museum of Art, in New York, called 'Corpus Hypercubicus,' the rest of the target pool comprising a Victorian postcard of a girl on a bicycle, a photograph of penguins, and a still-life of vegetables with a knife on a chopping-board. The target was judged to be correctly chosen as such based on this part of the receiver's mentation:

'. . . I think of guides, like spirit guides, leading me and I come into a court with a king. It's quiet. . . It's like heaven. The king is something like Jesus. Woman. Now I'm just sort of somersaulting through heaven . . . brooding . . . Aztecs, the sun God . . . High priest . . . fear . . . graves. Woman. Prayer . . . funeral . . . dark. Death . . . souls . . .Ten Commandments. Moses . . .'

Perhaps more than any other body of ESP studies, those involving the ganzfeld have forced many scientists to sit up and take notice. The methodology has been developed based on sound theoretical assumptions. In 1990, for the first time, a leading psychology textbook contained a section on parapsychology, focusing on the ganzfeld technique. The standing of parapsychology does not rest on one set of studies alone though, and while the ganzfeld continues to evolve and to be tested by different researchers, parapsychologists have been exploring ESP using other methods.

Applying Meta-Analysis

Researchers have begun to apply the statistical techniques used to analyze the ganzfeld studies to other sets of ESP studies. For a long time, parapsychologists have been faced with a fundamental difficulty: the small size of the ESP effect. In everyday life ESP can be quite dramatic, but effects in the laboratory are typically weak. This means that the chances of detecting the effect to a statistically significant degree in any one study can be quite small, especially if a study only has a few participants. However, recent developments in statistics have enabled the analysis of groups of similar studies, using techniques of meta-analysis. Often, an individual study can reveal an effect that is in the predicted direction, but that does not reach statistical significance. However, in many cases meta-analyses have shown that, taken together, such studies do have nontrivial effects; in other cases, meta-analyses have shown that effects are artificial.

The ganzfeld studies typically involve free-response telepathy methods; however, other methods exist. Between 1935 and 1987, sixty-two authors reported the results of 309 studies using forced-choice precognition methods, where the target material was randomly selected after the subject attempted to predict what it would be. More than 50,000 subjects performed almost two million individual trials, and the time delay in selecting the target ranged from under a second to one year. Overall, there was a very small but highly significant effect that was not due to just a few investigators. When the studies were coded for the number of methodological flaws they contained, it was found that the least flawed studies had the highest precognition effect size, contrary to suggestions by critics. Studies conducted with previously successful percipients were more successful than those with unselected percipients.

Extraverts and Introverts

The ganzfeld ESP studies showed that those receivers who were extraverted (that is, who were outgoing and comfortable in social situations) tended to have higher free-response scores than introverts (who prefer quietness and

solitude). Would this finding generalize to the wider body of ESP studies, including forced-choice research? Sixty studies by seventeen investigators were conducted from 1945 to 1983. For the free-response studies, there was a consistent and significant relationship between extra-version and ESP scores. At first there appeared to be a similar relationship for forced-choice studies, which use quite different techniques from the free-response studies. On closer inspection, though, it was discovered that the relation between extraversion and forced-choice was only found in those studies that gave the subjects feedback on their ESP results before they were tested for extraversion. When extraversion was tested before subjects knew their forced-choice ESP results, there was no difference between the performance of extraverts and introverts. In other words, if subjects are told they have done well at a forced-choice ESP task and are then tested for extraversion, this feedback seems temporarily to inflate their extraversion scores.

It has also been consistently found that if participants have practiced mental disciplines such as meditation, relaxation, or yoga, and if they have had previous ESP experiences, then they are likely to do well at ESP tasks. This is particularly the case if these individuals also show a particular profile when they take personality tests. Findings such as these are sufficiently reliable that parapsychologists can quite confidently predict in advance those participants whom they would expect to do well in ESP experiments.

One of the most consistent findings in experimental parapsychology is known as the 'sheep-goat effect:' subjects' beliefs in and attitudes toward ESP seem to be related to their performance. Those who doubt the existence of ESP and who do not think they could demonstrate the faculty under experimental conditions

(known as 'goats') often do badly at ESP tasks, scoring often significantly below chance expectation. In other words, the goats seem to be using their ESP to avoid hitting the target, so as to confirm their beliefs. The 'sheep,' on the other hand, who believe that ESP exists and that they can use it in the experimental task, tend to score positively. Like the goats, the sheep seem to be confirming their expectations of the experimental outcome.

The picture that is emerging of parapsychology in the 1990s is that, while laboratory psi effects are often small, they do appear with a variety of experimental techniques, and they are not dependent on a small number of 'star' subjects, experimenters, or laboratories.

The field of parapsychology has come a long way since the early days of investigating mediums who produced strange physical effects such as cold breezes, levitating tables, materialized spirits, and ectoplasm. Nowadays such phenomena are almost unheard of. Perhaps the greater sophistication of today's researchers into how such effects may be produced fraudulently has stifled the appearance of such dramatic phenomena. Today, effects are small-scale, usually only detectable with the aid of statistics.

Some researchers regret the loss of the early phenomena, and consider that the artificial conditions of the laboratory are 'throwing the baby out with the bath water.' On the other hand, the laboratory studies are helping parapsychologists to learn more about how ESP works, and the careful control of laboratory conditions enables them to be more confident in the validity of their findings.

The study of ESP in everyday life is still going on, and laboratory researchers must take care not to forget the natural manifestations of the phenomenon that give meaning to the findings of lab research. At the same time, there is a growing understanding of the ways in which individuals may deceive themselves, or be deceived by others, into thinking that they have experienced ESP. This happens most easily in the complex and often confusing conditions of daily life, and represents a valid topic of study in itself. Spontaneous psi experiences are quite common, and whether or not they represent the operation of 'genuine' psi, there can be no doubt that they have formed an important part of the human condition from the earliest times.

CAROLINE A. WATT

FURTHER READING: Alan Gauld. The Founders of Psychical Research. (Berlin: Schocken Books, 1968); J. B. Rhine et al. Extrasensory Perception after Sixty Years. (Wellesley, MA: Branden, 1940); H. L. Edge et al. Foundations of Parapsychology. (New York, NY: Routledge & Kegan Paul, 1986); Richard Broughton. Parapsychology: the Controversial Science. (London, UK: Rider, 1991).

Film

Cinema is itself supernatural; the unreality of what is happening on a movie-screen is fantastic. Somewhere in the back of the building, a machine with a magnifying lens, a light bulb, and a motor is passing from one reel to another a strip of celluloid, on which have been 'fixed' thousands of static images of scenes, scenes that have often been filmed in random order, and then painstakingly assembled to tell a story. The concept of a moving image is itself is related to the magical—the portrait that blinks an eye, the possessed landscape that has leaves shifting in the wind. Based as it is upon the hyper-natural technology of the camera, the film is unrivalled in representing supernatural phenomena.

Supernatural cinema pursues the metaphors and symbolism of goblins and fairies, mummies and zombies, God and the Devil, heaven and Hell, demonic (and sometimes alien) possession, death, reincarnation and immortality, angels, ghosts and saints, clairvoyance, telepathy and telekinesis, witches and warlocks, mediums and magicians, religion and mythology, demons, poltergeists and nameless evils, and metamorphosis into werewolves, fiends, and vampires.

Science fiction is inseparable from the supernatural. The genres follow many of the same lines, but instead of mummies we have aliens, instead of a God, the desolation of the agnostic unknown. The supernatural element comes from another dimension, whereas aliens arrive from another part of the galaxy. Fifty-foot women and giant crabs belong to science fiction: they can be looked on as Nature gone to extraordinary lengths. Very often a mad scientist or radioactive fallout is responsible or else some remote scientific possibility is brought into the here and now. Social realities are in this way examined and developed, exploring fantasies and ideologies.

The Birth of the Fantasy Film

Movie-making has two main points of origin. The first people to project moving pictures that had been made on a celluloid strip were the Lumière brothers, who gave the first showing of their Cinématographe in March 1895. Theirs was the cinema of realism: the films were advertised as 'Workers Leaving the Factory,' 'Watering the Gardener,' (a naughty boy treads on the hose), and 'The Arrival of the Paris Express'—which left audiences cowering in their seats as the train swept across the screen. Early cinema-goers marveled at the Lumières' spectral reflection of the world around them; their work was the foundation for documentaries and docudramas.

Also living in Paris was Georges Méliès (1861–1938), a magician who owned the Théâtre Robert-Houdin in Paris, where he staged miniature spectacles of conjuring and illusionism. He was so impressed with the Lumiere shows that he furnished himself with a camera and a projector, and began to create his own magic movie shows—for Méliès was a showman, a lover of music-halls and carnivals. His first trick film was *The Vanishing Lady* (1896). In it a woman, seated on a stage, is covered with a cloth by a magician. When he removes the cloth, the woman has gone—and a skeleton appears in her place. The magician replaces the cloth—and the woman reappears. An illusion of this kind is achievable, but only with great ingenuity, on the stage. In the film the effects could be obtained with relative ease by stopping the camera to adjust the scene being filmed.

Another of Méliès's films was the earliest vampire movie, *The Haunted Castle* (aka *The Devil's Manor*, 1896). A large bat flies into the castle hall and turns into Mephistopheles. From his cauldron there appears a girl in the company of a horde of skeletons, ghosts, and witches. One of them holds up a crucifix, and the devil disappears in a puff of smoke. Méliès again had the devil appearing as a bat in *The Devil in the Convent* (1899). These early vampire movies were not the horrific stories of later years, however, but amusing fantasy tales.

Méliès was not only the pioneer in the cinema of illusion and fantasy, but his methods became the basis of animation and early special effects.

Opposite page:
A bust of Nosferatu at Son Of Monsterpalooza held at Burbank Marriott Airport Hotel and Convention Center on October 27, 2012, in Burbank, California.

Beliefs, Rituals, and Symbols of the Modern World

Furthermore his stop-camera work was the direct forerunner of Ray Harryhausen's Dynamation stop-motion process, which created such screen classics as *Jason and the Argonauts* (1963), *Sinbad and the Eye of the Tiger* (1977), and *Clash of the Titans* (1981).

Frankenstein and Dracula

The early years of the century saw the first screen appearance of many horror stories and fantasy figures: apart from the first outing of the monster in *Frankenstein* (1910) and the horror-film 'personae' Dr. Jekyll and Mr. Hyde in the German film *Ein Selt-*

samer Fall (1914), there was the film debut of *The Werewolf* (1913), and *The Golem* (1914), a monster created when a statue is brought to life by magic. The 'classic' version of *The Golem*, by German director Paul Wegener (1874–1948), appeared in 1920, while the following year saw in Murnau's

A still from the 1984 film *Ghostbusters*, directed by Ivan Reitman and starring Dan Aykroyd, Bill Murray, Ernie Hudson, and Harold Ramis.

Nosferatu (1921), the creation of one of cinema's most powerful supernatural images, that of the arch-vampire Count Orlok, with his bald head, white skin, sunken eyes, pointed ears, and finger-length fingernails. Death also made an impressive appearance in *Der Meude Tod* (*Between Two Worlds*,

1921), when a young newlywed tries to reclaim her bridegroom from his gloomy realm.

From Gothic to the Gentle Ghost

The 1930s were the heyday of the horror film. Horror and thrills naturally incorporated supernatural monsters and horrific creations of science fiction. Monsters ruled the screen—many of them spawned by Universal Studios after the enormous success of Tod Browning's *Dracula* (1931) starring Bela Lugosi (1882–1956).

By the 1940s, with World War II in full progress, reality had overtaken the wildest fantasies. Cinema turned from Gothic horror to a gentler examination of the supernatural. Its themes were friendly ghosts and angels and the afterlife. Comfort in bereavement and the hope of ongoing 'contact' with deceased loved ones, or else a heavenly reunion, were what production companies realized their audiences needed.

The success of *Topper* (1937), in which Constance Bennett (1904–65) and Cary Grant (1904–86) play the ghosts of a sophisticated couple who come to the aid of a troubled banker-friend, paved the way for a host of ghost movies—including two sequels, in the first of which Cary Grant was replaced by a dog, because he had become too expensive. One of the best of the 'ghosters' is Frank Capra's heart-warming *It's a Wonderful Life* (1946), starring James Stewart (1908—97) as George Baily, a man contemplating suicide when his business collapses. Cuddly Clarence Oddbody, angel second-class, is sent down to earn his wings by showing Bailey how dreadful life for his friends and family would become if he died. Angel Dudley in *The Bishop's Wife* (1947) is an urbanely charming heavenly messenger who arrives in answer to the prayers of Bishop Brougham, his mission to solve the bishop's problems and restore his flagging faith.

Ernst Lubitsch's *Heaven Can Wait* (1943) has a devoted but distracted husband (Don Ameche) arriving in Hades, convinced that this is his hereafter home—but Satan decides the new boy is not nearly as naughty as he thinks, and sends him Upstairs.

Rains (1889–1967) crossed the line in 1946 to play a roguish Devil, in *Angel on My Shoulder* (1946), who promises a dead gangster a new lease of life if he will return to Earth to take over the body of a worthy judge who is trying to stamp out crime. Indeed, few stars escaped this life-and-death cycle. Ghostly parts were assigned to such unlikely contenders as Jennifer Jones (1919–2009), Rex Harrison (1908–90), Charles Laughton (1899–1962), Danny Kaye (1913–87), and Spencer Tracy (1900–67).

The Devil was played as sinisterly suave by Ray Milland (1907–86) in *Alias Nick Beal* (1941), and as a cunning 'hick' by Walter Huston (1883–1950) in *All that Money Can Buy* (aka *The Devil and Daniel Webster*, 1941).

As for angels, even Jack Benny (1894–1974) played one: the angel Athanael in *The Horn Blows at Midnight* (1945), in which he is sent down from heaven to blow the Last Trump. Comic Jacques Tati (1907–82) starred in *Sylvie et le Fantôme* (*Sylvia and the Ghost*, 1950), about a young girl who befriends the ghost of a man who died in the duel he fought for love of her grandmother.

The beginning of the 1950s had seen the end of the kitsch and charisma of harp–string movies; fear of the nuclear bomb—together with fear of McCarthyism—moved into the studios and cinemas in its place. In this environment, science fiction as a genre began to separate from the supernatural—instead of crazed scientists and their Frankenstiens, theatres began showing the monsters that resulted from nuclear fallout. For several years, far-fetched sci-fi and post-holocaust movies abounded, before a return to horror and the supernatural, in the form of films such as *I Was a Teenage Werewolf* (1957), an 'all-time, zero-budgeted schlock classic' that many directors and screenwriters claim as a seminal influence.

Japanese Ghosts

Kwaidan (1964) is a set of four Japanese ghost-stories directed by Masaki Kobayashi (1916–1996). One of the episodes, 'Hoichi, the Earless,' tells of a blind young monk who is a talented musician, summoned every night by the ghostly warriors of the Helke clan to sing the saga of their final battle, an ordeal that causes him to become weak and frail. When the other monks discover what is happening, they paint him all over with sacred writings, so that the ghost will not be able to see him. However, the other monks forget to paint his ears, which the angry ghost messenger tears from his head. The composer Toru Takemitsu (1930–1996) chose a different sound for each episode; wood being split, pebbles being struck together, the nonverbal vocal music that accompanies Noh drama, and the playing of the banjo-like *samisen,* which all add to the extraordinarily unsettling ambience of the film.

The popularity of ghost tales continues. Tim Burton's *Beetlejuice* (1988) became an instant cult movie. It tells of a ghostly couple haunting their old home, who are appalled by the crass family who move in. In desperation they seek the help of Betelgeuse, who is an 'alternative' exorcist—that is, he rids houses of unwanted humans.

Ghostbusters (1984) came up with a winning formula: a crackpot cast and story, a cheery line in comedy, gloriously disgusting ghosts, and a chart-topping title-track. *Ghost* was one of the hits of 1990. A loving couple is

separated when the man is murdered. However, he has to stay around to find a way of warning his beloved that she is in similar danger. Whoopi Goldberg (b. 1955) plays the medium who helps the lovers reconnect.

The demonic possession of a twelve-year-old girl was the plotline for one of the most commercially successful of all horror movies, The Exorcist *(1973).*

The Threat of Television

But for a time 1950s cinema was in trouble, and the problem was television. However, television was small-screen and black-and-white, and the cinema set about pulling people back into its seats. It toyed with the panoramic (but expensive) magnitude of Cinerama before settling for dazzling, action-packed epics in CinemaScope and VistaVision. It also re-introduced 3-D, mainly as a gimmick, and for a while everything on the screen appeared to be flying at the audience. King of supernatural tricks was the producer William Castle (1914–77). Like Méliès, he was a showman. *The House on Haunted Hill* (1958), a tricksy ghost story, featured 'Emergo:' as a skeleton rose from Vincent Price's cauldron of boiling acid, a 'live' skeleton rattled out over the audience's heads. For *13 Ghosts* (1960) Castle created 'Illusion-O.' Cinemagoers were given a card containing a red filter (a 'ghost viewer') and a blue filter (a 'ghost remover') for those too frightened to watch any more.

The 1960s, and the emergence of the 'permissive' society, saw the return of blood-and-lust vampire movies. Hammer Films, Britain's 'House of Horror,' followed up the success of *Dracula* (aka *House of Horror*, 1958),

starring Peter Cushing (1913–94) as the vampire hunter and Christopher Lee (1922) as the demonically dashing Count Dracula. Cushing came back to fight Dracula's disciples in *The Brides of Dracula* (1960). Neither actor appeared in one of Hammer's best, *The Kiss of the Vampire* (1962), but Lee returned in *Dracula Prince of Darkness* (1965), and turned in a powerfully evil performance—he more notable for his having no dialogue.

Lee went on to play other demons in British, US, West German, and Italian films. Italy was producing its own strong strand of vampire movies. Mario Bava (1914–1980) directed *Black Sunday* (1960, which made a cult movie star of English actress Barbara Steele (b. 1937)—*Black Sabbath* (1963) and *Planet of the Vampires* (1965).

In every land spoofs began to appear, such as *Munster, Go Home* (1966), Britain's *Carry On Screaming* and Roman Polanski's *Dance of the Vampires* (1967). He is now recognizeable to a younger group of moviegoers as Saruman, the White Wizard in Peter Jackson's film adaptation of *The Lord of the Rings* trilogy.

The popularity of vampire movies has continued and they became ever more erotic. Lesbian vampires abounded, as in the stylish *Daughters of Darkness* (1971) where it is never clear whether the glamorous Countess Bathory is responsible for the bloody murders that seem to surround her and her female lover.

Frank Langella (1938) provided a veritable pin-up of a Count in John Badham's beautiful but rather predictable *Dracula* of 1979, while George Hamilton (b. 1939) was handsome and funny in *Love at First Bite* (1979). This Dracula has to flee to New York when a People's Commissar from Transylvania commandeers his castle as a public gymnasium. Hamilton makes the most of a sparkling script.

Variations on the vampire theme proliferated. *Nosferatu the Vampyre* (1979) was a remake of Murnau's original (1922), with Klaus Kinski (1926–91) as the blood-stealer. Then there was *Blacula* (1972) in which an African prince is bitten by Dracula and imprisoned in a coffin that is shipped to Los Angeles, whereupon he emerges and does his bit for equal bite-rights. In *Deafula* (1975), a theology student, played by the film's writer-director Peter Wechsberg, is infected by Dracula before birth, and in due course turns into Deafula. Wechsberg's character is deaf, and the whole movie was filmed in sign-language with voice-over commentary.

Vampires Rampant

Teenage vampires have ruled the screen for decades. *The Lost Boys* (1987), the tale of a Californian teen-vamp gang, was very popular, though far from the best. Kathryn Bigelow's *Near Dark* (1987), about farm-boy Caleb who gets caught up with a gang of gypsy vampires, is thought to be far better.

In the 1990s, vampire films almost drove gangster movies from the screen. *DEF by Temptation* (1990) is, in effect, 'Rapula.' It was billed as 'the black rap chiller thriller of the decade,' in which a New York vampire sets out to seduce an innocent country preacher. *Sorority House of Vampires* (1992), a vampire tale with an ecological message, reveals that a major natural disaster (earthquake or tidal wave) occurs every time a vampire 'claims' a victim. It parallels vampirism with big business, claiming that both suck out Earth's lifeblood.

Then there was *The Addams Family* (1991), with Anjelica Huston (b. 1951) as Morticia, *Buffy the Vampire Slayer* (1992) which was remade into the popular late nineties television show, *Moon Legend* (1991) from Hong Kong, the two-and-a-half-hour *Bandh Darwaza* (1990)—an Indian vampire musical—Clive Barker's *Nightbreed* (1990) and, of course, Francis Coppola's *Bram Stoker's Dracula*. This hyper-promoted movie featured Gary Oldman (b. 1958) as a man seeking revenge for the death of his wife (in 1462) and someone to rekindle his heart in the present (1982). However, Van Helsing is always there to stop him. Following this came Neil Jordan's

English actor Christopher Lee as the blood-sucking Count in *Dracula* (1972)

Cillian Murphy in *28 Days Later* (2002)

adaptation of *Interview with the Vampire*, starring Tom Cruise (b. 1962) as the vampire Lestat.

Enter the Zombies

In the '70s, the undead were still a primary theme, but the flavour of the decade was the zombie. This would seem to have resulted from a fusion of a heyday in the development of special effects—especially 'splatter-movie' make-up—and a growing obsession with the body beautiful. Zombies had been around in movies for decades, but the '70s—continuing into the '80s—saw them getting out of hand. No longer were graveyards and tropical islands the only places stocked with sepulchral creatures who refused to die.

The zombie boom was triggered by *Night of the Living Dead* (1968), a painfully bleak and frightening film that was shot in grainy black and white. *Dawn of the Dead* (aka *Zombies*, 1979), in vibrant colour, takes place in the environment where the protagonists in their prezombie lives had known greatest happiness—a vast shopping mall. The second, *Day of the Dead*, is set in a bunker, the secret hideaway of a research team who are trying to domesticate zombies. In this film, most of the living are as devoid of soul as the undead.

Other ghoulish titles included *The Living Dead at the Manchester Morgue* (1974) and *Zombie Flesh Eaters* (1979), and the Canadian *Dead of Night* (aka *Death dream*, 1972),

in which a young soldier is killed in action but returns from the grave to cause havoc in his hometown.

The 1980s saw director Sam Raimi (b. 1959) well set on a zombie course. *Evil Dead* (1982) and *Evil Dead II* quickly became cult movies. Zombie films resurfaced again in the 2000s, with films such as *28 Days Later*, and the satires *Shawn of the Dead* and *Zombieland*, which poke fun at the zombie film tropes.

The Devil You Know

Being soulless, zombies hold no interest for the Devil. However, he can always find plenty to occupy him. In *The Devil Rides Out* (1967), one of Terence Fisher's finest films for Hammer Horror, based on the novel by Dennis Wheatley (1897–1977), Christopher Lee (this time the hero) constructs a magic pentagram to protect a family from demonic invasion. The nightlong battle against Satanic forces is an accomplished exercise in occult drama, and the film has, over the years, become an established cult favourite.

The following year produced another cult classic, Roman Polanski's *Rosemary's Baby* (1968), based on Ira Levin's Satanist thriller. It is a Faustian tale in which Rosemary's husband buys success from the Devil, not at the price of his soul but in exchange for his wife (played by Mia Farrow (b. 1945) giving birth to the Antichrist.

Rosemary endures a pregnancy full of pain and nightmares, with a growing terrifying realization that all is not as it should be with her husband and her invasively protective neighbours, the Castavets. Rosemary's attempts to retain a grip on her sanity is masterfully orchestrated by Polanski, and was a timely political piece during the Woman's Rights Movement about the fears of pregnancy.

Satanic Children

The demonic possession of a twelve-year-old girl was the plotline for one of the most commercially successful of all horror movies, *The Exorcist* (1973). As a result of the take-over, she levitates, spews up green bile, masturbates with a crucifix, spins her head round full-circle, 'persuades' the exorcist-priest Father Damien to throw himself out of a window—and caused many parents to gasp with horror while their offspring writhed with glee.

Another Satanic child, and another Damien also did very well at the box-office in *The Omen* (1976). This Damien is subtle about his demonic nature. He has himself adopted by a couple and kills off their expected baby—and anyone who suspects his devilish nature. Public enthusiasm led

to two sequels: *Damien—Omen II* (1978) and *The Final Conflict* (1981); and even sparked a 2006 remake.

Alan Parker's *Angel Heart* (1987) has a very different flavour. It follows the machinations of a powerfully persuasive Devil in the shape of Louis Cyphre, a compelling performance from Robert De Niro (b. 1943). He takes possession of detective Harry Angel, hiring him to track down a missing man, but the search draws Angel into a series of occult dramas and murders, until he discovers that the man he is searching for is himself.

Howling Horror

Lycanthropy is a different form of possession. A longtime teen favourite for the parallels between 'wolfing out' and puberty, the werewolf has always been a supernatural favourite, and continued to be so one the silver screen. After *The Werewolf* in 1913 there was a long lull until *The Werewolf of London* (1934). Then Lon Chaney Jr (1906–73) took over the role in 1941 as *The Wolf Man*. Werewolves appeared occasionally throughout the next three decades, but the '80s found them back in vogue. *The Howling* (1980) tells of a television anchorwoman who has a nervous breakdown following a traumatic episode. Convalescing in a rest home, she discovers that a colony of werewolves is also in residence there. This impressive supernatural thriller was director Joe Dante's run-up to *Gremlins* (1984).

An American Werewolf in London (1981) tells of two young Americans, David and Jack, who are hitchhiking across England when they are attacked by a werewolf. The beast tears Jack to pieces and he dies, but David is only wounded and wakes up three weeks later in hospital. There a horribly disfigured Jack 'appears' to suggest to David that he should commit suicide because he is about to become a werewolf. Special-effects makeup art-

ist Rick Baker (b. 1950) created Jack's hideous gaping wounds and David's subsequent furry, fanged persona.

Albert Finney (b. 1936) became entangled in full-moon frolics in *Wolfen* (1981). He played a detective convinced that a series of savage New York murders has been committed by wolves. He eventually discovers that the killers are the *wolfen*, a race of mutated Native American hunters who retreated into their own netherworld in despair at the bleak prospects for humankind.

Wolves, Witches, and Warlocks

In his adaptation of Angela Carter's novel, Neil Jordan (b. 1950), often a teller of grim tales, unfolds a wondrous fairy story in *The Company of Wolves* (1984). It spins the fable of a young girl's dreams and fantasies, of wolves, and of men whose eyebrows meet in the middle and who are hairy on the inside. This is a sensual and a sexual movie, and a triumph of costume, design, and special make-up effects.

Tangling with the demonic took on an altogether lighter tone in *The Witches of Eastwick* (1987). Three ladies—a brunette, a redhead and a blonde, discover they can pool their natural 'powers' to conjure up the man of their dreams. And who should that be but the devilishly charming Daryl Van Home? Soon each of the women is pregnant with a potential little devil. They decide to take control of the situation, and put their fallen angel in his proper place.

Witches, wizards, and warlocks turn up in unexpected places. From a coven hidden away in a seaside hotel, and led by the Grand High Witch (Anjelica Huston), *The Witches* (1989) intend to turn the children of Britain into mice. In *Warlock* (1988), Julian Sands (1958) plays an evil Satanic priest attempting to escape a witchfinder, who is getting too close for comfort, by switching centuries from seventeenth-century Massachusetts to modern Los Angeles. He 'arrives' in the apartment of a very surprised waitress, only to find that his pursuer has taken the next time-express and is right behind him.

In a lighter vein, Walt Disney (1901–66) had a soft spot for witches and wizards. Apart from the wicked-witch godmothers and stepmothers of his animated features, there is *Mary Poppins* (1964), who would have been a perfect Edwardian nanny if she could have kept the magic in her feet under control. *Bedknobs and Broomsticks* (1971) features Angela Lansbury (b. 1925) as an apprentice witch, and *Hocus Pocus* (1993) has three nasty reincarnated witch sisters who plan, at Hallowe'en, to steal the souls of trick-or-treating children so they can live forever.

In 2001, *Harry Potter and the Philosopher's Stone* was released, the first of eight films featuring the life of a young wizard and his friends, following Harry Potter from childhood through his education at the Hogwarts School of Witchcraft and Wizardry into young adulthood, culminating in the destruction of the arch supernatural villain in spectacular battle at the end of the final film. Presenting a world of magic and wizardry, heroes and horrors, the world of Harry Potter has created its own mythology, entrancing young and old alike.

Evidence of the sure place of the supernatural on the cinema screen in recent years can be found in the number of cinema and television films (more than thirty) based on the novels, stories, and original screenplays of Stephen King (b. 1947). It must be said that very few of these films in any way matches the power and inventiveness of King's original writing. Nevertheless, his stories provide themes that cover almost every aspect of the super-

natural, albeit in a horror context, and the fact that producers are so eager to make 'Stephen King' movies shows the ravenous appetite for the supernatural.

King's career was launched by Brian De Palma's movie of King's novel *Carrie* (1976, and remade in 2013), about a young woman who resorts to telekinesis when the world proves too unfriendly—as does the heroine of *Firestarter* (1984). *Salem's Lot* (1979) is a vampire-run New England Town; *The Shining* (1980) is the 'second sight' that a demonic hotel wants to steal from a little boy; *The Dead Zone* (1983) has a hero cursed with clairvoyance and telepathy; *Christine* (1983) is a demonic car which takes possession of her teenage owner; *Silver Bullet* (1985) is a werewolf tale; *Pet Sematary* (1989) boasts a zombie child (and a zombie cat); *Sleepwalkers* (1992) metamorphose from human to prefeline vampires; *The Dark Half* (1993) tells of an author pursued by the murderous reincarnation of the half of himself that he had buried—his thriller-writing pseudonym; and *Needful Things* (1993) has the Devil visiting Castle Rock, Maine, and turning good neighbours into vengeful murderers.

King's tales (with the exceptions that prove the rule) are firmly rooted in one of the major ingredients of successful supernatural fiction—everyday normality. Once the audience is safely settled in an ordinary little town, then, and only then, do doors start to creak.

Alien Invasion

A humorous and heart-warming take on a tired trope, came out in the early eighties the refresh the genre. An alien mistakenly left behind on Earth and his relationship with a small boy forms the core of the 1982 film, *E.T.—the Extra-Terrestrial*. The tenor of the film is gentle and humorous, focusing on loneliness and loss.

The film *Independence Day* dealt with the threat to life on Earth posed by the overt and enormous presence of alien spaceships hovering over major population centres apparently poised to launch a coordinated attack. Destruction of the alien presence is paramount as the US government struggles to organize a counter attack in this pro-military action film.

Suspended Disbelief

A film with a supernatural theme can employ devices unique to cinema and present changes and distortions of reality in an unparalleled fashion. It is a marvellous medium for representing alternative versions of reality and what lies above and beyond the natural. Movies and the supernatural have been bedfellows since the earliest days. And, over the decades, as the unbelievable has become commonplace, so new visions and versions of the supernatural have come into being.

Cinema has great advantages in dealing with the supernatural. Cinemagoers are isolated in the dark, yet sharing a common atmosphere of cosy vulnerability that is highly conducive to suspending disbelief and allowing the almost unimaginable to divert or terrify. Cinema has that mesmeric potential; and it has the ability to conjure up the intangible and unseen in concrete, visible, moving form—to turn the unreal into the reel.

As technology continues to grow by leaps and bounds, the tradition of the film medium has changed drastically. Instead of developing images on long reels the current trend is toward the digital. The supernatural effects of Méliès' films pale in comparison to the CGI that fills movies today.

Beliefs, Rituals, and Symbols of the Modern World

Computer generated images are a large part of today's supernatural films.

Even the medium of film has changed, from theatre to television set to computer screen. In this heyday of the Internet, media can be made and accessed with ease as never before, and the democratic era of YouTube has enabled innovations of all types. Yet the magic of entering a dark theatre and experiencing a film with a group of strangers still moves us, and keeps audiences coming back for more.

ANN LLOYD with
ELIZABETH LOVING

FURTHER READING: A. L. Zambrano. Horror. (New York, NY: Gordon Press, 1975); Carlos Clarens. Illustrated History of Horror Movies. (New York, NY: Putnam, 1967); R. Eberwin. Film and the Dream Screen. (Princeton, NJ: Princeton University Press, 1985).

Charles Fort

When Charles Fort's *The Book of the Damned* was published in New York in 1919, he declared: 'I am a pioneer of a new kind of writing that instead of heroes and villains will have floods and bugs and stars and earthquakes for its characters and motifs.' Most critics did not know what to make of it. 'I am a collector of notes upon subjects that have diversity,' he wrote, 'such as deviations from concentricity in the lunar crater, Copernicus, and a sudden appearance of purple Englishmen.'

Although *The Book of the Damned* was a radical critique of contemporary science, it was in an unprecedented style—fragmented, argumentative, and imaginative, it was by turns compas-

sionate, violent, poetic, ironic, and wise. It was also hilarious. Fort was lauded by the cream of US writers. Booth Tarkington (1869–1946) found the book 'vigorous and astonishing' and reveled in the author's 'gorgeous mad-man's humour.' 'Here indeed' he said, quoting Blake, 'was a "brush dipped in earthquake and eclipse."' Ben Hecht (1893–1964) wrote a review of the book in the Chicago Daily News in 1919. Fort, he said, 'has made a terrible onslaught upon the accumulated lunacy of fifty centuries . . . He has shot the scientific basis of modern wisdom full of large, ugly holes.' Hecht went on to coin the word, now used to describe an open-minded study of the widest range of anomalous phenomena: 'I am the first disciple of Charles Fort,' he said. 'Henceforth, I am a Fortean.'

A selection from Fort's writings would include such topics as spontaneous human combustion; unidentified flying objects; discoveries of the United States; lights on the moon; stigmatic wounds; 'mass hysteria' and panics; rains of stones, blood, or animals from the skies; people with paranormal abilities; wolf children and wild men; teleportations and poltergeists; sea serpents; and modern human artefacts exhumed from ancient rocks.

Fort went on to write three more books of encyclopedic diversity—*New Lands* (1923), *Lo!* (1931), and *Wild Talents* (1932)—in which he developed an objective viewpoint that was both constructive and capable of philosophical rigour.

Far from being a credulous man who would 'believe anything,' Fort cut at the very roots of credulity. Tentative acceptance, he thought, was more fruitful than belief. The difficulty of Fort's thesis wrongfooted the US press, who erroneously dubbed him 'the archenemy of science.' Fort's real target was scientific malpractice and blind dogma. His cynicism arose from observing how scientists argued for and against various theories, facts, and kinds of phenomena according to their own beliefs, rather than the rules of evidence. He was appalled at the way any datum that did not fit a particular scientist's view, or the collective paradigm, was ignored, suppressed, discredited, or explained away (which is quite a different thing from explaining). He called such rejected data 'The Damned' because they were excommunicated by a science that acted like a religion.

In *Lo!*, Fort called science 'the conventionalization of alleged knowledge.' His statement that 'nothing, in religion, science, or philosophy . . . is more than the proper thing to wear, for a while,' compares with Karl Popper's, that 'every scientific statement must remain tentative forever. It may indeed be corroborated, but every corroboration is relative to other statements which, again, are tentative.'

'Science has done its utmost to prevent whatever Science has done,' wrote Fort, pointing out that Voltaire (1694–1778) scorned the notion of fossils; Lavoisier (1743–94) delayed the acceptance of meteorites for forty years when he told the Academy of Sciences in 1769 that only peasants believed that stones fell from the sky, because, 'there are no stones in the sky'; spaceflight was considered 'utter bosh!' in the 1930s; and so on. Today we see old herbals plundered for new pharmaceuticals and the practices of witchdoctors for new therapies. Fort observed: 'Witchcraft always has a hard time, until it becomes established and changes its name.'

The Concept of Continuity

The reductive thrust of modern science—to define, divide, and separate the phenomenal—went contrary to the observed nature of phenomena, Fort reasoned. In its place he proposed the notion of 'Continuity,' a universal condition in which everything is in an intermediate state between extremes. This is summed up by Martin Gardner (1914–2010) in his *Fads and Fallacies in the Name of Science*: 'Because everything is continuous with everything else, it is impossible to draw a line between truth and fiction. If science tries to accept red things and exclude yellow, then where will it put orange? Similarly, nothing is "included" by science which does not contain error, nor is there anything "damned" by science which does not contain some truth.'

Like the Chinese, Greek, and other ancient schools of philosophy, Fort had notions of the universe-as-organism and the transient nature of all apparent phenomena. 'One measures a circle, beginning anywhere,' he wrote at about the same time that the hapless Paul Kammerer (1880–1926) was occupied with the related concept of meaningful coincidences he called 'seriality.' Both ideas prefigured the Jung-Pauli thesis of 'synchronicity,' which Jung (1875–1961) described as an 'acausal connecting principle.' Fort's idea of Continuity, however, was far more comprehensive; for instance: '. . . there is continuity between what is called the real and what is called the unreal, so that a passage from one state to the other is across no real gap, or is no absolute jump.'

'An Utterly Peaceable Man'

Charles Fort was born in Albany, New York, on August 6, 1874, to a prosperous family of Dutch immigrants. Escaping home at the age of eighteen, he spent a year as a journalist before hitch-hiking through Europe. In 1896 he contracted malaria and returned to New York, where he was nursed by Anna Filing, an English servant girl in his father's house. They married, to be separated only by Fort's death.

According to his biographer Damon Knight (1922–2002), Fort 'was . . . an utterly peaceable and sedentary man [who] lived quietly with his wife.' They settled in the Bronx to twenty years of dire poverty, sometimes having to break chairs for firewood. Beside his journalism, Fort wrote ten novels, only one of which—*The Outcast Manufacturers* (1906)—was ever published. He read every scientific book and journal he could find and amassed 25,000 pages of notes on the infallible public face of orthodox science. These he burned because 'they were not what I wanted.' He resumed what he called his 'grand tour,' through the world's major newspapers and scientific journals, taking notes in a cramped shorthand on small squares of paper filed in shoe boxes.

In 1916, when he was forty-two, Fort's luck turned—he came into a modest inheritance from an uncle, which was just enough to relieve him of the worry of earning his daily bread —and he began work on what became *The Book of the Damned*, which Dreiser bullied his publisher to put out in 1919.

The following year, in a fit of depression, Fort again burned his notes, and in 1921 set sail for London, where he and Anna lived near the British Museum. For eight years he took his 'grand tour' in the museum's library. He came to the conclusion that space travel was inevitable, and sometimes spoke on the subject at Hyde Park Corner.

During this period he wrote his least successful and most cranky book, *New Lands*— largely a satirical attack upon the pomposity of astronomers, who, he said, were 'led by a cloud of rubbish by day and a pillar of bosh by night.' In 1929 he returned to New York and began work on *Lo!*. A year later he completed his last book, *Wild Talents*, which dealt with occult or psychic abilities revealed during progressive blindness and weakness. On May 3, 1932, he was admitted to hospital, where he died within a few hours. He took notes to the end—the last one said simply: 'Difficulty shaving. Gaunt places in face.' He left 60,000 pages of notes, now in the New York Public Library.

In 1931, a year before his death, Dreiser, Tiffany Thayer (1902–59), and Aaron Sussman had founded the Fortean Society, which Fort refused to join. He had expressed his objection to such an organization: 'The great trouble is that the majority of persons who are attracted are the ones we do not want; Spiritualists, Fundamentalists, persons revolting against science, not in the least because they are affronted by the myth-stuff of the sciences, but because scientists either oppose or do not encourage them.'

Nevertheless, the Society enjoyed much success in its early years. Beside Dreiser, Hecht, Thayer, Sussman, and Tarkington, members included Clarence Darrow (1857–1938), Oliver Wendell Holmes (1841–1935), Havelock Ellis (1859–1939), John Cowper Powys (1872–1963), and Alexander Woolcott (1887–1943). Thayer, its secretary, championed ever crankier ideas—such as a flat Earth—and opposed others such as fluoridation of water supplies, and the Society, with its journal *Doubt*, petered out with his death in 1959.

> *Teleportation could account for the sudden appearance of animals far from their usual habitats, or the appearance of fish in a freshly-dug pond.*

Fort was one of the main influences upon the developing study of UFOs, not least because such writers as Eric Frank Russell (1905–1978) and Vincent Gaddis (1913–97) were original members of the society. Gaddis was writing articles about craft and lights in the skies well before the term 'flying saucer' was coined in 1947. Thirty years earlier, Fort had collected notes on lights and objects seen dancing, speeding, and hovering in the skies. He wondered then if they were alien vehicles or 'super-constructions' as he called them, or if some might be unknown forms of natural phenomena.

Teleportation

In *Book of the Damned*, Fort coined the term 'teleportation,' which he saw as a primary force that distributes, instantaneously, matter, objects, and life forms throughout the universe. He was aware of the phenomenon of 'apports' (objects that materialize in the seance room) and felt that this related in some way to reports of the things mysteriously transported or projected through the air during 'hauntings.'

In the beginning, he speculated, teleportation was extremely active, but as life and matter became more evenly distributed among inhabitable worlds, the need for such a force lessened. Eventually, it became vestigial, functioning erratically.

Teleportation could account for the sudden appearance of animals far from their usual habitats, or the appearance of fish in a freshly-dug pond. The teleportive force might also occasionally come under human control: poltergeist phenomena, levitation, bilocation, or psychokinesis could perhaps occur consciously. Many of these ideas were seized upon by US science fiction and fantasy writers.

Today oddity reports are mostly absent from the scientific journals—where Fort found most of his data—and are used as small filler paragraphs in the newspapers, written inaccurately and for laughs. Fort's work is continued in the United States by the International Fortean Organization (founded 1966), and in the United Kingdom by the magazine *Fortean Times* (founded 1973).

ROBERT RICKARD

Freud

The father of psychoanalysis, Sigmund Freud can be ranked with Darwin (1809–82) and Einstein (1879–1955), as one of the giants of the last 200 years whose work has radically changed Western concepts about the human animal, his environment, and the relationship between the two. The extent to which Freud revolutionized conventional thought is apparent in the way in which it is now axiomatic that there are large regions of the mind of which people are normally quite unconscious, yet which have a direct influence on their conscious behaviour. And yet in the nineteenth century it was equally generally accepted that a person's character could be adequately deduced purely from his outward actions and behaviour. When in the 1890s Freud dared to uncover hidden motivations and when moreover he linked these with sexual drives, his ideas were attacked for being not only impossible but also indecent.

This attitude, although deeply rooted at the time, has not always been the accepted one. The phenomenon of man's ignorance of the unconscious aspects of the mind, in terms of the whole of human history, is a brief aberration. To understand what happens at these normally unconscious levels has never been easy, but the fact that these levels do exist has seldom been so steadfastly ignored as it was at this period. For several centuries Europe had forgotten almost as thoroughly as if it had never known what the religious, mystical, and esoteric schools of East and West had always taught: that invisible and subtle levels of perception, even if not conscious, can influence human behaviour and states of mind; that the consciousness of these subtler or more fruitful perceptions can be obscured by a fog compounded of selfishness, fear, and willfully immature demands of the personality; that dreams are messages from those unconscious regions of the mind whose myths and symbols embody instructive material that can dispel the fog.

This has been the concern of various so-called religious and mystical schools throughout human history and this essentially is the nature of Freud's contribution. Considered from this point of view, therefore, Freud

was not the innovator and inventor of the ideas that have so captivated and caged twentieth century thought, but his achievement was rather to re-introduce certain concepts that had been forgotten and, most important, to be the first man to find a way to scientifically explore the working of the human mind.

Search for the Inner Mind

Sigmund Freud was born at Freiberg, Moravia, in 1856, the son of an unsuccessful Jewish wool merchant. He spent most of his life in Vienna, but in 1938 when the Nazis annexed Austria, he escaped to London where he died in 1939 at the age of eighty-three. He studied to be a doctor and specialized in neurology, making a name for himself by isolating a form of paralysis, later called after him, and by the co-discovery of the local anaesthetic effects of cocaine. In 1884 he became interested in the therapeutic uses of hypnosis, upon which he was to build his theories of psychoanalysis. In 1895 he and his colleague, Josef Breuer (1842–1925), published *Studies in Hysteria*, in which the two men examined the results of work in which they had used hypnosis to probe the minds of their patients. At the time this was a remarkably humane approach to hysteria, which was normally treated with a brutal lack of sympathy.

Shortly after the publication of this book, Freud quarrelled with Breuer and continued his research alone. He gave up the use of hypnosis in favour of 'free association,' in which patients were asked to relax on a couch and say whatever came into their minds, however absurd, unpleasant, or obscene it might appear by everyday standards. When that was done it seemed that powerful emotional drives swept the uncontrolled thoughts toward the area of psychological conflict. Great relief —'catharsis'—

seemed to follow and Freud noticed that frequently forgotten and painful memories were found to relate to unpleasant, buried sexual experiences in childhood.

At about this time he also discovered a fruitful source of emotionally significant ideas in his patients' dreams, and decided that there must be some truth in the ancient theory that dreams had symbolic meaning and that they appeared to be disguised forms of repressed desires and needs. 'Instead of dreaming about a penis,' writes G. A. Miller (1920–2012) in his recent book *Psychology*, 'the dreamer may substitute the image of a gun, a snake, a fountain pen, the number three, and so on. For masturbation the dream symbol may be climbing a tree or playing the piano. By recognizing these substitutions, therefore, it is possible to recover the true meaning of the dream.'

This passage indicates well the particular prejudice through which Freud filtered many of his ideas. The over-emphasis on sexual interpretation that he gave to almost every human motive from infancy onward may in fact have been the product of his own personal obsession; colleagues and contemporaries have noted that Freud himself was a puritanical and inhibited man. Perhaps he exaggerated partial truth to look like a universal state of affairs, and he would have been encouraged in this by having to contend with the sexual repressions of the times.

In the summer of 1897, after the death of his father, Freud decided to apply to himself the techniques he had formulated. Using his own dreams as the principal source of study, he worked to discover the unconscious processes that were responsible for forming them. He published his major account of this work in 1900 in *The Interpretation of Dreams* and it took eight years to sell the first 600 copies. Apart from a small group of 'disciples' no one seemed interested, yet today this book is considered his most important work, and the final chapter contains the theory of the human mind that he was to amplify and develop in the period ahead.

The practice of free association had led him to make discoveries about various psychoneuroses that threw light on the workings of the normal mind. The three most fundamental were: the existence of the unconscious and its effect on the conscious; the splitting of the mind into layers as the result of internal conflict, the most important of which is repression; and the existence and importance of infantile sexuality, producing a sexual attitude toward its parents, with its accompanying jealousy and hostility, which he termed the Oedipus complex, from the ancient Greek myth of Oedipus.

In his early work Freud used a simple twofold distinction between the conscious and unconscious mind.

Later he described the total personality as organized into three major systems—the id, concerned with the funneling of energies and tensions; the ego, which is the administrative, daily self that deals with the interactions of the personality with the environment; and the superego, which represents the conscious or the moral aspects of the personality, which passes judgments. Toward the end of his life Freud formulated two groups of instincts that provide energy for the id. One served the purposes of life and growth, and was called the libido. The second arose in the service of death—the 'death wish.'

The unconscious automatically 'represses' knowledge or feelings that upset the conscious mind, without necessarily being harmful to the personality. In some cases however, the repression seeks an outlet in a different form, frequently some type of inconsistent or unstable behaviour. The function of psychoanalysis in this case is to uncover and release the repression.

By the amplification of his elaborate theory on the development and maturing of the sexual instincts, he forced people to examine the idea that sex does not suddenly appear at puberty, but exists from infancy. He believed that the child's sexual gratifications came from different areas —'erogenous zones'—at different ages, and that in unfortunate circumstances, a child can become 'fixed' at an infantile stage, and by so doing develop personality traits corresponding to that particular level.

Freud and the Cabala

Although philosophers and poets in the past had guessed at the existence of the unconscious (indeed ten years before Freud's birth, Karl Carus (1789 –1869), court physician to the King of Saxony, had stated that the key to the understanding of the life of the mind would be found in the region of the unconscious), Freud, with his techniques of dream analysis, free association, attention to symbolism, and probing for buried memories, was the

Landscape from a Dream by **Paul Nash (1889–1946)**

first to discover a method of exploring this area. Undoubtedly his ideas were subject to influences in the climate of his time, including many forces that were later to be labeled 'Freudian.'

There was another more specific and powerful influence in his own background: the tradition of Jewish mysticism and the Cabala. David Bakan (1921–2004), in *Sigmund Freud and the Jewish Mystical Tradition* says:

Freud often wrote with obscurity . . . motivated consciously or unconsciously to hide the deeper portions of his thought, and these deeper portions were Kabbalistic in their source and content. The Kabbalistic tradition has it that the secret teachings are to be transmitted orally to one person at a time, and even then only to selected minds by hints. This indeed is what Freud was doing in the actual practice of psychoanalysis, and this aspect of the Kabbalistic tradition is still maintained in the education of the modern psychoanalyst.

Bakan attempts to show that many of Freud's unacknowledged sources were Cabalistic. He quotes a passage of the *Zohar*, a Jewish mystical book of the thirteenth century, and sets it next to a passage of Freud's work, pointing out as he does so that the differences between the two texts are readily explicable in terms of Freud's own theories of substitution and symbolism.

Even if Freud had been conscious of the role Jewish mysticism played in his work, as Bakan points out there were excellent reasons for not specifying the tradition. 'Anti-semitism' he writes, 'was so widespread and intense at the time that to indicate the Jewish sources of his ideas would have dangerously exposed an intrinsically controversial theory to unnecessary and possibly fatal opposition.'

Certainly, although Freud's theories were unequivocally materialistic and nothing approaching mysticism was allowed to disorder the psychoanalytic scheme of things, Freud himself showed an interest in subjects such as telepathy and extra-sensory perception. He looked for prophetic dreams in his patients—though found none—and was fascinated by the meaningful recurrence of certain numbers in his life. Several interchanges between Jung (1875–1961) and Ferenczi (1873–1933), men who were more interested in the occult than Freud, suggest that he may have cut short a growing fascination for the mysterious and magical because it would have interfered with the organization of his own theories. Indeed in a letter late in life to the psychical researcher Hereward Carrington (1880–1958), Freud went so far as to say: 'If I had my life to live over again I should devote myself to psychical research rather than psychoanalysis.'

Sigmund Freud and the Jewish Mystical Tradition

Apart from restoring the idea of the unconscious to Western culture, Freud's other important contribution was to produce a technical vocabulary more acceptable to his time—'repressions' and 'complexes' rather than 'devils' and 'spells'—with which to begin to isolate concepts and mental 'sets' that folklore and superstition encompassed but did not understand.

After the initial derision and opposition Freud's concepts became so cemented into the structure of contemporary thought that it was difficult to be sure if any concept was entirely uninfluenced by his ideas. They permeated everything, for the ideas he tapped were potent, and inevitably were not contained within the confines of medicine and mental disorders, which were his special field. They spread into every sphere of contemporary life, and influenced the way in which Western society came to regard the arts, the social sciences, social reform, child rearing, and every problem regarding human relationships.

Freud and the Jewish Mystics

We find a conception of sexuality which is startlingly close to Freud's in the Kabbalistic tradition . . . Never in the Jewish tradition was sexual asceticism made a religious value. The commandment to be fruitful and multiply was always taken extremely seriously in both rabbinical and mystical traditions. In contrast with other ascetic forms of mysticism, the Jewish mystics ascribed sexuality to God himself. The Jewish Kabbalist saw in sexual relations between a man and his wife a symbolic fulfilment of the relationship between God and the Shekinah . . . It is to be noted that the ideal form of sexuality is conceived of as heterosexual, and in particular as realized in marriage. Marital sexuality becomes the symbol of creativity. Thus Freud's use of the idiom of sexuality as the basic one for the expression of all the deeper and more profound problems of mankind is entirely in the spirit of the Kabbala.

David Bakan

It is only recently that it has become much clearer that Freud's explanations do not account satisfactorily for all human needs; that though his insights and techniques can be valuable, a deeper human hunger seems to lie underneath the levels of being with which he is concerned. Jung showed almost contemporaneously with Freud that if there are many things in our own personalities we are unconscious of, there are also lying beneath these, as it were, vast unknown areas which we hold in common.

PAT WILLIAMS

FURTHER READING: S. Freud. A General Introduction to Psychoanalysis's trans. James Strachey. (London, UK: Macmillan). J. Abramson. Liberation and Its Limits. (London, UK: Macmillan, 1984); B. Bettelheim. Freud and Man's Soul. (New York, NY: Knopf, 1983); S. Draenos. Freud's Odyssey. (New Haven, CT: Yale University Press, 1982); E. Fromm. The Greatness and Limitations of

Freud's Thought. *(New York, NY: Harper & Row, 1980)*; H. Kung. Freud and the Problem of God. *(New Haven, CT: Yale University. Press, 1980)*; G. A. Miller. Psychology: The Silence of Mental Life. *(New York, NY: Harper & Row, 1962)*; Lionel Trilling. Freud and the Crisis of Our Culture. *(Boston, MA: The Beacon Press, 1955)*.

Uri Geller

A young Israeli who sprang to prominence on television in 1973, Uri Geller (b. 1946) initiated a worldwide controversy that still continues. He claimed to be able to bend a range of metallic objects such as spoons and keys, and to be able to stop and start watches and clocks, solely by 'mind power.' He apparently successfully demonstrated this ability in the studio, and set off a wave of similar phenomena, particularly among children.

Most remarkable were the hundreds of claims that broken watches had started of their own accord, and household cutlery had been found inexplicably bent in many homes where his television performances had been viewed.

A number of distinguished scientists requested permission to investigate Geller under controlled laboratory conditions, and subsequently reported that his claims appeared to have been fully validated. Subsequent investigations into many of these experiments, however, suggested that his movements had not been observed with sufficient care, and the former stage conjuror James Randi (b. 1928), who had set himself up as a virulent investigator of psychic phenomena, was able to demonstrate, also on television, that he could replicate many of Geller's feats with ease.

Uri Geller was taken up by the parapsychologist Andrija Puharich (1918–95), and at one time claimed

that his powers dated from a day in his childhood when a 'dome of light' had landed close by him—a tale that he later denied in his autobiography.

Following the furore provoked by the claims and counterclaims of his supporters and detractors, Geller gave up his international stage demonstrations and retired from public view for a number of years. He later reappeared, apparently a millionaire, and claiming that he had earned his wealth by map-dowsing with a pendulum for mineral deposits such as copper and gold in distant parts of the world.

Germanen Order

The chief significance today of the Germanen Order, which flourished from 1912, lies in the fact that some of its members had connections with the early National Socialist Movement, and that it cherished so may of the myths that prevailed in extremist German nationalist circles. For instance, there was the delusion that the truly German master race (*Herrenvolk*) was descended from heroic Nordic ancestors who were fair haired and blue eyed, representing a racial ideal. Then there was the obsessive belief in the existence of a 'Jewish peril.' Jewry as a whole was said to represent a worldwide conspiratorial movement, and there were many who believed in the existence of a small, secret, and immensely powerful international group of Jews who sought to rule the world. Freemasonry was supposed to be dominated by Jews, so this also represented an international conspiracy.

There were several reasons for the decision to establish the Order on pseudo-masonic lines. Unconsciously, at least, there was the desire to use their opponents' 'magic,' in the form of rituals. Also, they supposed that secrecy was essential to prevent the Order being penetrated by Jews.

The founders of the Order were all obsessional anti-Semites. They included Theodor Fritsch (1852–1933), publisher of the anti-Semitic periodical *Hammer*, Philipp Stauff (1876–1923), an obscure journalist, Professor Heinrich Kräger (1870–1945), and Herman Pohl, who was probably a renegade Freemason.

Candidates for membership of the Berlin lodge of the Germanen Order had their skulls measured with a 'platometer' to make sure that they conformed to the Order's 'Nordic' racial ideals: thirty years later Heinrich Himmler (1900–45) organized a similar measuring operation on Russian prisoners.

The only known copy of an initiation ritual of the Germanen Order is preserved at the German Federal Archives. While the candidate waits in an adjoining room the Master and his two Knights take their places. They are clad in white robes and wear helmets adorned with Wotan's horns. 'The Master of the Music' sits at the harmonium and the Lodge members enter singing the Pilgrims' Chorus from Wagner's *Tannhäuser*. The candidate, who is blindfolded and wears a pilgrim's mantle, is brought into the Lodge room. He listens to a solemn address from the Master and is informed that what separates him from the Hebrews and members of other inferior races is 'our Ario-Germanic concept of the world and life.' The Bard ignites a sacred flame and the bandage is removed from the candidate's eyes. The Master takes Wotan's holy spear and holds it in front of him. His two Knights cross their swords upon it. Meanwhile the Music Master plays extracts from *Lohengrin*.

The Order was more or less inactive during the World War I. In 1916, Hermann Pohl made an undignified exit and founded a rival order. The original Germanen Order became active again in 1919; the Grand Duke

The Drummer of Tedworth. The tale of the Drummer of Tedworth (told by Thomas Glanville) recounted that local landowner John Mompesson discovered that his house was plagued by drumming noises at night, which were assumed to have been inflicted on the unfortunate landowner by the drummer through witchcraft. A possible early documented example of a poltergeist (c. 1681).

never a member of the Germanen Order and had no use for it. Indeed, when he came to power previous membership of the Order precluded an individual from attaining any rank in the National Socialist Party.

After 1922 the history of the Order is obscure. It is possible that it was obliged to dissolve or go underground.

ELLIC HOWE

Ghost Hunting

The enthusiastic pursuit of a quarry is an occupation as old as human history, but those who are involved in the activity of ghost hunting have as their target a phenomenon whose very nature renders it hard to capture and even harder to quantify.

Apparitions of various kinds are richly represented in both folklore and literature worldwide even featuring in operas such as Wagner's *The Flying Dutchman* and Benjamin Britten's *The Turn of the Screw*, based on a story by Henry James (1843–1916), which has a particularly malevolent and unsavory twist. The 1984 film, *Ghostbusters*, presented a comic treatment of the subject, and the large number of films dealing with paranormal experiences and investigations in the past thirty years have stimulated popular interest. Reports of ghost sightings are generally associated with specific locations, houses, and battlefields. For example, the sites of habitation or particular events, and the United Kingdom with its long and well-documented history is seemingly well endowed in this respect. The Tower of London, an ancient royal fortress that was also a prison, is reputed to be one of the most haunted places in Britain.

Dismissed as pseudoscience by the academic community, the subject of ghost hunting nevertheless continues to exert fascination. It has a long pedigree, and one of the earliest cases of

Johann Albrecht of Mecklenburg (1857–1920), a prototype German nationalist, was Grand Master. In 1920 the three 'secret chiefs' of the Order were General von Heimerdinger, Dr. Bernhard Koerner, a member of the former Prussian College of Heralds, and Eberhard von Brockhusen, a Pomeranian landowner. The latter was as much anti-Polish as anti-Semitic. It is clear from surviving documents that he and Koerner were followers of Guido von List (1848–1919), the Viennese occultist; also that much of the Order's lunatic teaching came from this source.

However, while the Order's leaders were conducting their eccentric ceremonies, links were being made with such right-wing conspiratorial groups as the notorious Organization Consul. At Munich early in 1919, members of Pohl's splinter group, led by Baron Rudolf von Sebottendorff, were deeply involved in the right-wing opposition to the short-lived Communist regime. Some of Sebottendorff's people had close links with the German Workers' Party, which Hitler (1889–1945) joined in 1919 and speedily transformed into the National Socialist German Workers' Party. Hitler was systematic investigation of supernatural events was written by Joseph Glanvill (1636–80), a young clergyman. In 1662, he was appointed to the living of Frome Selwood in Somerset, in the southwest of England. He had grown up in a period of extreme religious and political unrest—a civil war had resulted in the execution of the king and the abolition of the monarchy with the establishment of a republic in its stead. The restoration of the monarchy in 1660 ushered in a very different era: this was the beginning of the age of scientific enquiry, but it was also still an age of superstition and belief in witchcraft. Glanvill was elected to the Royal Society in 1664, a prestigious body of individuals distinguished in various branches of learning.

Glanvill wrote a detailed account of the case known as the Tedworth Drummer that was published in his in 1668 book *A Blow at Modern Sadducism In Some Philosophical Considerations about Witchcraft*. Now known as Tidworth, Tedworth, on the border of Hampshire and Wiltshire, was the home of a landowner, John Mompesson, who in 1662 was responsible for the arrest of a drummer who had attempted to obtain money falsely from the constable of a neighbouring village. The drummer was later freed but his drum was removed to Mompesson's house and it was then that the unusual and unexplained happenings began. Strange knockings were heard, both in and outside the building, objects moved, apparently of their own volition, and bedclothes were pulled off the bed of one of the servants while he was asleep. The activity became more intense and violent and at this stage Glanvill spent a night in the house. When the sounds began as usual, Glanvill went to investigate. He could find no physical explanation and decided that this was spirit activity of some sort, a form of witchcraft,

a conviction strengthened the next day when he went to collect his horse before leaving. He found the animal in a state of exhaustion as though it had been ridden all night; it died two days later. The case of the 'Tedworth Drummer' became so notorious that even Charles II (1630–85) sent two members of his court to investigate. By the end of the following year, the strange occurrences had ceased. Glanvill combined both a belief in unexplained phenomena with the intention that they should be subject to rational scrutiny.

The case of the haunting of a house at Hinton Ampner in southern England is set down in an account written by Mary Ricketts. Mary and her husband had taken a lease of the property in 1765 but their stay there began to be interrupted by a series of inexplicable occurrences. By 1769 Mary was living alone in the house with her children and servants, her husband William away on business. The sound of doors being shut noisily at night, the rustle of a woman's silk dress, loud footsteps, crashes, blood-curdling shrieks, what seemed to be many voices murmuring, and the glimpse of strange figures even in broad daylight became commonplace, and terrifying. When Mary's brother, Captain John Jervis (later Admiral of the Fleet and first Earl of St. Vincent, a distinguished commander who saw action in a number of theatres including the American War of Independence), came to stay, he was concerned by what his sister told him. Together with his valet and a neighbour, he decided to try and ascertain the truth of the matter and to get to the source of the disturbances—in effect to conduct a ghost hunt. The family then organized themselves so that every room in that part of the house under investigation was occupied. Night came, the doors were shut and locked to ensure that no one could enter from outside, and

the group waited. The sounds started as usual—doors opening and shutting, groans and footsteps—but the source could not be identified. Even Mary's sceptical brother was shaken. Mary and her family went to live elsewhere. Subsequently the house was revealed to have a history of unexplained happenings and apparent supernatural activity. Eventually it was demolished and another built some 150 feet away from it. There is some evidence that the events at Hinton Ampner provided the inspiration for Henry James' terrifying story, *The Turn of the Screw*.

In the mid-nineteenth century there was enormous interest in spiritualism and a number of small organizations were set up to investigate further. In 1882 the Society for Psychical Research was founded to objectively and scientifically enquire into the circumstances of unexplained phenomena. Its serious tone was evident in the choice of its first president, Henry Sidgwick (1838–1900), the Professor of Moral Philosophy at the University of Cambridge.

Modern ghost hunters arms themselves with a battery of electronic equipment including Geiger counters, cameras, and thermal imaging equipment in attempts to detect and measure alleged supernatural occurrences. The activity has provided a rich seam of inspiration for the entertainment industry, including a reality television series in the United States.

ELIZABETH LOVING

Gurdjieff

Born in Alexandropol, near the Persian frontier of Russia in about 1877, of a Greek father and an Armenian mother, George Ivanovitch Gurdjieff was brought up in an antique, patriarchal world where children were put to sleep at night with the story of

Gilgamesh, the great hero of Sumerian and Babylonian epic poetry. While he was still a very young man, Gurdjieff 'disappeared' into that cauldron of history, tradition, and ideas that we know as the Middle East. Indeed, in his second book, *Meetings with Remarkable Men*, he describes an even wider orbit, taking in the Gobi Desert, Mecca, and Tibet; but in this case the names may stand either for places or for symbols in his unremitting search for a 'real and universal knowledge.' 'I was not alone,' his disciple, the Russian writer P. D. Ouspensky (1878–1947) quotes him as saying. 'There were all sorts of specialists among us. We called ourselves "The Seekers of Truth."' Ouspensky recorded his first meeting with Gurdjieff as having taken place in the autumn of 1914. 'I realized,' he wrote, 'that I had met with a completely new system of thought surpassing all I had known before. This system threw quite a new light on psychology and explained what I could not understand before in esoteric ideas.'

During the first two years of the World War I, Gurdjieff elaborated his teachings to groups in St. Petersburg and Moscow but with the onset of the Russian Revolution, flight was inevitable. His journey with his followers through Russia to the Caucasus, then to Constantinople, and at last to the West, has all the elements of a modern thriller. It is given an epic quality and an extra dimension by the fact that Gurdjieff used the hardships and dangers—always for him the true stuff of existence—to exemplify his teaching, and required of his pupils that they should escape not merely with their lives but with their Life. It was not until 1922 that he succeeded in bringing to the West what he had found in the East, by establishing his pilgrim band at the Chateau du Prieure, near

Fontainebleau, where he founded his Institute for the Harmonious Development of Man.

Gurdjieff never openly disclosed the source of his teaching. By examining his writings and the numerous commentaries upon them it might be possible to discover parallels in various traditions but the fundamental features of his method cannot be traced to any one source. Ouspensky quotes him as admitting 'I will say that, if you like, this is esoteric Christianity.' In fact, there seems to be no reason to

His impact was tremendous. It was clear that he had come not to bring peace but a special kind of inner warfare . . .

reject this when one remembers that Christianity, as Gurdjieff knew it, was the heir to centuries of religious tradition and must have drawn into itself early pre-Christian Hittite, Assyrian, Phrygian, and Persian elements; and that there is nothing so explosive as old ideas restated in contemporary terms—as the Western world was to discover when Gurdjieff burst upon it.

Intentional Suffering

His impact was tremendous. It was clear that he had come not to bring peace but a special kind of inner warfare, and that his mission in life was to destroy men's complacency and make them aware of their limitations. Only by such means, by what he called 'Conscious labours and intentional suffering,' was it possible to bring about man's inner development. It very soon appeared that the Work, as his method came to be called, had been only too accurately named. Writers, artists, and men and women from all kinds of professions found

themselves digging wells, chopping down trees, and breaking stones by day, while at night they were required to take part in sacred dances or 'Movements,' or to assist at one of Gurdjieff's great feasts where, under the influence of good food, vodka, and the watchful eye of the Master, opportunities were provided for those who had the courage to come face to face with themselves.

By 1924, the Work was sufficiently well established for Gurdjieff to set out on the first of his visits to the United States where in January, in New York, a group of forty pupils gave demonstrations of his Movements. Two-thirds of these evenings were devoted to the sacred dances, and the remainder to what was described as 'Trick, Semi-Trick, and Real Supernatural Phenomena.' The audience was invited to distinguish between them and reminded that 'the study of the first two was held to be indispensable to the study of the third, since to understand the last a perfectly impartial attitude and a judgement not burdened by pre-established beliefs were necessary.'

It is clear from Gurdjieff's writings that hypnotism, mesmerism, and various arcane methods of expanding consciousness must have played a large part in the studies of the Seekers of Truth. But none of these processes had any bearing on black magic, which according to Gurdjieff 'has always one definite characteristic. It is the tendency to use people for some, even the best of aims, without their knowledge and understanding, either by producing in them faith and infatuation or by acting upon them through fear. There is, in fact, neither red, green, nor yellow magic. There is "doing." Only "doing" is magic.' Properly to realize the scale of what Gurdjieff meant by magic, one has to remember his continually repeated aphorism, 'Only he who can *be* can do;' and its corollary that, without 'being' nothing is 'done,' things simply 'happen.'

The US tour brought a new influx of pupils to the Prieure and, as usual, Gurdjieff, by deliberate indirection, set them to find directions out. 'The teaching,' wrote one pupil, 'was given in fragments—often in unexpected ways—and we had to learn to put the pieces together and connect them up through our observations and experiences.' It was in the late summer of 1924, that Gurdjieff, slowly reassembling his forces after a near-fatal car accident, began to put those separated fragments together in a book.

While helping the pupils who remained, Gurdjieff wrote incessantly at Fontainebleau, on his frequent motoring trips, or seated at a table in the Cafe de la Paix in Paris, where he had long been a familiar figure.

Called *All and Everything*, the book attempts to cover every aspect of the life of man. Into it Gurdjieff gathered the fundamentals of his teaching. Man, we are told, has a unique function in the cosmological scheme and enters into obligation by the very fact of being born. But the awareness of this is not a gift of Nature; and neither are individuality, consciousness, free will, or an immortal soul. These attributes, which man mistakenly believes he already possesses, have to be acquired by his own special efforts. Above all, the book repeatedly insists that man is asleep. It is only at the moment when he wakes, not merely to consciousness but also to conscience—indeed, for Gurdjieff, the words were synonymous—that his true evolution can begin.

Monsieur Bonbon

The manuscript, constantly revised, now became the focal point of the teaching, not only in France but also in New York during his two visits to the United States in 1929 and 1933. In the latter year, the Prieure was sold and his life entered another phase. Gurdjieff never stood still but was always growing, always experimenting, always searching. After enjoying his fame for nine years, he seems to have retired into the shadows, clearly for reasons of his own. 'He is no longer teaching,' said his older pupils when new people wanted to make direct contact with him. One of his pet tenets was that the Work was designed not to discover something new but to recover that which is lost, and an intrepid few set out to do just that. If Gurdjieff accepted them as pupils, they were put into small intimate groups, each member depending upon the others, like mountain climbers upon a rope, no group having any connection with the others. Gurdjieff's teaching was essentially intimate and personal, and his insistence that by the very nature of the Work he could not have many pupils, appears valid and inevitable.

The published reminiscences of various members of these small groups bear witness to the fact that he was, indeed, teaching in the '30s; but quietly, as though it were a question of holding his powers in reserve. Those who knew Gurdjieff as a teacher could gather only by rumour and hearsay that there were other Gurdjieffs: the healer of psychic illnesses, the curer of alcoholism, the business man, and the Gurdjieff known as 'Monsieur Bonbon,' an old eccentric gentleman whose sole mission in life, it appeared, was to dispense candy to local cronies and children.

In 1939 Gurdjieff again visited United States, a country that he held in affectionate regard because of its

Russian philosopher George Ivanovitch Gurdjieff (1877–1949)

'brotherliness.' On his return to Paris, war was close and when it broke out, Gurdjieff disappeared from the sight of all but his French pupils until the Liberation. It is said that he sustained himself during those lean years by putting about the rumour that he was heir to a Texan oil well. Nobody was more surprised than the French shopkeepers to find, when his British and US pupils streamed back and paid the bills, that the story was essentially true.

The year 1946 marked the beginning of the last phase of his teaching, a period that, for those who had known him earlier, was richer than any that had gone before. For a little over three years new adherents and old pupils who brought their own pupils and children, flocked to his small room to listen to a reading from one of his manuscripts, *All and Everything; Meetings with Remarkable Men; Life is Real Only When I Am;* to hear him play on his small, hand accordion the music he had composed for the different chapters; or to receive the bounty of his teaching in whatever form it might be given. 'If take, then take, no sipping, no trifling,' was one of his favourite aphorisms and for many the special nourishment that was offered in addition to the delicious edibles was indigestible, hard to stomach.

The exotic flavours and the vodka in which the famous 'Toasts to the Idiots' were drunk ('idiot' in this case having its original Greek meaning of private person) did not make things easier. But easiness was not the aim. The patriarchal host, massive of presence, radiating a serene power at once formidable and reassuring, dispensed this 'food' in various ways, always unexpected; sometimes in thunderclaps of rage, sometimes telling a story that only one of all the table would know was meant for himself, sometimes merely by look or gesture thrusting home the truth. Masks were mercilessly stripped off. Beneath the exacting benevolence of Gurdjieff's gaze everyone was naked.

Occasionally for those who could face their own situations, he would fleetingly let fall his own mask. It was possible then to see that behind the apparent mercilessness was sorrow and compassion. At such moments his 'humanity-ness' (a key word in his odd vocabulary) would radiantly declare itself. If his aim was to teach men how to rise to the possibility of saying 'I am,' he never forgot that 'thou art' and 'he is' complete the conjugation.

'Man Must Live Till He Dies'

In addition to the activities in his own apartment, Gurdjieff now instituted at the Salle Pleyel daily practices of the Movements that were so essential a part of his teaching. It was not only in Paris that the Work progressed so vigorously year by year. There were groups in England and the United States and others were now established in Holland, Sweden, Germany, and South America. During what was to be his last visit to the United States, on January 13, 1949, Gurdjieff announced that he was ready to publish *All and Everything.* At the same time, those English disciples who had joined the Paris groups after Ouspensky's death in 1947, arranged for the publication of *In Search of the Miraculous,* Ouspensky's long withheld account of his early years with Gurdjieff.

These two books, the first giving an added dimension to the second, and the second clarifying the first, opened up the teaching. Gurdjieff's health was now faltering but such was his powerhouse of inner strength that few could believe it. Throughout the summer, after his return from New York, the Work went on with added intensity. While serenely putting his own house in order, Gurdjieff used every moment as a moment of teaching, and

every aspect of his fading strength as a reminder to his pupils that 'Man must live till he dies.' In Gurdjieff's sense, to 'live' was consciously to labour and voluntarily to suffer. This he himself did, with constancy and deliberation, until October 29, 1949.

Since his death his chosen pupils have carried on his work, and groups are to be found everywhere in the Western world. The Movements have been accurately documented in a series of films; his second book, *Meetings with Remarkable Men,* has been published and the third is in preparation. The sittings of time are likely to prove that these records are his proper monument. In them the man and his myth are one.

P. TRAVERS

FURTHER READING: G. I. Gurdjieff. All and Everything. *(New York, NY: Dutton, 1964); G. I. Gurdjieff.* Meetings with Remarkable Men. *(New York, NY: Dutton, 1963); J. G. Bennett.* Gurdjieff. *(New York, NY: Harper & Row, 1974); S. C. Nott.* Teachings of Gurdjieff. *(London, UK: Routledge, 1961); P. D. Ouspensky.* Psychology of

Mans Possible Evolution. *(New York, NY: Knopf, 1954); F. Peters.* Boyhood with Gurdjieff. *(Santa Barbara, CA: Capra Press, 1980); C. Wilson.* The War against Sleep: the Philosophy of Guidjieff. *(York Beach, ME: Weiser, 1980).*

Hare Krishna

A common sight in Western cities in the 1970s, from San Francisco to New York, London, and Paris, was a small group of young people in saffron-coloured robes, shuffling and swaying to the tapping of a drum and the reedy music of a flute, holding out begging bowls while chanting 'Hare Krishna Hare Krishna Hare Rama Hare Rama Hare Hare Hare.' The young men's heads were shaven and the group, with their faraway gaze, often appeared undernourished. Regarded by many on-lookers as tiresome or deluded, they were in fact the most visible demonstration of the dramatic impact of Hindu *bhakti yoga* upon the West.

Bhakti is the principle of loving devotion to a deity, in this case the god Krishna, revered as the Supreme God, and the *mantra*, or verbal formula, which the group recites with self-hypnotizing effect, is intended to induce a profound inner peace. The movement looks back to the sixteenth-century Indian guru Chaitanya (1486–1534) as its founder. A holy man and devotee of Krishna, he was given to strange fits and uncontrollable outbursts of weeping, laughing, running to and fro, or climbing up trees. He taught that chanting the name of the god and dancing to simple musical accompaniment led to an ecstatic communion between deity and worshipper.

Baba Bharati Premand introduced the bhakti of loving devotion to Krishna to the United States early in the twentieth century and founded

temples in New York and Los Angeles. The Hare Krishna movement itself was taken to New York in 1965 by Bhaktivedanta Swami Prabhupad (1896–1977), who founded the International Society for Krishna Consciousness. Prabhupad had his headquarters in Bombay, India, and was believed by his followers to be 500 years old and a reincarnation of Chaitanya. Members lived simply in vegetarian communities, owning nothing, refraining from drugs and alcohol, practicing chastity and pacifism. By the late 1980s they were seen less often on the streets and the movement had lost impetus.

Harry Houdini

The stage name of the great magician and illusionist has become a byword for the apparently supernatural ability to escape restraint under seemingly impossible conditions. Born Erik Weisz in 1874 in the Hungarian capital of Budapest, then part of the Austro-Hungarian Empire, the early years of the man who became known simply as Houdini—a name adapted from that of the Frenchman Jean Eugène Robert-Houdin (1805–71), considered to have invented the modern art of conjuring—were marked by the need to escape extreme poverty. His father, Mayer Samuel Weisz (1829–92), immigrated to the United States in 1876 to be joined two years later by his wife and children.

In 1878 after two years' search for work, Mayer found a post as a rabbi in Appleton, Wisconsin, but four years later he was dismissed, a personal and financial catastrophe that brought the family to the edge of destitution. In the struggle to survive, Mayer's sons were forced to pick up what work they could, the family relocating to New York. At various times, the young Ehrich Weiss sold newspapers, cleaned shoes, became a messenger

boy, and later joined his father working in a garment factory. Significantly, he also began an apprenticeship as a locksmith—a boyhood fascination with locks and keys put to practical use when he discovered how to release a lock on a pair of handcuffs by means of a piece of wire instead of a key. By the time he was seventeen, Ehrich had devised a magic act with another factory employee, Jacob Hayman, the two performing under the name of the 'Brothers Houdini,' with Ehrich now calling himself 'Harry Houdini,' the first name derived from his nickname, Ehrie. The act split up, but Houdini was embarked on the path he was to follow for the rest of his life, exploring and refining the art of the illusionist to an extent and in a way that had never been done before.

Houdini's Jewish background was by no means inconsistent with his passion for conjuring and magic. Dramatic performance was part of Jewish cultural life—Yiddish theatre was a rich and established tradition—and by the late nineteenth century, there were a large number of Jewish stage illusionists working in the United States, mostly migrants from Europe; indeed, the father of one friend, Tobias Bamberg (1875–1963), had been the official conjurer to the Dutch court, Tobias being the sixth generation of his family to work as a professional magician.

Jacob's place was taken by one of Houdini's brothers, Theo, but this partnership was again short-lived. In 1894, Ehrich met and married Wilhemina Beatrice Rahner from an immigrant German Roman Catholic family. Bess, as she was known, also had a love for the stage and was part of a song-and-dance act. Their courtship was extremely brief, and the

Opposite page:
Harry Houdini, King of Cards poster

slightly built Bess took Theo's place in Houdini's stage act which was based on the illusion known as Metamorphosis, whereby the magician locked his assistant into a trunk only to swap places so that the audience were presented with the apparently miraculous sight of the magician bound and locked in the trunk in place of the assistant. Houdini and Bess worked with a traveling circus, Houdini taking every opportunity to learn from the other performers, including the notorious trick of swallowing a large number of needles and then pulling them, threaded, from his mouth.

The development of Houdini's act as an escapologist began in 1895 where he demonstrated his ability to release himself from handcuffs, ensuring maximum publicity for his act by issuing challenges to the police authorities to truss him up using their own handcuffs from which he would escape. Despite his abilities and innovative ideas, these were hard years for Houdini and Bess and they came close to giving up the idea of a professional stage career. In 1899, this changed abruptly when Houdini was taken on by Martin Beck, manager of a chain of vaudeville theatres, and by 1900 Houdini was beginning the first of his overseas tours, appearing in London as 'The King of Handcuffs.' Over the next few years, his act expanded to include escape from ropes, chains, and straitjackets. Refinements were added, such as escape after jumping into rivers bound and chained, and a routine known as the 'Milk Can Escape' where Houdini was submerged in water inside a large metal can. This developed into the Water Torture Cell act whereby the magician was suspended upside down with his feet locked into stocks and lowered into a glass box filled with water. Each development came with increased

risk of injury or death and this risk was used as part of the publicity. One photograph shows Houdini hanging upside down suspended from a crane confined within a strait jacket high above the city streets over the heads of an expectant crowd. Another image is of a sealed crate, containing the manacled Houdini, being lowered into New York Harbor, from which he was able to free himself, coming up to the surface of the water beside the crate.

> *The 'extravert' is one whose interests and emotions are directed predominantly toward the external world of Nature . . .*

The public nature of these acts ensured his increasing celebrity.

By the early part of the twentieth century Houdini was a master escapologist and possessor of both fame and fortune. He had escaped the uncertainty of his early life, and in 1913 he finally abandoned the name of Ehrich Weiss becoming Harry Houdini under US law.

His energy and creativity found other another outlet in the new medium of cinema. He appeared in several films including *The Master Mystery*, *The Grim Game*, and *Terror Island*, and started his own production company, but gave up after the failure of his film, *Haldane of the Secret Service*. He was also interested in the popular fascination with spiritualism, a fascination that had intensified with the huge loss of life on the battlefields of World War I, and the desire of grieving and vulnerable relatives and friends to contact the dead. As a professional illusionist, and one who had conducted 'seances' with Bess as part of his stage act in the early days,

Houdini understood how the public were often willing to believe the impossible if it was presented convincingly. After an encounter with the English writer Arthur Conan Doyle (1859–1930) who was a believer in spiritualism, Houdini went on to campaign vigorously against mediums as fraudulent individuals who were practicing deception.

In October 1926, while in his dressing room, Houdini received four hard blows to the abdomen delivered by a theology student who wanted to test the physical strength of the magician. Although Houdini apparently gave his consent to this, it seemed that he was unprepared for the assault. The next evening as he was sitting in a hotel lobby, he was punched again in the abdomen by a stranger, a completely unexpected assault. He collapsed after the show in Detroit and was taken to hospital where he was operated on for appendicitis. He developed peritonitis and died a few days later.

ELIZABETH LOVING

FURTHER READING: W. Kalush and L. Sloman. The Secret Life of Houdini—the Making of America's First Superhero. *(New York, NY: Atria Books, 2006); B. K. Rapaport.* Houdini: Art and Magic. *(New Haven, CT: Yale University Press, 2010).*

Jung

The most influential psychiatrist, after Freud (1856–1939), of the twentieth century has been Carl Gustav Jung. He was born at Kesswil, a Swiss hamlet near the falls of the Rhine in 1875. His grandfather, a Rosicrucian freethinker, was reputed to have been an illegitimate son of Goethe; exiled from Germany, he moved to Switzerland, and became professor of surgery at Basle. Jung's father was a pastor, whose hobby was philology. Jung took a medical degree at the University of Basle and then, like Freud before him, went to Paris to study psychological medicine. On his return he was appointed lecturer in the Psychiatric Clinic of Zurich University. His first important publication was a systematic report of a series of experimental studies, carried out by means of Galton's 'word association test' (during which the subject replies in turn to a disconnected series of words read out to him with the first word that comes into his mind). This led him to formulate the notion of a 'complex'—a cluster of emotionally toned ideas and memories all associated with some central theme and largely, if not wholly, unconscious.

In 1907 he met Freud, and for long remained his foremost disciple. However, his own psychiatric work soon led him to question some of Freud's fundamental principles. Freud, he believed, laid far too much stress on repressed sexual tendencies in the production of nervous disorders. Instead of seeking the main causes in forgotten infantile experiences, greater importance should be attached to the effects of emotional conflicts, and to the strains and stresses of the patient at the time of his breakdown. Jung's concept of the 'libido,' which in Freud's usage meant the energy of the sexual instincts, was that of a kind of general emotional energy, with sex, fear, anger, and the like as merely some of its specialized forms. His book on *The Psychology of the Unconscious* (1912) included criticisms too drastic for Freud to brook. This led to a final rupture a year later. Thereafter Jung preferred to call his theories and therapeutic methods 'analytical psychology,' leaving the older description 'psychoanalysis' to Freud and his more faithful followers.

Temperamental Types

Freud's aim was to develop a dynamical theory of mental structure and mental processes that would be universally applicable. Jung, on the other hand, largely as a result of his early experimental studies, became profoundly impressed by the influence of innate individual differences. These he sought to classify in terms of temperamental types. His first and best known distinction was between the 'extravert' and the 'introvert.' The 'extravert' is one whose interests and emotions are directed predominantly toward the external world of Nature and other persons; the 'introvert,' one whose interests and emotions are directed predominantly toward the inner world of the self and his own private thoughts and feelings. Later he proposed to subdivide mental processes into four primary activities—sensing, feeling, intuiting, and thinking. According as one or other of these activities tended to dominate the life of the extravert or the introvert, he was thus led to distinguish eight 'psychological types.' The contrast between the extravert and the introvert has since been abundantly confirmed by experimental and statistical research except that, instead of clear-cut 'types,' most present-day psychologists prefer to talk of 'tendencies,' varying in degree.

Perhaps the most characteristic feature in Jung's conception of the structure of the mind is his belief that below the 'personal unconscious' consisting of the half-forgotten relics of the individual's past experiences from infancy onward, there is the deeper layer of the 'collective unconscious,' which contains the persistent after-effects of the primitive experiences of the human race during the earlier phases of its evolution. Thus it includes not only what are commonly called instincts—the impulses of sex, fear, aggression, parental love, and the like—but also certain 'primordial

images' or ways of thinking, which Jung termed 'archetypes.' These he described as 'inherited complexes.' They may be discerned most clearly in the analysis of dreams; but they tend to mould all our attempts to interpret the universe as a whole—mythology, religion, philosophy, and even science.

One of the commonest archetypes is the so-called 'father figure,' often pictured as a wise and masterful old man, the representative of authority and power. Another is that of the Great Mother, the embodiment both of fertility and benevolent protection. The serpent or dragon commonly stands as a symbol of evil. As in heraldry, various animals—the lion or leopard, the sheep or lamb, the eagle and the raven—occur again and again as emblems of certain quasi-human characteristics. Some of the archetypal conceptions, however, are relatively abstract, for instance the polar opposites of male and female, hate and love, repulsion and attraction, which so often appear in both popular and scientific thought.

When Jung first developed his concept of innate archetypes, it was widely believed that acquired habits and ideas might eventually become hereditary, so that recurrent experiences of primitive man might be transmitted as part of our common racial inheritance. Today, almost every biologist rejects the theory that characteristics acquired by the individual can so affect the germ-plasm that they reappear in the offspring. There is no doubt about the frequent emergence of these symbolic concepts in the folklore, superstitions, and religions of widely separated races. Nevertheless, most contemporary anthropologists regard them as due, not to inheritance, but rather to the early diffusion of culture. Jung, in his later replies to biological critics, contended that his own theory of archetypes did not necessarily entail the direct inheritance of experience as such, and suggested that they might be an indirect effect of natural selection, operating during man's prehistoric evolution: as a result 'all human brains would to some extent be similarly differentiated.'

Secret of the Golden Flower

In the course of his therapeutic work Jung discovered that one of the commonest causes of nervous breakdown was 'loss of religious faith.' For this, the strictly materialistic and fatalistic outlook of Freud and his followers seemed to provide no cure. To combat this growing materialism Jung's main interest began to turn (as he expressed it) 'from therapy to the art of living.' Most of his later studies were concerned, not with psychiatry, but with topics that his colleagues and critics dismissed as 'antiquated superstition, unworthy of a genuine scientist's interest or attention'—alchemy, astrology, spiritualism, and popular folklore. Even if wholly false, so he maintained, the reasons for their widespread prevalence called for psychological investigation.

As a pastor's son, he had always been both interested in, and critical of, the traditional religion in which

he had been reared. Quite early in life his curiosity had been aroused by the accounts brought back by missionaries and others of the religions of the ancient East, particularly by the Chinese 'meditation school' and by Indian yoga, wondering whether they might be adapted for psychiatric treatment. In 1928 he published, jointly with Richard Wilhelm (1873–1930), an authority on Chinese philosophy, a book called *The Secret of the Golden Flower*. The 'secret' was the familiar conception that (in Jung's words) 'man is a cosmos in miniature, and is not divided from the Great Cosmos by any fixed limits; Tao, the Undivided, all-embracing ONE, gives "rise to two opposite reality-principles—Darkness and Light, Yin and Yang." The "Golden Flower" is a form of meditation aiming at their reconciliation. This suggested to him the idea of "individuation" as an aim both for psychotherapy and "the conduct of life."' 'Individuation' is his term for integrating the personality 'so that the person becomes in the true sense an "individual."'

But there seems to have been a more intimate reason for this radical change in the direction of his investi-

gations. In his autobiography *Memories, Dreams, and Reflections* (1963), he describes a quasi-mystical experience of his own during a serious illness at the beginning of 1944. When, according to his physician, he was actually at death's door, he felt himself caught up out of his body in a state of ecstasy into the remoter part of the heavens, and seemed on the point of entering an illuminated temple. 'The whole phantasmagoria of terrestrial existence was stripped from me; I became a historical fragment.' He wondered what would happen next and felt that as soon as he entered the temple he would receive the answer. At that moment he heard his doctor's voice recalling him to Earth. From the time of this experience he dated what he described as 'the second and most fruitful half of my long life.'

In the same book he related how he himself was apparently endowed with paranormal powers—telepathy, precognition, and psycho kinesis (psychic control over inanimate objects). Among other instances he recalls a discussion on parapsychology with Freud, who in those days rejected such ideas as nonsensical, though later he accepted them. On this occasion Jung twice demonstrated his powers to Freud; and an extant letter from Freud himself attests the 'poltergeist phenomenon' so produced. It was, he says, to gain a better understanding of his own mystical and paranormal experiences that he was driven to search for historical parallels. Suggestive explanations and examples he thought might be discovered in the writings of the early alchemists, such as 'the visions of Zosimos' (an Egyptian of the fourth century), and particularly the cryptic disquisitions of his own compatriot, Paracelsus. 'Here,' says Jung in his *Paracelsica*, 'seems to be the bridge that has led from early Gnosticism to the modern psychology of the unconscious.'

Portrait of the Swiss psychiatrist Carl Gustav Jung, who, in contrast to Freud, oriented his research toward the collective unconscious.

The Alchemical Heritage

'Alchemy,' he observes, 'has been called a dream of primitive medicine;' and, like ordinary dreams, he argued, its superficial or 'manifest content' might at once conceal and symbolize a deeper 'latent content.' It was by no means a mere bogus science practiced by mercenary charlatans. Philosophers such as St. Thomas Aquinas (1225–74), physicians such as Sir Thomas Browne (1605–82), scientists such as Sir Isaac Newton (1643–1727) had studied it. Like Gnosticism, alchemy appears to have originated in the Hellenistic culture of Alexandria in Egypt. The Egyptian metallurgists possessed the trade secrets of extracting and purifying the 'nobler metals,' gold and silver, for the wealthy, and cheaper imitations for those who could not afford the ornaments of the rich. The operations carried out in the laboratory were interpreted in terms of Aristotelian physics and Alexandrian Neo-Platonism (which also influenced early Christian doctrines). A leading conception was that the microcosm —the world of man—mirrored the macrocosm—the universe as a whole, with the heavenly bodies. Mesopotamian astrology thus became closely linked with alchemy. Each metal had its celestial counterpart: gold was associated with the sun, silver with the moon, quicksilver with mercury, and so on. To effect the 'great work' of transmutation, twelve successive laboratory processes, associated with the twelve signs of the zodiac, were necessary. And the astro-nomical symbols were borrowed to represent the chief chemical substances and processes.

As Jung points out, the explanatory theories, like those of the modern scientist, were often suggested by more or less fanciful analogies. Later alchemists were frequently physicians, and consequently thought of the chemical processes as analogous to those of human physiology and medicine. Just as lowlier animals had to be sacrificed, cleansed, and burned before they could live again as part of the human body, so the humbler metals had to be 'killed, washed, and fired' before re-emerging as nobler metals. Ideas were introduced from Chinese alchemists who regarded the transmutation of baser metals into silver and gold as of secondary importance; their own aim was rather to supplement the use of herbal medicines, which served to cure minor ailments, by a pill or elixir prepared from minerals and metals, which might confer immortality.

> *Each metal had its celestial counterpart: gold was associated with the sun, silver with the moon, quicksilver with mercury, and so on.*

All these ideas reappear in the writings of Paracelsus (1493–1541). Jung maintained that Paracelsus should be regarded, not only as the founder of iatrochemistry—the application of chemistry to medical theory—but also of psychological medicine, since he professed to cure not only physical but also psychical disorders as well. In its psychological aspect, he believed, Paracelsan alchemy is 'a path of salvation for the soul.' Jung was one of the first to emphasize the fact, which present-day historians of chemistry now fully recognize, that alchemy had both an exoteric or popular aspect and an esoteric or secret one. Exoteric alchemy was largely centered on the preparation of the Philosophers' Stone—a magical substance capable of converting lead, tin, and copper, not into a compound or alloy, but into 'purified' metals such as silver and gold; esoteric or mystical alchemy regarded these mundane transmutations as symbolic of a devotional system by which sinful man could be transformed into a perfect and immortal being.

Expressing the Inexpressible

Underlying the teaching of the esoteric school, so Jung contended, we can thus discern 'a profound philosophy, which is nothing if not practical, and therefore a religion rather than a science or a metaphysic.' The symbolism of the Judaeo-Christian religion was that of a sheep-rearing and agricultural community; and its symbols and rituals—bread and wine, the blood of the lamb, the sacrifice on the altar—seemed inappropriate to the bolder thinkers of the early Renaissance. They therefore sought to express their religion and their conception of the universe and man's destiny in what they took to be a more up-to-date and scientific symbolism. The reason why symbolism was necessary was not merely that the religious doctrines themselves would have been condemned as heretical, but because 'the inexpressible can only be expressed in terms of symbol and myth, parable and allegory.'

Jung made a couple of brief statistical studies to check predictions drawn from astrological horoscopes, and believed that on the whole the results confirmed them; but he fully recognized that his methods were too simple to carry conviction. Partly to explain the way in which celestial phenomena might affect human life, he put forward what he called the 'principle of synchronicity.' Natural science has commonly treated causation as the supreme explanatory principle; and causation implies temporal succession. However, events that are not successive but simultaneous may, he maintained, also be connected in a manner that appears intuitively meaningful. This supplementary principle

A portrait of Sir Isaac Newton, oil on canvas. By the English School (c. 1715–1720)

would furnish an explanation of such paranormal phenomena as telepathy and clairvoyance—examples of which he quotes, not only from the literature of psychical research, but also from his own experience.

In several of his writings he discusses the possibility of the survival of the individual mind or personality after death and of its preexistence in an earlier incarnation. On both these topics, he declares, he has no evidence of his own to offer. He thought it quite conceivable that the phenomena cited in support of such doctrines might really be no more than 'projections of the unconscious.' The most we can safely assert, he says, is summed up in a dictum of the US psychologist, William James (1842—1910): 'Whatever it may be on the *farther* side, the 'more' with which we seem to feel connected in religious and mystical experiences is on its *hither* side essentially a subconscious continuation of our own conscious life.'

CYRIL BURT

FURTHER READING:
H. Read, M. Fordham and G. Adler, ed. The Collected Works of C. G. Jung. *(Princeton, NJ: Princeton University Press, 1960-1979); C. G. Jung.* Memories, Dreams and Reflections. *(New York, NY: Random, 1965); V. Brom.* Jung: Man and Myth. *(New York, NY: Athenaeum, 1978); P. Homans.* Jung in Context. *(Chicago, IL: University of Chicago Press, 1979).*

Kirlian Photography

At some time during 1939, Semyon Kirlian (1898–1978), a Russian electrical engineer, was watching a patient in Krasnodar hospital receiving medical treatment by the use of a high-frequency electrical generator, at that time a new form of therapy. He noticed that, when the electrodes were brought close to the patient's skin, there was a glow of light, somewhat similar to that produced in a neon discharge tube.

Kirlian and his wife Valentina decided to investigate the phenomenon experimentally. They devised a simple set-up of two metal plates as electrodes, on one of which a photograph-ic plate was placed. Kirlian placed his hand between the two plates, and the high-frequency current was switched on. When the photographic plate was developed, it revealed the silhouette of Kirlian's hand with an aura of light surrounding the fingertips. The Kirlians then embarked upon an extensive series of experiments in which many materials, but particularly leaves and other plant matter, were investigated in the high-frequency field. They also

A fresh leaf produced an 'aura' full of light; but as the leaf died so the light went out.

devised an optical system that allowed them to observe the phenomena in motion.

Although the technique has now been attributed to Kirlian, it had been first reported in Russia forty years before, when the engineer Yakov Narkevich-Todko exhibited his 'electro photography' at the fifth exhibition of the Russian Technical Society in 1898. Even earlier, a Czech, B. Navratil, had coined the word in 1889; a French experimenter, H. Baravuc, produced electro-photographs of hands and leaves in 1896; and in 1939, still many years before the Kirlians published a report on their experiments, two other Czechs, S. Prat and J. Schlemmer, had published photographs of a similar glow surrounding leaves.

The principle lying behind what is now almost universally known as Kirlian photography is the corona discharge effect. When two plates, covered with a thin insulating material, are connected to a high-frequency oscillator such as a Tesla coil, the form of electrical discharge that occurs between them is not a spark but a generally distributed glow. This discharge can be affected by temperature, humidity, and other factors, and equally by objects placed between the plates.

The Kirlians first reported the results of their experiments in 1958, but their work remained virtually unknown until 1970, when the United States', Sheila Ostrander and Lynn Schroeder, published their book *Psychic Discoveries Behind the Iron Curtain*. This evoked only mild interest among scientific circles in the West, but sufficient to encourage the Russians to hold a conference on the subject at Kazakh State University in Alma-Ata in 1972.

What particularly excited delegates to the conference was the description by Kirlian of his observations on leaves. A fresh leaf produced an 'aura' full of light; but as the leaf died so the light went out. He also claimed that his methods had revealed the difference between a healthy leaf and one that was infected, although not yet showing any signs of infection.

The investigation was taken up early in the 1970s by Thelma Moss (1918–97) and Kendall Johnson at the Center for Health Sciences, University of California. They performed an extensive series of experiments, in the course of which they established that Kirlian photographs obtained from inanimate objects on separate occasions remained basically similar, but that living subjects produced widely varying results. This led them to postulate that there was a relationship between the corona and the physical or emotional state of the subject.

Support for this theory has come in recent years, as interest in the Kirlian phenomenon has grown. Experimenters have found that people's corona flares can change rapidly, becoming dramatic, for instance, when an attractive member of the opposite sex enters the room. And when subjects were given a glass of alcohol, in the words of one researcher, 'the flares lit up like a Christmas tree.' Following these investigations, claims have been made for the value of Kirlian photography to diagnose disease.

Various theories have been advanced to explain the phenomenon, with some enthusiasts comparing the corona flare with the etheric body or aura. The Russian experimenter V. M. Inyushin coined the term 'bio-plasmic body,' but this is little more than an attempt to give apparent scientific respectability to what remains, in effect, the concept of the human aura.

FURTHER READING: Robert Becker and Gary Selden. The Body Electric: Electromagnetism and the Foundation of Life. *(New York, NY: Quill/William Morrow, 1985); S. Krippner and D. Rubin.* Galaxies of Life. *(Newark, NJ: Gordon & Breach, 1973); S. Ostrander and L. Schroeder.* Psychic Discoveries Behind the Iron Curtain. *(Upper Saddle River, NJ: Prentice-Hall, 1970).*

Anton LaVey

The separation of Anton LaVey and his partner, Diane Hegarty, in 1988 became the subject of a legal dispute over the ownership of certain artefacts not commonly found in domestic interiors, including a coffee table

This photograph of two coins displays the dark blue so quintessential to Kirlian photography.

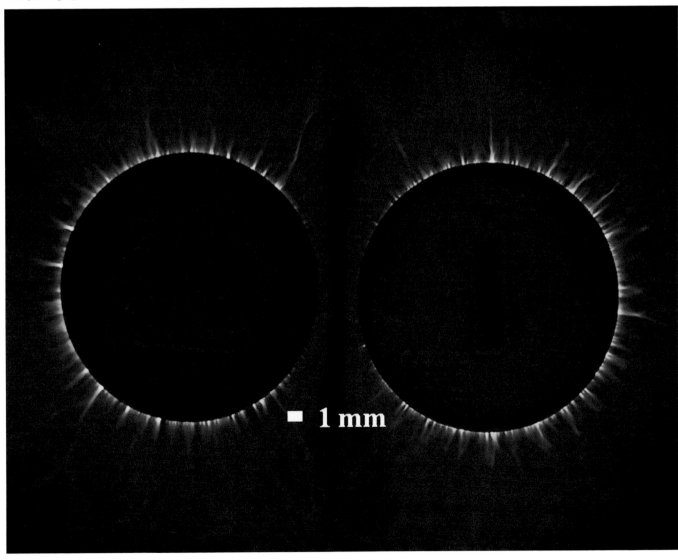

incorporating a stone tombstone, implements of medieval torture, and a shrunken head. LaVey was a controversial figure, having introduced a new and unsettling element into Californian counter-culture by founding the Church of Satan in a black-painted Victorian house in San Francisco, California in 1966, a public statement that was to define his persona and lead to him being known by journalists as the 'Black Pope.'

Anton LaVey was born Howard Stanton Levey in Chicago in 1930, his mother being of mixed Russian and Ukrainian parentage. The family moved to California where LaVey was educated. As a boy, he became interested in the supernatural. After leaving school at the age of sixteen he is reported to have worked as a lion tamer for a circus putting his head in the mouths of the animals, before nearly losing his life when a lion bit his neck. He later became a photographer and a musician. In 1950 he married Carole Lansing by whom he had one daughter; the couple divorced after ten years. He gave lectures on the paranormal and the year after founding an organization he called the Church of Satan, he presided at a Satanic wedding ceremony, an event that attracted media attention. He later conducted a Satanic baptism for his daughter by Diane Hegarty; a photograph of the event shows the child sitting by the feet of a naked woman while LaVey, wearing a headdress of horns, taps his daughter on the head with a sword.

Like the magician and follower of the occult, Aleister Crowley (1875–1947), LaVey cultivated a reputation that outraged and unsettled conventional morality. He was a showman and his appearance was arresting, with a shaven head (his head was shaved when he founded his church) and goatee beard. He preached hedonism and 'indulgence,' the fleshly desires were to be satisfied and not restrained.

His book, *The Satanic Bible*, containing the principles of the movement achieved great popularity, the dedications in early editions acknowledging the influence of a wide range of individuals on LaVey's thought, including Rasputin (1869–1916), Friedrich Nietzsche (1844–1900) and H. P. Lovecraft (1890–1937). *The Satanic Witch*, first published as *The Compleat Witch* in 1971, was LaVey's interpretation of the dynamics between men and women, describing the ways in which men may be manipulated by women. LaVey's publications and pronouncements gave him an increasingly broad media profile and by the time of his death in 1997, his name was synonymous with organized Satanism. His challenge to convention had become part of an alternative orthodoxy.

Concern about the spread of Satanism and various Satanic cults, in particular about alleged cases of ritual child abuse, gathered momentum in the United States and Britain in the 1980s and 1990s culminating in a number of high-profile investigations.

ELIZABETH LOVING

T. C. Lethbridge

Thomas Charles Lethbridge, always known as 'Tom,' listed his recreations in *Who's Who* as boats, natural history, water-colour painting, and curiosity. The last of these was not so much a recreation as one of the fundamental driving forces of his life. A distinguished University of Cambridge academic, a Fellow of the Society of Antiquaries, and an expert on Anglo-Saxon, Scottish, and Inuit archeology, he had a devouring curiosity about offbeat and, for an academic, highly eccentric subjects. They ranged from pendulum dowsing to ghosts, witchcraft, extra-sensory perception, Unidentified Flying Objects, and visitors from outer space—about all of which

he wrote quirky, original, imaginative, and provocative books.

Born in 1901 to an English family in the West Country, Tom Lethbridge was a student at Trinity College, Cambridge, then spent some time on archeological digs and, in the 1920s and 1930s, went on expeditions to Greenland and the polar regions. He was subsequently appointed Keeper of the Anglo-Saxon collections in the Cambridge University Museum of Archaeology and Ethnography. The post was unpaid, but he had a private income and the position suited his independent temperament. After service in World War II, he published his first book, *Merlins Island*, on the Anglo-Saxons, in 1945.

Gog and Magog

Lethbridge next published books on boats and Scottish archeology, and in the 1950s he became interested in the curiously named Gogmagog Hills, near Cambridge. Gog and Magog are the names of two notable giants in British legendary history (the names come originally from the Old Testament) and there was a tradition that a gigantic hill figure had once stood carved in the turf of an Iron Age earthwork in the hills, called Wandlebury Common. It was said that the giant had still been visible in the 1720s and that the Cambridge students named the hills Gogmagog in the figure's honour. It is a possibility that it was students who cut the figure in the chalk of the hill in the first place, although this was not the conclusion to which Lethbridge came.

Lethbridge searched for the giant by probing the ground with an iron sounding-bar and marking soft places at which it went in deeper. In this way he marked out the outline of what at first seemed puzzlingly to suggest a man in a bowler hat, but he persevered and eventually discovered what he believed were the outlines of three enormous figures that had been cut in the chalk, in the same way as the famous White Horse of Uffington or the Cerne Abbas Giant. All these hills are composed of the same easily worked chalk. The central figure, Lethbridge maintained, was that of Magog (the moon), a giant female on horseback, with a huge round owl-like face and goggling eyes, holding a round object in her left hand. On one side of her was a figure he identified as a sun god (Gog) and on the other was a sword-bearing warrior. There were also a horse and a chariot.

The huge female, he believed, was a representation of the Great Mother goddess of the pagan, pre-Christian religion of Europe. This was the same goddess whom Margaret Murray (1863–1963) had claimed to find behind the records of the witchcraft persecutions. Lethbridge came to agree with her theory that witchcraft in medieval Europe was not a cult of the Devil, nor even a fantasy of the persecutors, but the survival of 'the old religion' of pre-Christian times. Murray's ideas, however, have since been rejected by most scholars and writers on the topic.

Undeterred, Lethbridge expounded his conclusions in *Gogmagog: The Buried Gods*, published in 1957. Even Lethbridge's admirers have reservations about the book and it did not go down at all well with academic archeologists and Lethbridge's colleagues at Cambridge, who declined to believe in either his chalk figures on Wandlebury Common or the Murray theory of witchcraft. Lethbridge, disgusted, left Cambridge and spent the rest of his life in Devon, England.

Future Memories

Early in the 1960s, Lethbridge published books on witchcraft and ghosts. Meanwhile, he had met a neighbour who was a practicing witch and who revived his early interest in dowsing.

Years before on Lundy Island, off the North Devon coast, he had successfully located dykes with a divining rod. He now tried his hand with a dowsing pendulum. Using pendulums of different lengths, he found that they seemed to respond to different materials, which enabled him to establish what he called the 'wavelengths' of different substances. He also believed that he could pick up emotions, such as anger or fear, by pendulum dowsing.

His results persuaded Lethbridge that objects retain the impression of events and emotions in which they have been involved—hence the ability of some psychics to describe the character of a long-dead person from an object that that person owned. Lethbridge suggested that ghosts may similarly be impressions of people and events at a place, which a sensitive person visiting the place becomes aware of, like 'recordings' being replayed.

Other results with his pendulum suggested to Lethbridge that he was exploring a world beyond death, or possibly more than one world. He thought that some dreams, too, give entry to other dimensions of reality, and his interest in prophetic dreams and trances, revealing what he called 'future memories,' led him to ponder on the nature of time. His book on these matters, *The Power of the Pendulum*, was not published until 1976, five years after his death.

Also published posthumously, in 1972, was *The Legend of the Sons of God*, in which Lethbridge suggested that the megalithic stone circles and sites of Europe were laid out to guide descending craft bringing visitors from outer space—the 'sons of God' who appear in the Old Testament and other mythologies. Here he was treading much the same ground as Erich von Däniken (b. 1935), whose internationally renowned *Chariots of the Gods* had come out a few years before, but Lethbridge had reached

his conclusions independently of von Däniken.

Tom Lethbridge died in 1971, aged 70. The writer on the paranormal Colin Wilson (1931–2013), an enthusiastic admirer who said that Lethbridge had 'a mind that bubbled with ideas like a glass of champagne,' thought that if he had lived longer he might well have become a cult figure of the New Age.

FURTHER READING: T. Graves and J. Hoult ed. The Essential T. C. Lethbridge. *(London, UK: Routledge, 1980).*

Ley Lines

One summer day in 1921, Alfred Watkins (1855–1935), a sixty-six-year-old local businessman with antiquarian interests, was sitting in his car near the village of Bredwardine in Herefordshire, England, looking at a map. Suddenly he had a vision. He saw a network of straight lines running across the countryside and linking together natural and man-made landmarks. The vision came on him, he afterward said, like 'a flood of ancestral memory.' Following it up on maps, he found that prehistoric burial mounds, standing stones and stone circles, old settlements, holy wells, wayside crosses, churches, old marker stones, crossroads, beacon sites on hilltops and notches in hills, as well as pools, fords, and clumps of trees, seemed to lie in straight lines.

Watkins christened his lines *leys* (pronounced to rhyme with maze), derived from the word 'lea' or 'leigh,' which he thought meant a green track. He was not entirely happy with the name and later dropped it. He believed that the leys were originally prehistoric tracks, dating from a time far in the distant past when traders made their way across the country by going straight from one landmark to another. He described them poetically in his book *The Old Straight Track* in 1925. 'Imagine a fairy chain stretched from mountain peak to mountain peak, as far as the eye could reach, and paid out until it reached the "high places" of the earth at a number of ridges, banks, and knolls. Then visualize a mound, circular earthwork, or clump of trees, planted on these high points, and in low points in the valley other mounds ringed round with water to be seen from a distance. Then great standing stones brought to mark the way at intervals, and on a bank leading up to a mountain ridge or down to a ford the track cut deep so as to form a guiding notch on the skyline as you come up.' He suggested that some of the leys were orientated to the sun or the stars.

The Old Straight Track was a classic of its kind, though professional archeologists dismissed it as absurd and the archeological periodical *Antiquity* refused even to accept an advertisement for it. Orthodox archeology at that time could not conceive that the prehistoric inhabitants of Britain could have organized any development as taxing as the laying out of a network of 'old straight tracks.' The idea caught on, all the same, and people started to go out into the countryside hunting for leys. A Straight Track Postal Portfolio Club was founded to organize field trips and inform members of new discoveries; it lasted until 1948. Watkins published his other major book, *The Ley Hunter's Manual*, in 1927.

Similar ideas were stirring in Germany meanwhile, quite independently of Watkins, and a clergyman named Wilhelm Teudt (1860–1942) announced his discovery of a network of 'holy lines' connecting ancient sites. In his book *Germanische Heiligtümer*, published in 1929, Teudt suggested

that prehistoric German sacred sites were strung together like pearls on a necklace of invisible lines, and were astronomically orientated with remarkable accuracy. His ideas were later taken up by Heinrich Himmler (1900–45) and the Nazi-funded *Deutsche Ahnenerbe*, or German Ancestral Heritage organization.

Watkins died in 1935, but his spirit has continued to inspire enthusiasts who have discovered thousands more alignments. His explanation of the leys as prehistoric tracks has been abandoned, however, as it has become evident that early travelers in Britain

> *It has been noticed more recently that where ley lines do coincide with ancient tracks, the line tends to run along the side of the track, not along the middle of it . . .*

did not march sternly across country along straight roads, but sensibly followed the lines of least resistance. Genuine ancient tracks, such as the Ridge way in southern England, do not run straight.

It has been noticed more recently that where ley lines do coincide with ancient tracks, the line tends to run along the side of the track, not along the middle of it, as if the track function was somehow a side-effect or afterthought. In addition, the track theory did not really explain why so many manmade features of much later dates should lie exactly on leys.

Corridors of Sanctity
Obviously some features on a map may lie in a straight line entirely by coincidence and ley-hunters normally require at least four significant points in a distance of 10 miles or so to qualify a line as a ley. A particularly

well-known example runs straight from a prehistoric burial mound a mile northeast of Stonehenge, through Stonehenge itself, and on south to the massive hill fort of Old Sarum, then through Salisbury Cathedral and down to two more prehistoric sites, Clear bury Ring and Franken bury Camp, along a total length of over 18 miles.

Another example, on a much smaller scale, is the so-called 'corridor of sanctity' in York. It runs in a straight line from the former private chapel of the archbishops of York, through the massive central tower of York Minster, to the centre of the medieval city, and the churches of St. Samson, All Saints and St. Mary in succession, and then on to the Norman keep of Clifford's Tower on its high mound, to end finally on the site of the Knights Templar chapel of St. George, which is no longer standing. Another remarkable alignment is to be found in Cambridge, where the sites of five churches founded before the Norman Conquest lie in a straight line, close to a north-south axis through the town.

Patterns on the Ground
Some of the lines appear to be astronomically orientated. For example, if the midsummer sunrise axis of Stonehenge is extended to the southwest, it runs to the prehistoric settlement at Gravely Castle and the famous Cerne Abbas Giant hill-figure and goes on to finish on the Dorset coast at Puncknowle Beacon. Going the other way, northeast from Stonehenge, the line runs past the edge of the Sidbury Hill earthwork to the Ink Pen Beacon hilltop and the Winterbourne Camp earthwork.

Some ley lines seem to form equilateral or isosceles triangles. Stonehenge, Old Sarum, and Groveley

Castle lie in an equilateral triangle whose sides are 6 miles long. The grandly christened Great Isosceles Triangle of England has its apex at the Arbor Low stone circle in Derbyshire and its other points some 150 miles away to the south, at Other Church close to Glastonbury in Somerset, and West Mersea on the coast of Essex. And the famous White Horse of Uffington on its Oxford shire slope is said to form an isosceles triangle with two other white horses cut into hillsides at Pewsey and Cherhill in Wiltshire.

The Pewsey and Cherhill white horses were made centuries later than the Uffington one, which raises one of the main difficulties about ley lines. They often connect features that are hundreds or even thousands of years apart in date. There is no independent evidence to suggest, for example, that those who chose the site of Salisbury Cathedral in the thirteenth century decided to plant it on the line of a far more ancient alignment with Old Sarum and Stonehenge, or that they had any knowledge of such an alignment.

The answer often given by believers in leys is that they are 'lines of force,' or electromagnetic energy, which were originally created in the immeasurably distant past as the newly-formed Earth cooled. Certain places, such as Stonehenge and Arbor Low, where a number of lines converge, are *ley-centres*—geological power stations, where huge amounts of energy are concentrated. The lines of force are also lines of 'psychic energy.' The people of prehistoric times, living far closer to nature than modern humanity, had far better psychic faculties. They were aware of this network of energy, which they marked out on the ground with standing stones and circles, ramparts and mounds, and they were able to use it. As time went by, conscious knowledge of the lines was lost, but subsequent generations responded unconsciously to them, and sited churches or other features along them.

The concept of 'lines of force' has been traced back to a novel, *The Goat-Foot God*, written in 1936, the year after Watkins's death, by the occultist Dion Fortune (1890–1946). One of the characters, advising the hero how to select a suitable location for invoking 'the old gods,' draws on a map a straight line connecting the great prehistoric stone circles at Avebury with other ancient sacred places and tells him to look for 'the lines of force between the power centres.' It has been suggested that Dion Fortune may have found the germ of the idea in a book by W. Y. Evans Wentz, *The Fairy Faith in Celtic Countries*, published in 1911, in which an Irish 'seer' is mentioned, who 'regards 'fairy paths' or 'fairy passes' as actual magnetic arteries, so to speak, through which circulates the earth's magnetism.' It is interesting that Alfred Watkins described his visionary network of lines as 'a fairy chain.'

Paths of the Dead?

Since the 1960s, interest in ley lines has grown substantially, spreading to North America in the 1970s and 1980s, as has the use of dowsing and pendulum dowsing to identify and explore them. In his influential book *The View Over Atlantis*, which came out in 1969, John Michell (1933–2009) related leys to the ancient Chinese system of geomancy and its concept of energy flowing along the surface of the ground. It was also John Michell, in 1974, who published the first thorough systematic study of alignments in a single area, in his book *The Old Stones of Land's End*. He confined himself to the West Pen with peninsula of Cornwall, England, and to prehistoric sites, in which the area is rich. He found twenty-two exact alignments of what he described as 'rifle-barrel accu-racy' between the centres of fifty-three sites, running over distances up to 6 or 7 miles.

It certainly looks as if prehistoric standing stones and circles were aligned with natural features in straight lines, at least over comparatively short distances, though for what purpose is still a mystery. One sugges-

tion is that it had to do with the spirits of the dead, and perhaps other spiritual entities. At Rösaring in Sweden, for instance, there are various burial mounds of the Bronze Age and the Iron Age, and a stone labyrinth. Early in the 1980s, a perfectly straight road leading to the site was excavated, lying exactly on a north-south axis, dating from the Viking Age and thought to have been used for the burial of a chieftain. Was the straight road a path for the dead man's spirit and the labyrinth intended to contain it?

It is the lines of force concept, however, which dominates speculation about leys. In the 1970s at the Roll Right Stones in Oxfordshire, a stone circle with a sinister reputation, a team of dowsers led by Tom Graves claimed to have identified lines of force running above ground—Graves called them 'over grounds'—from the circle to outlying stones. He estimated that there were probably more than a hundred of them—like telephone lines radiating from an exchange.

Stonehenge, a prehistoric monument in Wiltshire, England, a UNESCO World Heritage Site. A ley line runs through Stonehenge.

Beliefs, Rituals, and Symbols of the Modern World

In 1988, when the Alexandra Palace on its hilltop in North London was rebuilt after a major fire, it was publicly announced that the building stood at a ley line intersection point. The authorities decided to install copper rods in the structure as a precaution to cope with any consequent danger. Ley lines were being taken seriously at last.

FURTHER READING: A. Watkins. The Old Straight Track. (London, UK: Garnstone, 1970, reprint); N. Pennick and P. Devereux. Lines on the Landscape. (London, UK: Robert Hale, 1989); T. Graves. Needles of Stone Revisited. (Glastonbury, UK: Gothic Image, 1986).

H. P. Lovecraft

H. P. Lovecraft's short story, *The Call of Cthulhu*, first published in 1928, has achieved a success that its author could not have foreseen. As well as being made into a film nearly eighty years after its publication, it has provided the inspiration for the highly popular role-playing games, *Call of Cthulhu*, and *Arkham Horror*. Although Lovecraft died in relative obscurity he is now widely acknowledged as a pioneer in the genre of horror and science fiction writing, and he has achieved a recognition that eluded him during his lifetime.

Born in Providence, Rhode Island in 1890, Lovecraft effectively lost his father at the age of three, when Lovecraft senior was confined to a psychiatric institution where he died five years later. His mother was later treated in the same hospital. Lovecraft suffered ill health as a boy and the death of his maternal grandfather in 1904 heralded a downturn in the family's fortunes, resulting in a move from the family home. Leaving full-time education at the age of eighteen, his early adulthood was marked by isolation

and economic inactivity, but in his twenties he began contributing essays and poetry to amateur magazines and reviews. His short stories were published in the pulp fiction magazine, *Weird Tales*, set up in 1923, which remained the main outlet for his work until after his death in 1936. In 1927 he wrote an overview of horror fiction tracing its development through the Gothic novel, a plea for the 'dignity of the weirdly horrible tale as a literary form.'

ELIZABETH LOVING

Mankind United

The socio-religious movement called Mankind United was the creation of Arthur L. Bell, an American businessman. Although little is known of his earlier career, Bell claimed to have been born in New Hampshire in 1900, to have grown up in poverty, and to have completed only four years of school. Immigrating to California in his teens, he sold real estate and insurance during the booming '20s and became a Christian Science practitioner and a devotee of various theological and Utopian writings. He was badly hit by the economic crash of 1929, and subsequently divorced his first wife and married, at the age of thirty-four, a fellow Christian Scientist—a woman in her early sixties.

Evil of Mad Ambition

Financially supported by his wife, Bell conceived the movement, and at his own expense published its text, *Mankind United* (1934). In its 313 repetitious pages, Bell sought to answer the ancient questions of why the world is dominated by war, poverty, greed, and hate, when so many long for it to be otherwise; and how it might be changed so that everyone could live in economic abundance and happiness under the Golden Rule of Christ:

'Whatever you wish that men would do to you, do so to them' (Matthew, chapter 7. 12).

According to the text, on Christmas Day 1875, a small group of wealthy and humane persons had assembled to ask themselves these same questions. In their opinion, poverty, war, and other evils were totally unnecessary since technology was capable of producing more than enough for all. These evils continued only because 'a worldwide organization composed of a small group of families in possession of fabulous wealth' was stifling the economic and moral well-being of mankind in order to bring it to total enslavement. In their mad ambition to control all wealth and power, these 'World's Hidden Rulers' or 'Money Changers' were the root of all evil.

Wanting to save mankind, this group pledged their fortunes and lives to overcoming the Money Changers and to instituting a world economy of equality and abundance. They called their organization The International Institute of Universal Research and Administration. Bell referred to them, more simply, as 'the Sponsors.'

In the following years, the Sponsors gradually expanded their numbers, spied upon the Money Changers and engaged in the development of fantastically advanced techniques of economic production. Since the World's Hidden Rulers would destroy the Sponsors if they knew of them, the latter had to work in secrecy.

By 1919, the Sponsors' research department had assembled exhaustive proof of the Money Changers' existence and nefarious aims, and had worked out a plan for a worldwide economy in which, working only four hours a day, four days a week, eight months a year, everyone could live in astonishing prosperity. Since then they had been waiting for the most propitious moment to make their discoveries and plans known, and to prepare for this 'unveiling' the Sponsors had formed a group called the International Legion of Vigilantes. Bell claimed that he was recruited to this organization when it was set up in 1919 and that by 1934 he had been working as a secret agent for fifteen years.

Thirty Days of Proof

Recognizing that their claims might seem incredible to the public at large, the Sponsors planned a rapid thirty-day program during which time the Institute's well-guarded sixty years of discoveries and carefully prepared recommendations will be freely offered to the human race.' In two-hour programs repeated day and night, twelve times each twenty-four hours, five days a week, irrefutable and exhaustive proof would be offered as to how the Money Changers worked and how Utopia was possible.

The book *Mankind United* was merely a 'bulletin' announcing the imminence of the thirty days of proof. It did not in itself offer proof of anything, but was intended as an 'invitation' to those who saw it to take part in the thirty days, and at the end to vote on 100 recommendations. However, the Sponsors had determined that if the enormous power of the Money Changers was to be overcome, it would be necessary to have at least 200 million people listening and voting. Until that number had agreed to participate, the thirty days of proof could not begin. It was in order to register the requisite millions that a part of the Sponsors' secret organization had become public. Once the 200 million had voted for the Sponsors' program, the Universal Service Corporation would be formed and would thereafter conduct all economic production and distribution. Membership in the corporation would increase rapidly, and within a few years the World's Hidden Rulers would be completely out of business.

A migrant agricultural worker's family. The mother, aged thirty-two, sits with her two hungry children in Nipomo, California. The poverty of the Great Depression drove many to Salvationist schemes.

Arthur L. Bell, the argument of the text continued, was selected by the Sponsors to be the first 'public' vigilante, and California was to be the first area in which registration was to occur. In his role as a mere functionary of a large and powerful secret organization, Bell disclaimed the authorship of *Mankind United*, and the title page proclaimed that the book was 'published by the International Registration Bureau (Pacific Coast Division of North America).'

Equipped with his wife's money, an ideology, and an attractive physical presence, Bell set out to build a movement. It was to have an active life of only seventeen years (1934–51), but it provides an intriguing study in the ingenious responses of a leader to changing and adverse circumstances.

Promise of Utopia

During the 1930s California, deep in the depression, was overrun with Salvationist schemes. It was into this highly competitive market that Bell introduced Mankind United. Membership involved merely the purchase of the book, a promise to pass it on to friends, and a willingness to listen and vote during the forthcoming thirty-day program. In return for this minimal effort, members were promised a fantastic future gain. At the height of the movement's popularity, in 1938–9, frequent mass meetings were held throughout California and it is estimated that upward of 250,000 West Coast citizens read the book, registered themselves, and attended at least a few meetings. Bell encouraged the formation of local clubs dedi-

General Eisenhower talking with US paratroopers as they prepared for the Battle of Normandy. Bell assumed that World War II was an economic plot of the Money Changers.

cated to promoting the book and, as they grew in numbers, Bell organized them into an elaborate bureaucracy of dedicated workers. As many as 30,000 were actively engaged in the goal of registering 200 million 'educated and religious people'—precisely the people, Bell said, whom the Money Changers most urgently wanted to annihilate.

The bulk of the membership was drawn from the working and lower 'white-collar' classes, was primarily between the ages of forty and sixty, and had completed some secondary education. Females slightly outnumbered males. By and large, the members came from those worst hit by the depression—groups who were neither poor in 1929 nor sufficiently wealthy to weather the decade in reasonable

comfort. Specifically, Bell sponsored his movement among those portions of such groups that were religiously inclined but disenchanted with established religion. His doctrines were as much economic as religious but his scheme to make 'do as you would be done by' a reality on Earth was promoted among persons who were more religious than they were economically or politically sophisticated.

Levy of Half Their Income

When war came to the United States in 1941, Bell condemned it as another of the Money Changers' plots to worsen mankind's situation. Communist, fascist, and capitalist leaders alike were merely puppets of the Money Changers, and the latter were pulling the strings to further their plan for world

dictatorship. By 1939, the Federal authorities had infiltrated the movement and Bell had begun to retrench by discontinuing sale of the book and insisting upon the close screening of members.

As support for the US government increased, membership declined, and in response Bell instituted a series of measures designed to commit the remaining followers. A program to train 'instructors' and 'election supervisors' to conduct affairs during the imminent thirty-day program was instituted. Initially this involved a payment of only $20 per member, but a variety of other monetary requests followed. These culminated in a requirement made in 1943 that members become part of the 'fifty-fifty fund' by giving fifty percent of their gross earnings to the movement. The successive demands were made in the context of extreme secrecy and urgency: the thirty-day program would begin at any moment, if only the latest monetary goal could be reached. But each time, Bell announced, the members failed and each time he sent them headlong toward a new financial goal that had to be achieved if the War was to be prevented (in 1940–41) or stopped (1942–43), and Utopia begun.

In pursuit of these elusive monetary goals and in scurrying about on a variety of additional and inexplicable 'missions' at Bell's bidding, the members lived with an inflated sense of self-importance and a vivid sense of the urgency of their tasks. The extent of this 'urgency' was made clear in December 1942 when Bell and sixteen leaders were arrested on charges of sedition. They were found guilty in May 1943 but, following appeal, the decision was reversed on procedural grounds four years later. None of them actually ever served any time in prison.

The best defense being offence, in the face of declining membership and government prosecution, Bell adopted a bold but logical strategy to save and consolidate the movement. In 1943, he announced to the membership the 'literally unheard-of opportunity' to become 'student ministers' in 'training schools' for those who would form the foundation of the forthcoming Universal Service Corporation. Incorporating a new organization, Christ's Church of the Golden Rule, Bell pressed his followers to give over all their worldly goods to the Church and to begin work in one of the large number of businesses he was in the process of acquiring.

Fewer than two years later, by the summer of 1945, he had assembled nearly $4 million worth of property in California, including a number of office buildings, hotels, ranches, laundries, garages, and the like. Bell's following, however, was now down to about 850 people, so that only part of these vast new holdings were run by members as Utopian 'Laboratories of Abundant Living.' Bell faded from public view. Members grew few and old, operating a few remaining businesses, among which was a laundry and a motel. By 1956, fewer than one hundred members remained and the end of Mankind United was reached.

JOHN LOFLAND

> *At sixteen, he found that he could write and draw automatically, producing drawings in the style of . . . such artists as Dürer, Beardsley, Matisse, and Picasso.*

Matthew Manning

Born in Cambridgeshire in 1955, Matthew Manning is known as 'the most scientifically investigated healer in the world.' His first paranormal experiences came at the age of twelve, when the Cambridge poltergeist investigator, Dr. A. R. G. Owen, concluded that the young Matthew was the focus of some of the most interesting poltergeist activity he had ever encountered.

This type of disturbance, which followed Matthew to boarding-school, continued intermittently for several years. At sixteen, he found that he could write and draw automatically, producing drawings in the style of—and in some cases apparently signed by—such artists as Dürer (1471–1528), Beardsley (1872–98), Matisse (1869–1954), and Picasso (1881–1973). His automatic writing included languages with which he had no known familiarity, such as Greek and Arabic.

In 1974 Manning saw a television broadcast by Uri Geller, following which he also was able to demonstrate metal-bending. Such a wealth of paranormal talent attracted media attention, and in the same year he was examined by a panel of scientists. Three years later he took part in an extensive series of tests at the Mind Science Foundation in San Antonio, the University of California at Davis, and the Washington Research Center in San Francisco.

Dr. William Braud, who supervised the Texas research, reported in the *Journal of the Society for Psychical Research* (1979) that 'Matthew Manning was able to exert significant psychokinetic influences upon a variety of biological systems.'

It was while on holiday in the Himalayas during the course of these experiments that Manning decided to become a healer. In 1983 he was asked to explain his technique to the Royal College of Surgeons in London. He said: 'I just give people permission to heal themselves . . . If there is any outside help, I just say it comes "from the boys and girls upstairs."'

Men in Black

One of the curious by-products of the developing interest in UFOs during the 1950s and '60s was the regularly reported phenomenon of the 'men in black.'

Typically, an observer who claimed the sighting of a UFO would submit a report of the experience to one or other of the organizations concerned with collating such reports or, occasionally, to an official bureau; he or she would not have mentioned the matter to the media, or to more than one or two close friends.

Within a few days, the observer would be visited by a team of three men, dressed in the dark suits, plain white shirts with plain dark ties, and black hats favoured, in the popular imagination, by members of the FBI and other government organizations they were described as 'dressed like funeral directors.' They would sometimes make a prior telephone call to establish that the observer was alone, and arrive silently in an elderly but immaculate black Cadillac, its plates bearing a registration that could not be checked in any records.

The facial features and complexions of these men would be described later by the observers as 'foreign.' They were either pale or deeply tanned, and some appeared to be wearing lipstick, while their hair, if they removed their hats, was either nonexistent, or thin and irregular. They walked in a curiously disjointed manner; their voices were unnatural in timbre; and they sometimes complained that their strength was fading, and that they must leave at once.

The message of all these strange visitors was the same. The person visited, who had reported UFO phenomena, must immediately cease talking about the matter, destroy all records (including photographs) of the observation, and on no account discuss this unexpected visit. Frequently there were threats of what would happen to the observer, or to other members of the family, if the orders were not obeyed.

Although there is, of course, no way of telling whether anybody obeyed these orders to the letter, a number of people disregarded them, and in due course—either within a few days or after the passage of years—reported their experience of the mysterious visit. None, apparently, ever suffered

the punishment with which they were threatened. For this reason it is impossible to be sure that these are not 'copycat' reports.

There are, however, many significant differences in detail. In mid-September 1976, for example, Dr. Herbert Hopkins, a fifty-eight-year-old physician and practicing medical hypnotist, was engaged in the investigation of a reported UFO incident in Maine. One evening, he has said, when his wife and children were out of the house, he received a telephone call from a man who said that he was vice-president of the New Jersey UFO Research Organization, and that he would like to discuss the case.

Dr. Hopkins agreed, and immediately after, on opening the back door of his home, was surprised to find a man already climbing the porch steps. 'I saw no car, and even if he did have a car he could not possibly have gotten to my house that quickly from any phone,' he later remarked.

The man was dressed in the usual black suit and hat, the suit unwrinkled and the trousers sharply creased. When he removed his hat he was seen to be completely hairless: not only bald, but without eyebrows or lashes. His skin was white, but his lips bright red and, when he later brushed his mouth with the grey gloves he was wearing, Dr. Hopkins observed that the gloves appeared to be smeared thickly with lipstick.

The two discussed the UFO incident for some time, and the visitor told him that he must erase all tapes of hypnotic sessions he had held in connection with it. Then he remarked that Dr. Hopkins had two coins in his pocket—which was indeed the case —and asked him for one. He held it in his hand, and it vanished. 'Neither you nor anyone else on this plane will ever see that coin again,' he said. The speech of the man in black appeared to be slowing down. He rose

unsteadily to his feet and said: 'My energy is running low—must go now—goodbye,' and walked uncertainly to the door. Dr. Hopkins saw a bright light shining in the driveway, which he assumed to be the visitor's car, but he neither saw nor heard it drive away.

A few days later, on September 24, Dr. Hopkins's son John and daughter-in-law Maureen allegedly received a visit from two people, a man and a woman. Both were in their mid-thirties, but dressed in curiously old-fashioned clothes, and both walked with very short steps, leaning forward as though afraid of falling.

The two strangers asked a number of questions about the married couple's domestic habits, while at the same time the man was fondling his female companion, and asked if he was doing it correctly. When John Hopkins left the room for a moment, the man asked Maureen 'how she was made,' and whether she had any nude photographs of herself.

Soon after this, the couple rose to leave. The man was between the woman and the door, and she asked John: 'Please move him, I can't move him myself.' The man then left suddenly, followed by the woman. Both walked 'in straight lines,' and neither said goodbye.

This is just one of a considerable number of reports that have puzzled investigators. Experts in folklore and the history of witchcraft have drawn parallels between these incidents and earlier stories of the appearance of the Devil, who was often described as a tall man dressed in black. Although the men in black—referred to by collectors of UFO reports as MIB—are usually associated with these particular phenomena, they have also been recorded in connection with alleged sightings of monsters and other nonhuman entities. The subject has excited interest among psychologists, and many symptoms of contemporary paranoia are exhibited by those who would otherwise laugh at any suggestion that the Devil exists. The American Tony Kimery wrote in 1970:

'The mysterious MIB and the entire collection of their thugs, henchmen, and highly trained intelligence officers, are a big part of the complex UFO phenomena. It is known that projects by them are now under way for the complete control of . . . political, financial, religious, and scientific institutions. They—the MIB—have a very long background and history that stretches back for centuries, indicating a massive build-up of concentration to where it is today.'

Men in Black were known to dress not dissimilar to funeral directors

Messianic Movements

The distinction between a messiah, or saviour, and a prophet who foretells doom and offers ways of escaping it, is not always easy to draw, but in the strict sense the term 'messianic' is confined to movements whose leader claims to be God or a representation of God, or which arise in firm anticipation of such a god-man's appearance. The term is often used loosely for religious movements that expect the end of the world and the establishment (usually for believers only) of a new dispensation of peace, plenty, and pleasure. These are more accurately called millennial movements but some movements, of course, are both messianic and millenialist, when the messiah's role is to lead the faithful into the millennium. Early Christianity, and movements expecting the Second Coming of Christ, can be called messianic but current usage tends to restrict the term to groups whose messianic beliefs are outside the Bible.

Claimants to messiahship were common in Jewish history before Christ, and were by no means uncommon in the Middle Ages among Jews, Christians, and Muslims. In modern times, the messianic figures who have commanded the greatest following have appeared in non-Christian countries. An example is Hung Hsui-chuan (1814–64), the son of a Chinese peasant household who emerged as a visionary, after repeatedly failing the Civil Service examinations, and inspired the Taiping rebellion, which began in southern China in 1851 and lasted until 1864, with Nanking as its capital for most of this period.

Younger Brother of Christ

Hsui-chuan had been influenced by a US missionary and the content of his visions was in many respects Christian, but he became convinced that his destiny was to restore the true faith to China, and that this would be achieved only with the overthrow of the Manchu imperial dynasty. Thereafter *Ta'i-p'ing t'ien kuo*, the heavenly kingdom of great peace, would be established. The name 'Ta'i-p'ing' had been used to describe an era of peace in the Chinese past, but the rest of the title was coined to express the Christian concept of a heavenly kingdom. Hung Hsiu-chuan did not make outright claim to be God, but rather to be the younger brother of Jesus; however, some scholars believe that he produced, in place of a Trinitarian system, a fourfold concept of the deity.

His followers were seen as a Chinese version of the children of Israel seeking the Promised Land.

As the movement grew and drew around it more conventional rebellious elements, Hung Hsiu-chuan's role was overshadowed by more militant and political leaders. He had been the early focus of attention for many who were discontented in southern China, where the peasantry had been reduced to the status of tenants, where population growth had produced new pressure on arable land, and where, in Hunan province in particular, famines and catastrophes had been frequent. Hung Hsiu-chuan's ideas were alien to Chinese thought, and this has been seen as a factor that may have limited the support that he commanded. His message combined the unreconciled elements of Christian eschatology, promising both a new kingdom on Earth with resurrection of the dead, as well as the prospect of salvation in the otherworld. He is reputed to have dwelt very much on sin and to have made men anxious about its consequences, demanding regular prayer for forgiveness, and obedience to the Ten Commandments. In the early days of his activity some of his followers had ecstatic and convulsive experiences. In spite of the unfamiliarity of these things, the new ideology mobilized an effective following who rose in armed rebellion on an impressive scale, until the movement suffered defeat largely through the agency of General Gordon.

Gordon's role in life seemed destined to be that of opponent of messianic claimants, for he is linked more intimately in the public mind with the struggle against another modern messiah—Mohammed Ahmad, the Mahdi who inflamed the Sudan in the 1880s.

Ahmad proclaimed himself the Imam, successor of the Apostle of God, the expected saviour, the chosen one who would reconquer the Muslim world and restore the community that Mohammed the prophet had brought into being. He took the title Mahdi, the 'guided one,' although, since the Sudan was of the Sunnite division of Islam, he did not claim to be the Hidden Imam, long awaited by Twelver

> *Believing himself to be possessed of the Holy Spirit, his sermons became increasingly heretical . . .*

Shi'a Muslims. Ahmad was widely accepted, and his personal piety and high reputation made plausible his claim to be the Mahdi. He quickly built up a new state that was a theocratic despotism, the success of which lasted for more than a decade after his own death in 1885, even though there were strong tensions between the different groups among his followers.

'Why Shouldn't God Smoke?'
One of the more colourful, although a somewhat shadowy messianic leader was Lou, born Louwrens van Voorthuizen in north Holland, who spent the middle years of his life as a fisherman. Lou, as he preferred to be called, declared himself to be God in 1950, and drew around him a small and somewhat contentious body of followers, *Lou-mensen*, who were united essentially by their complete devotion to him. Lou maintained that his role was the equivalent of that of Christ, but whereas Christ had won a spiritual victory over the Devil, he, Lou, would defeat the Devil in the body.

Lou rejected conventional moral obligations, as having no relevance for salvation. (He made much of his liking for cigars: 'Why shouldn't God smoke?' he asked.) Salvation was to be attained only through him. His followers were to regard themselves as the sons and daughters of God, and needed no wills of their own. They should surrender themselves gratefully to Lou, God.

The Bible was entirely superseded now that God was on Earth again incarnate and, in the pamphlets that some of his middle-aged women votaries sold on the streets of Amsterdam, Lou derided both the Bible and the clergy who preached it. He preached that the time of the end was at hand, when all his followers would triumph over death. The message was never widely disseminated. As a result of disputes amongst his followers, Lou and his partner moved to Belgium where, despite the claim to immortality, he died in 1968. At this point about one-third of the followers left the movement. For a time the remainder continued as a group, but appear to have dispersed subsequently.

A figure about whom even less is generally known is Georges Roux (1914–1999), the Christ of Montfavet, near Avignon in France. Roux was a postmaster who had practiced as a faith healer for some time when, in the early 1950s, he announced that he was Christ. To read his works in simplicity of heart, it was claimed, was to accept his mission as the reappearing Christ. Roux's small following, whose churches took the name *L'Eglise chrétienne universelle*, was found mainly in Paris and the south of France.

The Abode of Love
The nineteenth century produced the most spectacular recent claimants to

messiahship in Britain. Among these were two men, one of whom 'inherited' this claim from the other. Such a transfer of a status as unique as that of messiah must be unprecedented (short of a belief in the transmigration of souls) and yet the group known as Agapemonites, created in the 1840s by an Anglican priest, Henry James Prince (1811–99), accepted, after his death, a new immortal messiah in the person of John Hugh Smyth-Pigott.

Prince was renowned at St. David's, Lampeter, where he had studied for the Anglican priesthood, as a particularly pious student, and soon after taking up his first curacy at Charlinch in Somerset, he gained a reputation for powerful sermons and a strong personal magnetism, particularly for women. Believing himself to be possessed of the Holy Spirit, his sermons became increasingly heretical; after some time his relations with the Church of England became strained, and he opened his own chapel in Brighton.

With donations from his supporters, among whom were a number of wealthy women, he bought a large house and grounds, together with a farm, at Spraxton in Somerset, and there established his community, the Abode of Love. He had set forth his teachings in a number of tracts, and styled himself 'the Beloved One' and 'the Messiah.'

At Spraxton, Prince assumed complete control of his followers, making it clear that his will was the will of God, which none might question. Some of the women who joined the community bestowed all their property on Prince, and well-wishers in Brighton, Weymouth, and elsewhere contributed to its support.

From the beginning a luxurious style of life was adopted, with emphasis on recreation (the chapel itself was furnished with a billiard table). Prince drove a carriage with footmen, and was later remembered as having traveled through the neighbouring town of Bridgwater, with his footman sounding a trumpet and announcing him as the messiah.

The most distinctive feature of the Agapemonite life was Prince's teaching of 'spiritual wivery.' Surrounded by 'sisters,' he took a 'bride of the Lamb' from among his following, declaring that 'in name you see Christ in the flesh, in my flesh.' The successive sexual adventures of Prince, which were undertaken in the name of the highest spirituality, caused some of his followers to withdraw, but those who stayed at Spraxton, other than his own paramours, led chaste and upright lives. The teaching that allowed Prince to affirm that he was above sin, no matter what he did, was for the leader, not for the following.

Messianic Succession

Prince fathered several children, and also found himself involved in a number of lawsuits when some of his female adherents made attempts to recover their surrendered property. Although his sexual practices were exposed in these proceedings, and although Prince himself was unfrocked as an Anglican priest, the community continued; undoubtedly most of its members had implicit faith in their messiah. Prince preached that he and his followers were immortal and deaths within the community were explained as the consequence of lapses into sin. His own death, in 1899, might have been expected to see the collapse of the Agapemonites: instead it produced a new messianic claimant.

Shortly before his death, Prince had sponsored the building of a church in Clapton, London, known as the Church of the Ark of the Covenant. This development was all the more surprising, since in his later years the Agapemonites had done little in the way of evangelization. It is uncertain whether the founding of this church, at which sympathizers with the Spraxton community occasionally met, had any direct connection with the choice of Prince's successor, or whether Prince had any interest in the continuance of his sect after his death. But it was at this church that, in 1902, John Hugh Smyth-Pigott declared himself to be Prince's successor.

Smyth-Pigott had been ordained an Anglican clergyman in 1882 and for a time had been curate at St. Jude's Church, Mildmay Park, not far away from Clapton. In the period following Prince's death he was leading a mission in Dublin. By some means he came, or had come, into contact with the Agapemonites and, after his pronouncement at the Church of the Ark of the Covenant, was accepted by them as their new leader. Some among them came to believe that he had been specifically designated as such by Prince himself—improbable, in the nature of messianic claims, as that must seem.

At Spraxton, Smyth-Pigott quickly established himself over the community, and continued many of the features peculiar to Prince's regime. He retained the division into three classes: the lowest comprised those who were the domestic servants of the rest, and the highest were the most spiritual group from among whom he would choose his soul brides.

Young women were still recruited to the community, and in 1904 Smyth-Pigott brought in a 'chief soul bride,' a Miss Ruth Preece. He had three children by Ruth. His wife, who had borne him no children, appears to have accepted the situation with equanimity, as indeed did most members of the community. The local Anglican bishop, however, eventually felt constrained to have the Spraxton messiah unfrocked. Producing illegitimate children, rather than the well-publicized claim to messiahship, was what finally caused the Bishop of Bath and Wells to have Smyth-Pigott's case brought before a Consistory Court. The messiah took other brides in later years, and Ruth was displaced, following an elaborate ceremony, for disobeying the messiah's will.

The numbers at Spraxton, sometimes reinforced by visitors from a Norwegian sister house which Smyth-Pigott frequently visited, steadily declined, and the messiah's death in 1927 reduced the numbers further. Without a leader the community slowly dwindled, until in the 1950s Ruth also died, and within a short time the community disappeared.

Movements that arise around a self-styled messiah are, in the modern age, unlikely to be revolutionary movements in any militant sense. The legal monopoly of coercive force in the modern state virtually precludes the possibility of a messiah actively fulfilling the implications of his claims to supernatural and omniscient power. In effect, therefore, the messianic leader operates more as if he were simply a wonder-worker. His miracles tend to be small miracles, tokens of power rather than manifestations of power in anything like the dimensions in which it is claimed. The reputation for small miracles is often enough for the faithful, and on such miracles rested a great deal of the reputation of one of the best-known of modern messiahs.

Father Divine

Like many claimants to messiahship, Father Divine had a career of active evangelism before he accepted the title of God. As George Baker, he had been a missionary among African Americans in parts of the United States, but in 1930, at Sayville on Long Island, New York, Baker took the suggestive title, Father Divine. It was one among a number of such names assumed by other revivalists ('Daddy Grace' was a contemporary rival of Baker's).

At Sayville he established the first of his Peace Missions, communities that became known as 'heavens' for those who lived in them. They were organized on cooperative lines, and to them were attached members who were nonresident but who joined the residents for religious services.

Father Divine conceived the idea of a well-organized social service for his adherents. He found jobs for the unemployed and cared for the poor and, since many of those who joined the sect were incapable of much organization on their own part, there was a very real sense in which Father Divine was their saviour, in this world at least, if not in the next.

Like most messianic leaders, he had no developed eschatology: salvation was indeed here and now, since God was here and now. In common with other messiahs, he taught that his members should not and would not die: death was a shameful thing within the movement and not to be spoken about. Nor had Father Divine much use for the Bible, which was clearly a superseded book. Since God was available to speak for himself, the written record of his acts, long ago, and for a remote people, was of little interest.

The Peace Mission espoused a rigorous ethical code and this may in itself have been part of its formula for success. Members were weaned away from those habits that caused debility and degeneracy among large sections of the population. Smoking and drinking were prohibited. Honesty was a strict requirement. Sexual continence, even between those who were married, was rigorously enjoined, and the ill consequences of a large progeny were in this way avoided.

Father Divine taught his followers to accept his will as their supreme good, and he forbade them to accept government welfare or to take out insurance policies. He himself could work all the miracles that they needed.

He gave lavish banquets on a scale and in a style far beyond the previous experience of his adherents and, as they did not pay for these directly, his provision appeared as a miracle. He could pour innumerable cups of coffee from one small coffee pot, it was frequently affirmed of him. His followers believed that anyone who spoke or acted against him in any way would surely suffer, and took this as certain evidence of his divine power.

It is not easy to assess the numbers who believed in Father Divine when he was on the tide of success in the late 1930s, but there were perhaps hundreds of thousands. After World War II the movement seemed to have passed its peak, as more militant forms of black religion, and in particular the Black Muslim movement, displaced the essentially peaceful Father Divine cult. The movement may have suffered after Divine took a (white) second wife toward the end of his life, and because he was gradually less and less disposed to appear in public. He died in 1965, but the movement continued, although at a less impressive level than formerly.

Lion of Judah

Not every messianic movement arises round a self-styled messiah. Some select as their divine saviour an individual who makes no such claims on his own behalf. One of the most remarkable modern examples is the Rastafarian movement in Jamaica, whose messiah was the former Emperor of Ethiopia, Haile Selassie (1892–1975).

A central theme of the movement is hatred of the whites who have dominated, first politically, and still economically, the life of the West Indies. In Haile Selassie the 'Rastas' acclaimed a saviour who would bring black men into their rightful heritage—the ownership of the African continent—and who would help them to win black supremacy.

The movement had its origins after World War I, in the strong impression made on many Jamaicans by the pronouncements of Marcus Garvey (1887–1940) a militant Jamaican who was active in the United States. His attempts to establish African Americans as a power in their own right included a prophecy that black people should 'look to Africa when a black king shall be crowned, for deliverance is near.' Not long afterward, in 1930, Ras Tafari, as the Ethiopian crown prince was known, became Emperor, and many West Indians applied Garvey's words to him.

The Italian invasion of Ethiopia in 1935 strengthened Rastafarian enthusiasm in Jamaica, for it seemed clear that an armed struggle of black men against white had begun. Christian ideas were now abandoned by supporters of Ras Tafari and the movement became a semipolitical religious belief in the power of a black saviour. Some extremists withdrew to the plantations, grew 'ganja' (marijuana) and established a colony of militant antiwhites, while there were leaders who traded on the bizarre fantasies of some of the followers, promising that planes would soon arrive to airlift them all to Africa and cynically turning a profit on the sale of worthless 'passports.'

An inquiry into the activities of the Rastafarians in the late 1950s led the newly independent government of Jamaica (to which the Rastafarians were as opposed as to the whites) to permit a delegation to visit Africa. They visited Liberia, Nigeria, and Ethiopia; and were received in Addis Ababa by Haile Selassie, who presented them with a token plot of land in his country. The Rastafarians were, however, disappointed in the possibility of migrating to Africa, and seem to have received no positive encouragement from any of the governments they visited. In 1956 Haile Selassie paid a state visit to Jamaica and,

although he presented medals to some of his would-be subjects at a formal garden party, he made no mention of the possibility of satisfying their dream of settling in Ethiopia.

Haile Selassie's reign in Ethiopia ended in 1974, when he was overthrown by a military coup, and he died the following year. By this time the Rastafarian movement was strongly established in Jamaica and in Jamaican immigrant circles in Britain and North America. New cult heroes emerged, such as the musician Bob Marley (1945–1981), famous for his distinctive reggae sound, who was a prominent and devoted Rastafarian.

Cyanide at Jonestown

Between the 1960s and 1970s in the United States the short-lived Jesus People movement blended rock music

and a hippie-style emphasis on love and 'letting it all hang out,' with a fundamentalist belief in the Bible's literal truth and confident expectation of the imminent Second Coming of Christ. Since then, two dramatic episodes have brought other messianic cults to public notice in the West.

The first occurred in 1978 in Guyana on the north coast of South America, when hundreds of people were involved in an extraordinary case of murder and mass suicide. They were members of a US group, the People's Temple, founded in 1957 by a former Methodist minister from San Francisco, the Rev. Jim Jones (1931–78). Jones claimed to be a reincarnation of Jesus Christ, the Buddha, and Lenin.

In 1974 he settled his followers, who were largely poor and black, in a commune named Jonestown, on

The revolutionary preacher Father Divine in his later years

27,000 acres of land given by the Guyana government, some 150 miles inland from Georgetown, the capital of Guyana. He later considered moving the commune to the Soviet Union and made the study of Russian compulsory in Jonestown.

Reports soon began to circulate in San Francisco of savage beatings, torture, and conditions of virtual slavery in the commune and, in November 1978, a Californian congressman, Leo Ryan (1925–1978), and a team of journalists flew to Jonestown to investigate matters. Ryan and three journalists were shot dead when they attempted to leave again by air with some members of the sect who had decided to quit the commune.

Jones then ordered more than 900 of his faithful followers to kill themselves and their children, an act that they had already rehearsed several times before. A large tub was filled with Kool-Aid fruit drink laced with cyanide. The adults and children were ordered to drink the poison, which was tipped down babies' throats. Anyone who refused to drink was forced to comply by armed guards or was injected with cyanide in the arm. It took them about five minutes to die. Jones told his people that this was not suicide, but 'a revolutionary act.' His own body was found with a bullet in the head among the corpses.

The activities of the group known as Heaven's Gate was brought to the attention of the world's media by the discovery of thirty-nine bodies at a mansion in San Diego in 1997.

Another episode hit the headlines in 1993, when FBI agents and police set siege to the headquarters of the Branch Davidian sect near Waco, Texas, in a compound called Mount Carmel. Eventually, in April, the FBI stormed the complex, which caught fire, and some seventy members of the cult were killed. Among them was their leader, David Koresh (1959–93), who called himself the Seventh Angel or the Lamb and claimed to be the Son of God, with a mission to bring the world to an end.

He had started life as Vernon Wayne Howell in Houston, Texas, where he grew up as a Seventh Day Adventist, but broke away to join the obscure Branch Davidian cult in the 1970s. He recruited followers in Britain and Australia before taking over the Waco compound at gun point from the previous leader in 1987. He exercised total control over his followers' lives and had fifteen or more 'wives' and innumerable children.

Despite occasional outbreaks of this kind, the militant and ecstatic type of movement may be a waning phenomenon. Social disorder seems likely to manifest itself in other forms as societies move into the technologically advanced modern world.

Heaven's Gate

The activities of the group known as Heaven's Gate was brought to the attention of the world's media by

The Branch Davidian compound near Waco, Texas, burns on April 19, 1993. The fire apparently started inside the compound several hours after federal agents began pumping tear gas into the headquarters of the cult led by David Koresh.

the discovery of thirty-nine bodies at a mansion in San Diego in 1997. Together with its founder, sixty-six-year-old Marshall Herff Applewhite (1931–97), a former teacher, the members of the group had committed suicide in the belief this was the means by which they could leave Earth and travel in a spaceship attached to the comet Hale-Bopp thus achieving the 'Level Above Human.' Applewhite's cult was a strongly repressive and controlling one that suppressed individuality. Members were required to be celibate and lived a frugal and simple communal life. (Applewhite and several of the men in the group had undergone castration.) Obedience was held to be a key component of the group's complex theology that saw human beings as 'vehicles' that required reprogramming through mental training, the vocabulary of the computer age in a group that rejected capitalist and consumer culture.

Aum Shinrikyo

A religious group originated in the 1980s in Japan under the leadership of Ashara Sholko (b. 1955) who accorded himself messianic status as the possessor of the 'supreme truth.' The group attracted support as well as large sums of money from many young well-educated Japanese. However, the cult had more in common with a criminal or terrorist fraternity: members of Aum Shinrikyo were held to be responsible for gas attacks on the Tokyo subway system that killed twelve people and injured nearly 6,000 in 1995.

Ashara Sholko was convicted of being the mastermind behind the attack and given a capital sentence.

BRYAN WILSON

FURTHER READING: A. Fauset. Black Gods of the Metropolis. *(Pennsylvania, PA: University of Pennsylvania Press, 1971); S. Harris and H. Crittenden.* The Incredible Father Divine. *(London, UK: W. H. Allen, 1954); Donald McCormick.* Temple of Love. *(Peterborough, UK: Jarrolds, 1962); Katrin Norris.* Jamaica: The Search for an Identity. *(New York, NY: Oxford Univeristy Press, 1962); Bengt Sundkler.*

The Morning of the Magicians

An unlikely collaboration between two individuals of widely differing backgrounds produced a large and best-selling book popularizing concepts about history, myth, science, and belief that went far beyond conventional approaches. First published in France in 1960 as *Le Matin des magiciens*, the title appeared in the United States as *The Morning of the Magicians*. Russian-born Jacques Bergier (1912–78) had immigrated to France with his family in 1925. He trained as a scientist and met Louis Pauwels (1920–97) in Paris in 1954. A former teacher, Pauwels was then working as a journalist. Both men were attracted by science fiction and ideas about other worlds not susceptible to modern scientific rigour. Their book found resonance with a large number of people whose curiosity was aroused by its far-ranging theories including the possibilities that visitors from other worlds may have come to Earth, and that some members of the human race may have mutated into what they called 'superior beings.' The book appeared at a time when there was a growing interest in the West in alternative spiritualities and culture that was to develop into the New Age movement. Bergier died in 1978. In the 1970s, Pauwels launched a magazine supplement for the newspaper *Le Figaro*. He later converted to Catholicism.

ELIZABETH LOVING

Morphic Resonance

The theory of evolution by natural selection, first propounded by Charles Darwin (1809–82) and now regarded as dogma by most biologists, maintains that new species of living organisms develop gradually over many generations. A small, and presumably chance, genetic change results in a modification of the organism, which is subsequently transmitted to its offspring; if this modification is favourable to its survival, giving it an advantage over its relatives, and is succeeded by additional favourable modifications, it will result in the organism's eventual domination. This is taken, for example, as the explanation for the long neck of the giraffe, which allows it to reach leaves high on trees that are denied to other species.

It can be seen that there are objections to this theory. The giraffe is also capable of browsing on lower leaves, and its superiority in reaching its food supply should, if the Darwinists are correct, have resulted in the eventual extinction of all other browsing species in its immediate environment. Yet the other species are still with us.

Infinite Variety

There are other objections. In the plant kingdom, for instance, there are species with a wide variety of flower and leaf that appear to survive together in the same environment. And in the bird world many species have evolved which are apparently ill-adapted to their surroundings: birds with huge decorative feathers that hinder their movements, or birds that find great difficulty in launching themselves into the air once they have landed on the ground.

Geneticists regard the ancestors of these species as freaks or 'sports' that developed by accident, and that somehow managed to survive in an environment where they encountered little competition.

This is clearly in contradiction of the theory of gradual evolution. Darwin himself favoured, to a degree, the theories of the earlier Lamarck (1744–1829), who believed that adaptation to circumstances in one generation could be transmitted to succeeding generations—a suggestion that modern Darwinists deny. Thus the ancestral giraffe could be supposed to be an animal that managed to stretch its neck sufficiently to reach higher leaves, and this ability was passed on to its offspring.

The modern British biologist Rupert Sheldrake (b. 1942) has advanced a theory, to which he gave the name 'morphic resonance,' which attempts to reconcile these conflicting views. He drew upon the concept of 'morphogenetic fields,' proposed by certain embryologists. This theory supposes the existence of some kind of force field surrounding the developing embryo that determines the emergence of the different features of the body.

Sheldrake pointed out that the evolution of marsupials in Australia closely reflected the evolution of placental mammals in the rest of the world. There are (or were) marsupial wolves, cats, anteaters, moles, and other species. It was as if they had 'tuned in' to some worldwide force that had determined the development of their shape and appearance. Sheldrake suggested that the morphogenetic field could be envisaged as extending, not only through space but also through time, which would explain the sudden reappearance of atavistic forms, such as horses born with two toes like their primeval ancestors.

New Laws of Science?

Morphic resonance, as Sheldrake termed it, would explain how an embryo developed to resemble the physical example of other members of the species in its vicinity. It would also explain an observed phenomenon: that different populations of the same species, widely separated geographically, can suddenly, and without any apparent reason, develop similar peculiarities of behaviour. For instance, tits (a nonmigratory species) have discovered in Britain how to remove or pierce the caps of milk bottles; similar behaviour has been observed hundreds of miles away in Germany.

The astrologers were the first to have trouble with the authorities, who equated their science with fortune-telling.

Sheldrake postulated that accepting the existence of morphic resonance could help to explain many psychic phenomena such as telepathy, precognition, and psychokinesis. 'If the hypothesis of morphogenetic fields could be confirmed by experiment,' he wrote, 'it would involve the discovery of a new set of laws providing connections between things across space and time—laws that have not yet been recognized by science.'

Nazism

It is impossible to estimate the extent of the influence upon the nascent Nazi Party, during its first years in 1920's Germany, of the doctrines of such occultists as Lanz von Liebenfels (1874–1954), Hermann Pohl and the *soi-disant* Rudolf Freiherr von Sebottendorff (1875–1945).

Lieberfels was the founder (by his own account in 1894, but certainly by 1907) of the Order of the New Templars, a rabid racial eugenist who proposed many of the principles of the German 'master race' later taken up by Heinrich Himmler (1900–45) in the S. S., and among the first to use the swastika as a symbol of German nationalism. Pohl was the founder (in 1911) and first Chancellor of the Germanen Order, planned as a Teutonic answer to Freemasonry, which was held to be dominated by an international conspiracy of powerful Jews.

In 1916 Pohl broke with the Germanen Order and formed a splinter group, the 'German Order Walvater of the Holy Graal.' Shortly after this, he made the acquaintance of Sebottendorff—an adventurer and astrologer whose real name was Adam Alfred Rudolf Glauer—and appointed him Grand Master of the Order's Bavarian Province. In January 1918 Sebottendorff began publication of *Runen*, a periodical devoted to Nordic mysticism and anti-Semitism. He was assisted by Walter Nauhaus, who was another member of Walvater, and head of a study circle known as the Thule Society, whose arms also incorporated the swastika.

In July 1918 Sebottendorff purchased the Franz Eher Verlag, publishers of a bankrupt newspaper; under its new title of *Münchener Beobachter und Sportsblatt*, he filled its pages with a mix of anti-Semitism and horse-racing tips. Soon after he changed its name again, to *Volkische Beobachter*, later to become world famous as the official journal of the Nazi Party.

The Workers' Party

The chaos in Germany that followed the armistice of November 11, 1918, excited Sebottendorff and his fellow members of the Thule Society to feverish activity. They decided that the Marxist philosophy being promulgated among the workers in Bavaria needed a strong counter-influence, and one of their number, Karl Harrer, (1890–1926) accordingly founded the Deutsche Arbeiterpartei (German Workers' Party) on January 5, 1919. A year or so later this party added the all-embracing phrase 'National Socialist' to its title becoming the NSDAP—abbreviated to Nazi Party.

Among the journalists working for Sebottendorff was Dietrich Eckart (1868–1923), an alcoholic, morphine addict, and anti-Semite; in 1919 he began publication of an anti-Jewish periodical, *Auf Gut Deutsch* (In Plain German). Closely associated with Eckart was a certain 'Tarnhari,' an occultist who claimed to be the reincarnation of the chief of the ancient Teutonic tribe, the Volsungen. Tarnhari was a disciple of Guido von List (1848–1919—who had been the very first in Germany to make use of the swastika symbol—and published a magazine called *Swastika Letter*.

Adolf Hitler (1889–1945) had developed his anti-Semitic opinions some eight years earlier as a starving art student in Vienna, almost certainly under the influence of issues of von Liebenfels's *Ostara*, the so-called 'Pamphlets of the Blond Fighters of the Rights of Man.' According to August Kubizek (1888–1956), a friend of Hitler at the time, his interests also included 'oriental religion, astrology, yoga, hypnotism, and other aspects of occultism.'

The Evil Swastika

Hitler left Austria for Munich in the spring of 1913, and two days after declaration of war in August 1914 he volunteered for service in a Bavarian regiment. In September 1919, while still a serving corporal, he became the fifth member of the DAP, following in the footsteps of Captain Ernst Röhm

(1887–1934) and Dietrich Eckart. Under their influence he met other members of the Thule Society, and absorbed much of their ideology of Teutonic mysticism, though he deprecated their political ineffectiveness. In 1920, when he became Führer (leader) of the nascent Nazi Party, he insisted on the adoption of the swastika as its symbol—but, significantly, in its left-handed form, which many occultists regarded as a sign of evil and black magic. The party flag was designed by Dr. Friedrich Krohn, an occultist who was a member of both the Thule Society and the Germanen Order, and at about the same time, the party purchased the *Volkischer Beobachter*, 'at great sacrifice,' as its newspaper.

This is not the place to go into the history of the rise of the Nazi Party, the formation of the Sturmabteilung (SA—shock troops) under Röhm and their subsequent purge in 1934 by the S. S., and the consequent rise to power in the party of Heinrich Himmler. What is notable, however, is that in 1933, despite the avowed interest of both Himmler and the deputy Führer, Rudolf Hess (1894–1987) in occult matters, Hitler turned violently against those whose influences had helped to bring him to power.

When Hitler became Reich Chancellor on January 30, 1933 there was no easily identifiable German occultist movement. There were, however, countless groups concerned with esoteric traditions and theories, some of them large, such as the Theosophical and Anthroposophical Societies, and a great many small ones.

At that time Rudolf Hess was interested in a number of 'fringe' subjects, including neo-Paracelsian medical theories, and he was far from sceptical concerning astrology. Heinrich Himmler had not yet begun to rely upon astrological advice, but had a growing interest in Germanic or 'Nordic' occult subjects, such as the Edda sagas

and rune symbolism. Finally, since the Nazi Party by now included a wide cross-section of the German population, most occultist groups must have been represented among members.

The Germans now encountered the new phenomenon of *Gleichschaltung*, the purposeful integration of every conceivable organized activity according to the National Socialist philosophy of life. In some cases this meant no more than the immediate exclusion of Jews or individuals who were thought to be unsympathetic to National Socialist ideology. In the case of other organizations, where recognition by the authorities was desirable, the situation could become complicated.

The Freemasons were immediate candidates for official harassment. There had always been the supposition that Masonry was a department of occultism, but the major reason for its suppression was the belief that it represented a Jewish-dominated international conspiracy. Previous membership of a Masonic Lodge now prevented any former Mason from holding Party rank. This also applied to members of the Germanen Order, some of whom had been among Hitler's earliest supporters.

The astrologers were the first to have trouble with the authorities, who equated their science with fortune-telling. During the months before January 1933 there had been a spate of ill-informed and inaccurate speculation and prognostication in the popular astrological weeklies, and a lot of nonsense had been printed about Hitler and his astral prospects.

The Astrologers Protect Themselves

The leaders of the two most important astrological associations, both of which had large memberships, were soon taking steps to find a Party umbrella. They supposed, not without reason, that without protection the whole astrological movement might be in jeopardy, because an unrecognized science of this kind could soon find itself in an anomalous position in a totalitarian state. It is indicative that very few references to Hitler's horoscope were published after the summer of 1933 and none at all after the spring of 1934. Public speculations of this kind had become too dangerous.

Claims to represent the astrological movement led to an unseemly quarrel. The principal contenders were the Astrological Society in Germany, whose headquarters were in Leipzig, and the Central Astrological Office in Düsseldorf. The Leipzig group was controlled, by Hugo Vollrath, a bogus commercial occultist and owner of the Theosophical Publishing House. Vollrath had been making a living out of occult literature since about 1908, and had a vested interest in astrological books. He quickly joined the Party and reconstituted the Society on approved National Socialist lines.

Dr. Hubert Korsch (1883–1942), the President of the Central Astrological Office at Düsseldorf, also

hastily joined the Party as a protective measure. During the summer of 1933 both groups were busy lobbying Party offices in order to obtain official Nazi patronage, but without success. In the meantime Vollrath's monthly *Astrologische Rundschau* published articles refuting astrology's Babylonian, and hence Semitic, origins and asserting that it was an ancient Nordic science.

Furthermore, *Mensch im All* (Man in the Universe), an independent astrological monthly, as a matter of political expediency, effected a temporary merger with 'Professor' Ernst Issberner-Haldane's *Die Chiromantie* (Cheiromancy). Issberner-Haldane (1886–1966) was a well-known Berlin palmist. He was also a pathological anti-Semite and a prominent member of Lanz von Liebenfels' racialist and occult Ariosophical movement and of the Order of New Templars.

In the autumn of 1933, the police presidents in Berlin, Hanover, and Cologne instructed the local newspapers to refuse all advertisements from professional astrologers, and during

the spring of 1934, the Berlin police president banned all forms of professional fortune-telling. In Berlin and elsewhere the police began to confiscate booksellers' stocks of occult and astrological literature, although on an uninformed and haphazard basis. These measures affected the economic well-being of a number of specialist publishers and it was they, rather than the disorganized astrologers, who persuaded the Reich Chamber for Authors and Publishers to appoint an official censor for astrological books. Serious textbooks could still be published but the trash disappeared.

At the end of 1938, *Zenit* and *Astrologische Rundschau*, the two leading astrological monthlies, ceased publication. No explanation was offered to their readers. Furthermore the Theosophical Society, with which the *Astrologische Rundschau* was linked, was banned. After the annexation of Austria in 1938, Lanz von Liebenfels was forbidden to write for publication, although he considered himself to be one of National Socialism's spiritual fathers. When World War II began,

Reich eagle and swastika on the side of an electric locomotive in a Nuremberg museum, Germany

on September 1, 1939, the German occultist movement had already been driven more or less underground.

An Astonishing Prophecy

During the autumn of 1939, Dr. Goebbels' Propaganda Ministry was keeping a close watch on the two surviving astrological periodicals, *Stern und Mensch* and *Mensch im All*, since it was suspected that they might be the source of undesirable rumors. On November 10, Goebbels (1897–1945) ordered that the few surviving astrological almanacs be carefully scrutinized for anything that could be construed as a prediction of the mysterious attempt to assassinate Hitler at the Munich Burgerbrau beer cellar on November 8.

An astonishing prophecy in this connection, made by Karl Ernst Krafft (1900–45), a Swiss astrologer living in south Germany, had aroused considerable interest in exalted circles in Berlin. Krafft had written on November 2 to his friend Dr. Heinrich Fesel, who was employed in Himmler's department, to suggest that Hitler's life would be in danger between November 7 to 10. Dr. Fesel, unwilling to become personally involved, filed the letter and kept quiet. When on November 9 the newspapers and radio reported the assassination attempt, Krafft despatched a telegram to Rudolf Hess at the Reich Chancellery in Berlin and drew attention to his prediction. Fesel was now obliged to produce the letter. Krafft was immediately arrested at Urberg, a remote Black Forest village, and brought to Berlin for cross-examination. He was released a few days later.

In the meantime the credulous Heinrich Himmler was unsuccessfully trying to establish the identity of the would-be assassin by consulting a Viennese trance medium, who had been summoned to his Berlin headquarters.

Krafft's involuntary visit to Berlin coincided with Goebbels' new interest in the sixteenth-century prophetic verse quatrains of Nostradamus (1503–66) as a source for psychological warfare purposes. It was necessary to find a Nostradamus expert who could supply the Propaganda Ministry with appropriate material for processing. Krafft's name was first mentioned in this connection early in December 1939 and this led to an invitation to move to Berlin. He began work there during the first week of January 1940.

Although Krafft ostensibly worked for the Propaganda Ministry, his pay came from Hitler's department. Goebbels and his people were completely cynical as far as Nostradamus was con-

> Rudolf Hess's sudden flight to Scotland on May 10, 1941 had disastrous results for hundreds of Germans . . . identified with one or other department of occultism . . .

cerned. Not so Krafft, who sincerely believed that prophecies concerning Germany's victory over all enemies, present and future, could be decoded from Nostradamus's obscure quatrains. Tens of thousands of pamphlets based upon Krafft's 'discoveries' were circulating in French, Dutch, Italian, Serbo-Croat, Romanian, Swedish, and English by the middle of 1940.

A letter from Krafft, mailed from Berlin in February 1940, was sent by order of Himmler's department to M. Virgil Tilea (1896–1972), the Romanian Minister in London. Romania was still neutral but M. Tilea's anti-German sentiments were well known in Berlin. The letter was nothing less than an exercise in psychological warfare, and in that respect failed to influence Tilea, but had one unexpected result. Tilea, who

had a slight acquaintance with Krafft and somewhat grudgingly respected his prophetic abilities, concluded that, since he now unexpectedly wrote from Berlin, he must be advising Hitler or other highly placed Nazis.

Tilea showed Krafft's letter to a number of eminent gentlemen in London and suggested that, since Hitler was undoubtedly employing Krafft, it would be reasonable to engage a highly skilled astrologer whose task would be to deduce, from astrological evidence, the nature of the advice that Krafft was presumably giving to the Führer. Various departments of British Intelligence became involved and this led to the appointment, around September 1940, of Louis de Wohl (1903–61) as the 'Secret Service astrologer.' In London it was soon considered ineffective, and de Wohl was quietly dropped. He was later employed on a casual basis in London and the United States on psychological warfare projects that involved faked astrological predictions and bogus Nostradamus prophecies.

Krafft's own employment in Berlin did not last beyond the spring of 1940, although he subsequently wrote on a freelance basis a book that was published in French, Danish, and Portuguese. Its purpose was to demonstrate that Nostradamus had predicted an inevitable victory for Germany and the consolidation of Hitler's 'New Order' in Europe.

'Aktion Hess'

Rudolf Hess's sudden flight to Scotland on May 10, 1941 had disastrous results for hundreds of Germans who were known to be identified with one or other department of occultism, and with astrology in particular. Hess's disappearance greatly embarrassed the Nazi bosses, the more so since it had somehow to be explained to the German public. A solution was quickly found. It was proclaimed that Hess had been in poor health for many years and had latterly had resource to hypnotists and astrologers.

The subsequent 'Aktion Hess' led to the arrest of hundreds of occultists, with the astrologers at the top of the list. There were reasons for suspecting that the date of Hess's flight had been fixed on the basis of astrological considerations. Ernst Schulte-Strathaus, who was a member of Hess's personal staff at Munich, was an enthusiastic astrologer and his local expert on occult subjects. Schulte-Strathaus was arrested immediately, but denied that he was aware of Hess's plans or that he had given Hess any advice.

The 'Aktion Hess' was organized on a nationwide basis and practically all the arrests were made early on June 9, 1941. The victims included many Party members. Apart from the astrologers the Gestapo arrested a wide range of occultists: clairvoyants, radiesthetic practitioners, faith healers, and Nature-cure pundits, Ariosophists of the Lanz von Liebenfels school, members of the Christian Community (an Anthropo-sophical sect), anti-Semite Ariosophical Cabalists, and so on. The Gestapo's main attention was focused upon the astrologers, to identify whoever might have been in touch with Hess. It is unlikely that the 'missing astrologer' was ever found, if only because he or she probably never existed.

In the majority of cases, those arrested were released within a few days or weeks, although there were some important exceptions. Before being set free all were required to sign a declaration that they would neither practice astrology or any other occult science nor discuss the subject with anyone. All publishers'

and booksellers' stocks of occult literature were seized and many private collections were confiscated. Among those arrested and never released were Dr. Hubert Korsch and Karl Krafft. Although the men were acquainted, there was no connection between their respective cases. The Gestapo suspected Korsch on account of some anonymous articles that he had published about Hitler's horoscope, long before the latter came to power, and their main concern was to discover who had written them. The author's identity was never revealed, and Dr. Korsch was probably murdered at the Oranienberg concentration camp near Berlin on April 24, 1942.

The ritual festivals of the S. S. were derived from the calendar of the Nordic pagans . . .

However, even after the 'Aktion Hess,' the Nazis were apt to use astrology and other occult procedures when it best suited them. There was, for instance, the organization of the 'Pendulum Institute' at Berlin during the spring of 1942. It was directed by Captain Hans Roeder, of the German navy. British submarine-hunters were destroying an increasing number of U-boats, and it was supposed that they must be using a new detection technique. Roeder had proposed that the British were identifying the positions of U-boats by the use of pendulums.

Swinging the Pendulum

The pendulum operator, it was suggested, sat with a chart of the Atlantic ocean in front of him. He would then 'search' the map and, when the position of a German submarine had been reached, the pendulum would begin to swing in the prescribed manner. Cap-

tain Roeder hoped to employ German naval personnel in the same way.

The purpose of the Institute was to discover the correct techniques so that naval pendulum swingers could be trained to locate British convoys. A number of German radiesthetic practitioners, and some alleged 'sensitives' with no previous experience, were recruited under conditions of the strictest secrecy. For days on end they untiringly swung their pendulums, but apparently to no very useful purpose. With few exceptions they had previously been arrested in the course of the 'Aktion Hess' and had been released. Some had nervous breakdowns and others managed to make their escape upon one pretext or another. The experiment was a complete failure.

The assistance of the occultists was again recruited after Mussolini (1883–1945) was arrested by the Badoglio government on July 25, 1943. Hitler had peremptorily demanded that the Duce should be found and brought back to Germany. The problem was, however, that the Germans did not know where Mussolini was and, when their military intelligence service failed to produce any useful information, the occultists were again called in to help—not by the military but by Himmler personally.

Once again previous victims of the 'Aktion Hess' were assembled, including Wilhelm Wulff (1892–1979, an astrologer who had previously spent a brief and disagreeable period at the Pendulum Institute. According to Walter Schellenberg, the sceptical head of Himmler's foreign intelligence department, a pendulum expert correctly suggested that Mussolini would be found on an island to the West of Naples. The Duce had, in fact, first been taken to one of the small Ponza islands that he indicated. A little later he was transferred to the mainland

and a small German airborne force eventually abducted him from his mountain eyrie.

Himmler's personal involvement with astrology came to a head in 1943 when Felix Kersten, who gave him remedial massage for stomach cramps and other ailments, steered Wilhelm Wulff in his direction. During 1944–5 Wulff had frequent meetings with the Reichsführer and was still being consulted by him when the Third Reich was on the verge of defeat in April 1945.

Death's Head Cult

Himmler's other occult interests, however, had found expression in the mythology of the S. S.. He regarded himself as the reincarnation of Heinrich the Fowler (875–936), who had founded the Saxon royal house and driven the Poles eastward, and on the thousandth anniversary of the king's death he had sworn an oath to continue Heinrich's 'civilizing mission in the east.' Thereafter, he made a pilgrimage each year to the king's tomb and spent some time in silent meditation.

The ritual festivals of the S. S. were derived from the calendar of the Nordic pagans, with midsummer as one of its high points, and marriages, baptisms, and funerals were carried out by local S. S. leaders. At weddings, the couple exchanged vows and rings, and then received a gift of bread and salt. The first child of such a marriage received a silver-plated mug from Himmler, and the fourth child a silver candlestick inscribed: 'You are but a link in the endless chain of the clan.'

The centre of the cult was situated in the castle of Wewelsburg, near Padersborn in Westphalia. Himmler purchased this in 1934, and during the following nine years spent a vast sum on its restoration. The banqueting hall was furnished with a large table, around which stood thirteen throne like chairs; here Himmler and his closest subordinates would sit, silently meditating on the 'race soul.' In the crypt below, twelve stone pedestals awaited the ashes of the coats-of-arms of the chosen of the death's head cult.

ELLIC HOWE

FURTHER READING: Ellic Howe. Urania's Children: The Strange World of the Astrologers. *(London, UK: William Kimber, 1967). Francis King.* Satan and Swastika. *(Cranston, RI: Mayflower, 1976); W. Wulff.* Zodiac and Swastika. *(London, UK: Arthur Barker, 1973).*

Neo-Pagan German Cults

The first neo-pagan German religious sects emerged at the beginning of the twentieth century. All of them were by-products of the German *völkisch* movement, a confused and complicated ideological phenomenon, stemming from the ideas of the late Romantic movement and German nationalism. As a social group, the *Völkischen* were mainly middle class, and identified with a passionate and, indeed, irrational belief in the sanctity of everything that was specifically German or 'Germanic;' they reflected the most extreme and chauvinistic form of German nationalism. The Völkischen, with their countless leagues and associations, were politically ineffective but nevertheless constituted an active and often vociferous pressure group.

The Völkischen were universally anti-Semitic. They believed that the Jews, whether of German or any other nationality, represented dishonest, decadent, and racially inferior qualities. In contrast, the Germanic race was noble, heroic, honest, and possessed of all the attributes proper to a *Herrenvolk* or master race.

Germany was ostensibly a Christian country, predominantly Protestant in the north and largely Catholic in the Rhineland and south. Only a small proportion of the population can have been identified with neo-pagan beliefs, but the phenomenon is of historical and sociological interest because of the Nazis' ambivalent attitude to Christianity after their rise to power in 1933. Their anti-Semitism was directly inherited from the pre-1914 generation of Völkischen.

Many members of the various völkisch groups were opposed to conventional Christian beliefs. A major reason for their hostility to Christianity was that Jesus himself was a Jew; so they put forward the hypothesis that since he was a great spiritual teacher he *must* have been an Aryan. The Old Testament was dismissed out of hand as Jewish folklore and therefore contemptible nonsense. And so, there were people who wanted to create a Germanic form of Christianity, from which all Jewish elements were eliminated, and others who completely rejected Christianity in favour of a wholly Germanic religion.

A number of widely read nineteenth century German writers had paved the way for the first German neo-pagan sects. The philosopher Schopenhauer (1788–1860), who was sympathetic to Buddhism, had protested against Christianity's 'optimistic Jewish tendencies.' The philosopher Nietzsche (1844–1900) had asked why 'the strong races in northern Europe had not rejected the Jewish god and created a new one.' Felix Dahn (1834–1912), a popular historical novelist proclaimed that 'whatever is Christian is not Germanic, and whatever is Germanic is not Christian . . . there is also an ethical ideal in the old pagan morality; rough and manly, but by no means barbaric.' Dahn's enthusiasm for his Germanic ancestors and their virtues led the Roman Catholic

Church to accuse him of fostering the revival of a Wotan cult. In his book *The Jewish Question* (1880) a sociologist, Eugen Dühring (1833–1921), suggested that the ancient Nordic gods were still alive, and had remained so during the period when they were driven underground by Christianity.

Houston Stewart Chamberlain (1855–1926), British by birth but German by choice and Wagner's son-in-law, was without any doubt the most influential of the anti-Christian publicists. In *Foundations of the Nineteenth Century* (1899) he categorically stated that Christ could not have been a Jew. He suggested that the Germans would find salvation only in a religion corresponding to their essential nature. And the latter could only be Germanic.

Hence the ancient Germans represented something closer to the roots of what was morally and ethically desirable than did their early twentieth century successors. Old Germanic religious beliefs, in so far as they could be identified, reflected a source of primeval strength. It followed, then, that ancient symbolism, such as the runes and swastika, and old legends, such as the one surrounding Mitt-gart, said to be the home of the original Nordic gods, had an immediate significance. The *Edda*, a collection of ninth to eleventh-century Scandinavian sagas, became the equivalent of Holy Writ for the völkisch neo-pagans.

Splits and Schisms

The internal history of the German neo-pagan sects is extremely complicated because of their continual fissions and regroupings. Membership statistics were almost invariably for

View of the 'Crypt' designed in one of the Wewelsburg Castle's towers by Himmler. The circular crypt had a gas pipe in the floor for an eternal flame and a swastika on the ceiling.

private circulation only. It is possible, however, to distinguish three groups.

The first was the loosely-organized *Germanische Glaubensgemeinschaft* (Community for Germanic Beliefs), which was founded in 1907 by Professor Ludwig Fahr-enkrog (1867–1952) of Barmen. In 1911 Fahrenkrog and his followers joined forces with O. S. Reuter (b 1876), the author of *The Mystery of the Edda*, and his German Religious Fellowship. Dr. Ernst Wachler, a well-known figure in völkisch circles, and his Wotan Society also became affiliated with the

Fahrenkrog group in 1913. At about this time Fahrenkrog's sect changed its title and became the Germanic Belief Fellowship. Meanwhile, Reuter and his followers broke away, and founded yet another sect. This group became the esoteric 'inner circle' of Reuter's *Deutsche Orden*, the German Order, which later organized a völkisch rural settlement called 'Donnershag,' after the Germanic god Donar.

A third group, the *Volkschaft der Nord-ungen*, or 'Nordungen Fraternity,' originated in German youth movement circles, c. 1913. Here again there was an eventual affiliation with the *Deutsche Orden*. The emphasis was on the revival of the values supposed to be inherent in the ancient Germanic civilization. 'The aim and significance of our every action is Nordland' (the North-land or Nordic-land). Apart from these three major groups there were a fair number of very small ones, none of them well documented.

Neo-pagan 'Christening'

Candidates for admission to Fahrenkrog's sect had to attest that they had no non-Aryan blood in their veins: 'In marriage I will keep my blood pure and educate my children in this sense.' In the household, the father was to assume the role of priest and to officiate at 'Germanic' christenings, confirmations, marriages, and funerals. Local groups met annually to celebrate the summer solstice (which was always an important festivity in völkisch circles). The sect had no religious system; there was merely a mystical identification with a whole series of very hazy concepts—blood, race, Germanic virtues, and so on. All this applied to Reuter's 'Fellowship,' whose members were required to 'strive for the Volkisch and moral rebirth of the German *volk* (race) in a Germanic spirit, namely on the basis of German godliness.'

These people did not merely study the *Edda*. Their literary canon included the writings of Meister Eckhart (c. 1260–c. 1327), one of the profoundest speculative thinkers among the German mystics, Paracelsus and Jacob Boehme, and also Johann Fichte (1762–1814) and Paul de Lagarde (1827–81), whose intellectual influence on the Völkischen was profound. Readings from these and other acceptable, that is Germanic, authors were common to the meetings of all sects.

The same 'festivals' were celebrated by the various neo-pagan fellowships. The principal ones were the *Oster* (Easter) feast, named after the Anglo-Saxon goddess Eostre, followed by High May (observed at Whitsun), the feast of the May Queen or May Bride and her partner. The *Jul* (Yule) feast was held at Christmas. The Christian Good Friday was observed as a day of remembrance for the 4,500 Saxons said to have been slaughtered by Charlemagne at Verden an der Aller in 772. The Christian Feast of the Ascension was replaced with one associated with the myth of Thor's hammer.

The völkisch periodical *Rig* contains an account of a 'christening' ceremony held in the Forstenrieder Park near Munich. 'In the centre of five old oak trees we made a table from boulders. On the table is placed a bronze hammer and a bowl of water from the pond close to the beech trees. . . . The mother lays the child at the father's feet. The father bows and takes the child in his arms, saying: "I recognize you as my own, take you into our kindred and give you a name. I sprinkle you with the pure water of the German spring. May all that is un-German be alien to you . . ."'

Fahrenkrog's plan to build a cathedral was never fulfilled. There were to be three aisles and where they met an altar of stone; behind it a table on which were to be placed a copy of the *Edda*, Thor's hammer, and a ring upon which solemn oaths were to be sworn. The sermon was to be based upon a text from the same work. At the end of the service a small pile of wood, previously placed upon the altar, was to be ignited with a tinder and flint.

In 1931–32 these groups united as the Nordic Religious Working Community. They appear to have been neither encouraged nor attacked by the Nazis after 1933.

While there were undoubtedly some Germans who actually indulged in a form of Wotan worship, most authorities are inclined to believe that the groups in question were both few and small. There are stray allusions to a Sun Religion sect that existed during the early 1900s, but once again it cannot be adequately documented.

Fahrenkrog revived his sect, although on a very small scale, after 1945, but it must be remembered that the old pre-1914 völkisch movement was already in a state of decline by 1933. Hitler himself despised these sects because they were politically ineffective; of the major Nazi leaders, only Himmler appears to have been vaguely influenced by the völkisch tradition. Fahrenkrog died in 1952 and his sect with him; and there is no evidence of neo-pagan religious sects in Western Germany today.

ELLIC HOWE

Teresa Neumann

A visionary and bearer of the stigmata, Teresa Neumann was born in 1898 and lived all her life at her birth-place,

> *On her bed, in her home in Konnersreuth, she appeared to witness and to some extent reenact the various scenes of the passion of Christ.*

Konnersreuth, a village in Bavaria not far from the Czechoslovakian border. After leaving school she worked at the local inn and during World War I, she helped on a farm. On March 10, 1918, during a fire at a neighbouring farm, she injured her back. This event was the prelude to a complicated medical history. After her return from hospital, uncured, there followed a progressive deterioration in her health and she became bedridden, suffering from temporary blindness and deafness, appendicitis, convulsions, paralysis of the legs, and purulent sores on her back and feet. In 1923 she regained her sight on praying to St. Teresa of Lisieux (whose beatification occurred on the same day that year). In 1925 she renewed her prayers to the saint on the day of her canonization, and recovered the use of her legs; her other ailments also disappeared. She now enjoyed some semblance of health, though the original medical diagnosis, made before there was any question of preternatural phenomena, suggested that the illness was largely hysterical; this introduces a doubt into the whole affair.

Wounds of the Passion

In mid-Lent, 1926, she began to exhibit the phenomenon of stigmtization: the reproduction on the body of the wounds of the Passion of Christ, particularly (but not exclusively) the wounds on hands, feet, and side. In Teresa Neumann's case, as with others in the past, it was accompanied by other manifestations, including abstinence from food, precognition, and visions of the Passion.

On her bed, in her home in Konnersreuth, she appeared to witness and to some extent to reenact the various scenes of the passion of Christ. For some years this was a weekly occurrence when, beginning on Thursday night, her stigmata would bleed, she would pass into a state of trance, and utter cries as if suffering pain or witnessing distressing events. The bleeding appeared to be profuse and occurred not only from her hands, feet, and side, but also from her forehead, as if from a crown of thorns. She seemed to exist on a spoonful of water daily; after September 1927 she gave this up also, and her only sustenance was the daily reception of Holy Communion.

In the late '20s and '30s, despite the reserved attitude of the Church authorities, Konnersreuth became a place of pilgrimage. Crowds flocked there at all seasons of the year, and especially at Easter. Immediately after the World War II many US soldiers found their way there. The phenomena were received quite uncritically and to question their supernatural origin was to invite obloquy from the very active 'Friends of Konnersreuth' who bitterly opposed those who, in their view, wrote against Teresa Neumann. Toward the end of her life, Teresa's phenomena seem to have diminished—certainly in 1951 some who made the journey to Konnersreuth were disappointed on at least one occasion—and in the last five years of her life little was heard of her. She died in 1962.

She was not of course by any means the only example of such phenomena. There are upward of 300 recorded cases of stigmatization, beginning with Francis of Assisi in the thirteenth century, and continuing in every century since then down to Padre Pio, who died in 1968. By far the greater majority of them have been women, and the only two cases of complete stigmatization in men are the two just mentioned: St. Francis and Padre Pio. Father Herbert Thurston (1856–1939), who made a life-long study of these phenomena, wrote:

'The impression left upon me has been that the subjects who were so favoured or afflicted were all suffering from pronounced and often hysterical neuroses. Many of them were intensely devout (of course it is only in the case of people whose thoughts were concentrated on religious motives that one would expect to find this type of manifestation) but in others piety was combined with eccentricities and with apparent dissociations of personality which were very strange and not exactly edifying. I find it difficult to believe that God could have worked miracles to accredit such people as his chosen friends and representatives.'

How are we to judge Teresa Neumann and account for her strange phenomena? When Louise Lateau, the stigmatist of Bois d' Haine, in Belgium, died in 1883, the prevailing opinion among her coreligionists was

that the extraordinary phenomena in her case were marks of divine favour, and that to doubt their preternatural character was to display a lack of faith. Nowadays, with the greater resources of modern medicine and, perhaps, with a clearer notion of all the implications, a more cautious attitude is commoner.

Analysis of Blood

In the case of Teresa Neumann, there were too many unanswered questions for a categorical assertion that all the phenomena really occurred as they were usually reported. Teresa's fast was never rigorously controlled to the satisfaction of the Church authorities or the medical men that they called in to advise on the case; too many of the allied phenomena resembled too closely those that have been observed to occur in other paranormal but non-religious contexts; the blood observed on the stigmata by one expert witness was never seen to flow from them but appeared on the wounds after Teresa had escaped observation beneath the bedclothes, or when the witnesses had been sent out of the room (it was the same observer, Dr. Martin, who alleged that some of the blood proved when subjected to analysis to be of menstrual origin).

Whatever the truth of these matters, it seems certain that, to the Church authorities, what is important is the life of the subject under examination. In the case of Gemma Galgani, who died in 1903, for instance, the Roman Catholic Congregation of Rites, which deals with canonizations, in declaring her to be a saint explicitly refrained from giving any verdict on the preternatural character of her stigmata and allied phenomena, saying that it was a matter 'upon which no decision is ever given.' In other words, the stigmata and allied phenomena are unimportant, and we should look to the teaching and lives of the mystics

and leave on one side what, on a last analysis, is their occupational disease or at least their occupational hazard.

LANCELOT SHEPPARD

FURTHER READING: S. J. Herbert Thurston. The Physical Phenomena of Mysticism. *(London, UK: Burns & Oates, 1952); S. J. Herbert Thurston.* Surprising Mystics. *(London, UK: Burns & Oates, 1955); Hilda Graef.* The Case of Therese Neumann. *(Cork, Ireland: Mercier Press, 1952); Paul S. J. Siwek.* The Riddle of Konnersreuth. *(Dublin, Ireland: Browne & Nolan, 1954).*

New Age

A growing dissatisfaction with contemporary materialism, and a re-awakened interest in spiritual matters, began to be expressed during the 1960s. At first no more than an alternative 'fringe' movement, it gradually drew into its orbit such an eclectic range of beliefs and practices, promulgated by a remarkable mix of thinkers and seers, that it merited identification as an emergent cultural philosophy. Drawing upon the fact that the point of the Spring equinox was moving out of the sign of Pisces, with the consequent 'dawning of the age of Aquarius,' the ethos quickly earned itself the title of 'New Age.'

Those who subscribe to New Age beliefs hold that 'science, technology, and a higher standard of living, for some, do not necessarily produce happier human beings or make the world a better place;' they subscribe to 'a shared belief in a different way of being that is life enhancing, and the conviction that we have far more potential than we are realizing and that, in changing ourselves, society as a whole can be transformed.'

New Age philosophy is characterized by a renewed interest in non-Western beliefs—the *chakras* of Hinduism, Chinese *tao*, the tenets of Zen Buddhism, even the mythology of the North American First Nations peoples—combined with a belief in the most esoteric aspects of Western occultism. A syncretic philosophy is being developed in which body, mind, and spirit are regarded holistically: ayurvedic theories are equated with medieval European herbalism, Chinese medical practice is combined with the most unorthodox branches of modern psychology, and the use of the Tarot pack and the horoscope share equal significance with the Dreamtime of the Australian aborigine or the Spiritualist seance. 'Fundamental to New Age belief is the idea that the awakening of the Higher Self is the goal of human life, and that the process of awakening is transformation.'

Lanz claimed Hitler, above, used his theories on race to develop his own ideologies.

New Templars

Viennese occultist, racial theorist, and founder of the Order of New Templars, Dr. Jörg Lanz von Liebenfels (1874–1954) was a representative member of what has aptly been described as the European 'intellectual underground.' The son of middle class but apparently well-to-do parents, he was born at Vienna on July 19, 1874 as Adolf Lanz. Nevertheless, he claimed that his father was Baron Johannes Lancz de Liebenfels and that he was born at Messina, Italy, on May 1, 1872. The incorrect birth date was intended to mislead astrologers who might be interested in his horoscope. His doctorate, however, existed only in his own imagination.

In 1893 at the age of 19, he became a novice at a Cistercian monastery at Heiligenkreuz (on the present Austro-Hungarian border) but was expelled six years later for 'worldly and carnal desires.' Shortly afterward

he founded his Order of New Templars, which had a strongly 'racial-religious' emphasis. In 1934, a year after Hitler (1889–1945) came to power, he wrote that the Order was 'the first manifestation of the Movement (i.e. Hitler's), which now, in accordance with the law of God, is most powerful in history and unrestrainedly sweeping over the world.' Lanz was not the only founder of a Central European sect to claim that he had anticipated Hitler's racial and other theories.

The Master Race
The largest and the most persistent bee in Lanz's bonnet was the necessity to defend the purity of the 'Ario-heroic' white master race. This could be achieved only by the maintenance of strict eugenic standards. Lanz was not exclusively anti-Semitic and was equally apprehensive about the sup-

posedly baneful effects of 'Germanic' intermarriage with people of Slav or non-white descent. Thus candidates for admission to his Order ideally had golden hair, blue or grey-blue eyes, a rosy complexion, a narrow skull and face, a high-bridged and narrow nose, and slim hands and feet.

Since this was the racial type that Lanz wished to perpetuate, it was necessary to breed such people. Hence his advocacy of the establishment of breeding colonies where one man might, if necessary, inseminate several women. Since he was eternally a theorist rather than a man of action he never personally implemented this design, but one or two somewhat similar experiments were made in Germany before 1933, although not under Lanz's auspices. Heinrich Himmler (1900–45) later proposed something of the kind for his S. S.

At least theoretically, Lanz anticipated all or most of the Nazis' repressive racial measures, such as the eradication of 'unsatisfactory' racial types or groups by castration or sterilization, starvation, forced labour, and other means. Nevertheless, it is unlikely that he would have countenanced the 'gas chamber' solution if he had been in a position to implement it. Lanz and his followers belonged to the fringe sector of the pre-Nazi Pan German movement.

The Order of New Templars represented the most esoteric of Lanz's multifarious activities as a racial publicist and 'authority,' and membership of its inner circle was limited to carefully selected initiates. The Order acquired its first Temple in 1907 when Lanz purchased and equipped Burg Werfenstein, a ruin high above the Danube River. It is recorded that he hoisted a flag incorporating a swastika there in that year, when Hitler himself was only eighteen years old. Lanz was an early user of the swastika symbol, which was soon to become associated with a score or more of *völkisch* or German nationalist groups in both Austria and the Reich. Other Temples were consecrated later at Marienkamp, close to the Plattensee, at Staufen near Ulm, and at Rügen on the Baltic coast. The Order also had cells at Salzburg and in Hungary.

Secret Bible

The New Templars never represented a mass movement and its existence probably remained unknown to all except an enthusiastic minority. With the exception of the dramatist August Strindberg (1849–1912), with whom Lanz was on friendly terms, no widely-known personalities were members.

The Order's initiates held 'Grail Celebrations' at Burg Werfenstein and elsewhere, and in duly impressive surroundings, garbed in white robes,

practiced the Order's rituals, all of which were written by Lanz.

Lanz created a vast ceremonial and pseudo-liturgical literature. This included *The Psalms in German, The New Templars' Breviary* in two volumes (1915–16) and selections of historical, moral and mystical readings for members of the Order, all taken from the literature of 'Ario-heroic' peoples of all eras. The *Hebdomadarium*, a collection of weekday prayers, was intended for use with the readings. Finally there was Lanz's *Bibliomystikon*, or 'secret bible for the initiated' in ten volumes. It is thought that Lanz's published works, largely forgotten today, amount to more than 15,000 printed pages.

Lanz was also the creator of an esoteric system known as Ariosophie, to which almost everything could be referred, particularly racial hygiene. There were a fair number of Ariosophists in Germany and Austria after 1918 and some of them were also members of the New Templars. An Ariosophical monthly published in Germany by Herbert Reichstein (1892 –1944), one of Lanz's most devoted supporters, reflects the sect's interest in most branches of occultism or pseudo-science: astrology, phrenology, the Cabala, fringe medicine, diet reform, and so on. Lanz himself wrote untiringly on all these subjects although 'race' was always his major preoccupation. By this he meant the superiority of the 'blond' race and its eternal battle with inferior races, which represented the powers of evil.

'The World Will Tremble'

In 1958 W. Daim (b. 1923), a Viennese psychologist, published a study of Lanz with the intriguing title *Der Mann, der Hitler die Ideen gab* (The man who gave Hitler the ideas). Daim tried to establish that Lanz's influence on Hitler was a substantial one. Hitler had one brief meeting with Lanz at Vienna in 1909, when he called at

his office to collect some back numbers of the latter's periodical *Ostara*. Hitler was then about twenty years old. In a letter written to a member of the New Templars in February 1932, Lanz proposed that 'Hitler is one of our pupils . . . you will one day experience that he, and through him we, will one day be victorious and develop a movement that makes the world tremble.'

However, when the Nazis finally came to power in 1933, Lanz supposed that his work as a pioneer racial eugenist and early protagonist of National Socialist ideology would be acclaimed in Germany, but this never happened. He was forbidden to write for publication when the Germans invaded Austria in 1938 and the Order went underground.

Hitler had realized as early as 1924, when he was writing the first volume of *Mein Kampf*, that men like Lanz were politically ineffective. In *Mein Kampf* he summarily dismissed them as *völkisch* wandering scholars, absurd figures without any positive influence, who had fought for forty years for a so-called idea without achieving the slightest success.

It would therefore be a mistake to overestimate Lanz's influence on Hitler or, indeed, his later genocidal policies. Lanz was but one of scores of Austrian and German writers and publicists who concerned themselves with the concept of 'race.' However, none of them, not even Heinrich Himmler, could match Lanz's obsessional identification with eugenic theories and racial mysticism.

Lanz died at Vienna on April 22, 1954. His wish to be buried at the monastery at Heiligenkreuz was refused. However, a rumour was current in New Templar circles that the monks were so anxious to have the mortal remains of their 'greatest son' that they secretly disinterred the body and removed it to the monastery at Heiligenkreuz for reburial.

ELLIC HOWE

Padre Pio

Francesco Forgione, the celebrated stigmatic affectionately revered by multitudes of Roman Catholics as Padre Pio, was born in 1887 in Pietrelcina, an out-of-the-way town in southern Italy. The man who was later to be crassly saluted by the *National Review* as 'the hottest thing in mysticism in the twentieth century' grew up in humble circumstances as the son of a farmer, and suffered from frequent bouts of ill health. It was realized early on that he had a vocation for the Church and he joined the Capuchins in 1903. Ordained priest in 1910, he spent most of his adult life in the friary at San Giovanni Rotondo on the slopes of Monte Gargano, near Foggia.

As a young friar Padre Pio was frequently ill and also alternated between intense spiritual exaltation and profound depression—not an uncommon experience among mystics. He prayed earnestly to participate in Jesus's suffering on the cross and in 1910 he appeared with puncture wounds in his hands, which he said Jesus and the Virgin Mary had given him in a vision. He was embarrassed by the wounds, which eventually disappeared, but they reappeared a year later, accompanied by pain in the feet and side. Again the wounds vanished, but now Padre Pio began to experience diabolical visions, in which he was menaced by a monstrous black cat, saw alluring naked women, was attacked by demons, and beaten by torturers. Sometimes the blows left visible bruises.

In 1916 he joined the small community at San Giovanni Rotondo. He suffered from vomiting attacks and severe fevers, with temperatures high enough to break the thermometer. There were reports of his being seen in two places at once and of his seeing ghosts. He was thirty-one when, in 1918, alone in the chapel, he saw a vision of the crucified Christ, radiating shafts of light that pierced the friar's hands and feet. He came round lying on the floor, bleeding from the five wounds of crucifixion in his hands, feet, and side. A photograph taken in 1919 shows the marks of the stigmata in his hands. He found them very painful, and in normal circumstances he kept them covered by mittens.

The Church, as is its custom, viewed Padre Pio's stigmata with conspicuous reserve. As word spread of what had happened in the remote friary, however, excitement mounted. So many letters arrived that a special room had to be set aside for dealing with them, and pilgrims appeared in numbers that swiftly swelled into thousands. When Padre Pio's clothes were sent out to be laundered, they were cut up and sold. Tradesmen hawked pieces of cloth smeared with chicken or rabbit blood as relics stained with the blood of the holy man's wounds. People pushed aggressively into the friary, carried off chairs they thought he had sat on, and tried to pull the clothes off his back.

It appeared that Padre Pio had supernatural powers of healing and prophecy, which did not diminish the excitement. The touch of a glove he had worn cured a woman of stomach cancer in 1921, and there were other apparently miraculous cures. Many people testified to the fragrance emanating from his wounds, sometimes described as like violets or other flowers. He seemed to have extra-sensory powers, often knowing things about people or events at a distance that he could not have discovered by normal means. There were more stories of bilocation. On one occasion, for instance, he was found in his room, unconscious, and shivering violently with cold, though it was a warm day. It was later reported that at that same time he had been hearing the confession of a dying man up in the snow on the mountain.

Small, squat, and bearded, known for his matter-of-factness and practical common sense, Padre Pio was not comfortable with the awe in which he was held. He had a strong sense of humour and a talent for mimicry and practical jokes. He died aged eighty-one at San Giovanni Rotondo in 1968 and more than 100,000 people attended his funeral, many of them in tears. Pilgrims still visit his tomb.

Psychical Research

It is not easy to define psychical research. The purpose of the Society for Psychical Research (SPR) is 'to examine without prejudice or prepossession and in a scientific spirit those faculties of man, real or supposed, which appear to be inexplicable on any generally recognized hypothesis.' That psychical research is a 'science' in the sense that most psychical researchers attempt to investigate certain classes of phenomena, real or imaginary, 'without prejudice or prepossession' may indeed be granted; though it must be borne in mind that some of the groups which have called themselves societies for psychical research are in effect Spiritualist organizations.

Problems arise when one attempts to demarcate the alleged 'faculties of man' that constitute the special subject matter of psychical research. They cannot be just those faculties that are 'inexplicable on any generally recognized hypothesis,' because most human faculties are far from properly understood, and psychologists diverge as to how they should be explained.

Are they then faculties whose existence, rather than whose explanation, is in doubt? If that were so then, to the extent that the phenomena investigated were satisfactorily demonstrated, the subject itself would disappear. Furthermore, psychical research would include topics that are generally held to lie outside its scope (such as the question of whether or not humans may be sensitive to the direction of the earth's magnetic poles).

Could it be simply a historical accident that certain alleged 'faculties of man' are commonly held to constitute the subject matter of psychical research, while others are excluded? A case could be made out on these lines. The immediate ancestry of modern psychical research is to be found in certain aspects of the mesmeric and Spiritualist movements that spread across Europe and the United States during the early and middle nineteenth century. Some of the early mesmerists believed that mesmeric subjects might exhibit, not merely heightened faculties and heightened

responsiveness to the commands of the operator, but faculties that seemed to be almost unknown in unmesmerized persons. Accounts of thought transference, of clairvoyance, and 'eyeless vision,' of clairvoyant diagnosis and mesmeric cure of ailments, and of hypnosis at a distance, were in circulation quite early in the history of French and German mesmerism—in fact before the end of the eighteenth century. In the first part of the nineteenth century accounts of some of these kinds of phenomena became commoner in continental Europe; and in the 1830s and 1840s the mesmeric movement, and with it alleged instances of such phenomena, spread to the United States and Great Britain.

The mesmeric movement paved the way for the Spiritualist movement of the second half of the nineteenth century. It accustomed the public to

the idea that certain especially gifted persons might, when in a state of trance, exercise clairvoyant, and other paranormal faculties, and even to the idea that some mesmeric subjects might become aware of, and perhaps communicate with, the spirits of departed persons. The mesmeric trance developed, by an easy and natural transition, into the mediumistic trance, in which the medium's 'interior vision' might have imposed upon it scenes and personalities from the next world; and the rapport that was thought to exist between mesmerist and subject provided an analogy for the process by which departed spirits were thought to control the hand or vocal apparatus of a medium. A public that had digested the leading ideas of mesmerism had little difficulty in assimilating the beliefs of Spiritualists.

There can be little doubt that the central body of material commonly studied by psychical researchers comprises those seemingly novel faculties that were apparently revealed by the experiments of mesmerists, plus the developments of, and super additions to, those alleged faculties that took place in the context of the modern Spiritualist movement. The first 'psychical researchers' were in effect those persons who first attempted a dispassionate examination of these supposed faculties. One might mention, in particular, Sir William Crookes (1832–1919), whose *Researches in the Phenomena of Spiritualism* (1874) described his instrumental recordings of the phenomena produced by D. D. Home (1833–86) and other physical mediums.

Although it seems quite possible that the supposed paranormal faculties and phenomena that constitute the subject matter of psychical research have been grouped together largely for historical reasons, it could nonetheless be argued that, whatever the reasons for associating the phenomena, many

Portrait of Padre Pio found in Our Lady of Sorrows Church, Poland

of them do in fact together form a unitary class—a class to which similar laws and similar kinds of explanation will ultimately be found to apply. Whether psychical research can be marked out as a distinct branch of inquiry, or as a distinct branch of psychology, on grounds such as these, only time and sustained investigation will show.

Founders of the SPR

The history of modern psychical research can be roughly divided into three periods: from 1882 to 1914; from 1914 to 1945; and from 1945 to the present day. A great impetus was given to psychical research by the foundation, in 1882, of the SPR. Prominent amongst the founders and early members were Sir William Barrett (1844–1925), professor of physics at the University College of Dublin; Henry Sidgwick (1838–1900), professor of moral philosophy at the University of Cambridge; his wife Eleanor (1845–1936), later principal of Newnham College, Cambridge; F. W. H. Myers (1843–1901), poet, essayist, and classical scholar; Edmund Gurney (1847–88), a keen student of psychology and philosophy; Richard Hodgson (1855–1905), Australian by birth and one of Sidgwick's pupils; Walter Leaf (1852–1927), eminent both as a banker and a classical scholar; Frank Podmore (1856–1910), the historian of the Spiritualist movement, and a man of keenly sceptical mind; and Sir Oliver Lodge (1851–1940), a professor of physics at Liverpool University.

A number of these people, and their associates, most of them religious by upbringing, were of the opinion that recent scientific developments had not merely undermined orthodox religion, but were in danger of rendering any form of religious belief impossible. They felt there was just a chance that they could meet science with

English philosopher Henry Sidgwick (1838–1900), in c. 1890, who was one of the founders and the first president of the SPR

science, and by conducting strictly scientific inquiries into the more puzzling phenomena of mesmerism and Spiritualism, achieve not, perhaps, new religious insights, but at any rate the overthrow of the 'materialist synthesis' that had seemed imminent during the 1870s. To that end they gave unsparingly of their time and money and of their very considerable abilities; and within twenty years a great many data had been collected and the main outlines and the main problems of modern psychical research had become clear.

A comparable society was founded in the United States, following a tour

of that country in 1884 by Sir William Barrett. Its first president was Professor Simon Newcomb (1835–1909), the astronomer, and its leading early light was Professor William James (1842–1910), the philosopher and psychologist.

For the spectacular physical phenomena associated with Spiritualist mediumship, the S P R found at first little evidence, indeed, certain investigations whose results the S P R published seemed, by revealing the extent to which even honest and intelligent persons could be misled by deliberate conjuring, to cast doubt on the reality of any of the alleged physical phenomena. In 1886 S. J. Davey, a member of the SPR who was a skilled amateur conjuror, was introduced as a medium by Richard Hodgson, and succeeded in reproducing many of the feats of William Eglinton (1857–1933), one of the better-known physical mediums of the time. It was not until 1908 that the SPR was able to obtain evidence for 'physical phenomena' under anything like satisfactory conditions. Three of its most experienced members, Hon Everard Feilding, Hereward Carrington (1880–1958), and W. W. Baggally, had a series of sittings at Naples with a well-known Neapolitan medium, Eusapia Palladino (1854–1918). Eusapia had been detected in fraud by the three investigators; nonetheless, she many times produced for them seemingly inexplicable movements of objects, and materializations of hands, in fair light and under satisfactory conditions of control.

Reports were also received, and investigations conducted, of a number of poltergeist cases. The principal investigators of these cases were Sir William Barrett, who came to believe in the genuineness of some of the phenomena, and Frank Podmore, who concluded that fraud was probably always responsible.

The most striking experimental results published by the SPR in its early years were probably those obtained in certain experiments on telepathy. The design of many of these experiments would not nowadays be considered satisfactory; nonetheless, some of the results remain puzzling. Particularly curious were experiments on the telepathic transmission of drawings conducted during the 1880s by Mr. Malcolm Guthrie and Sir Oliver Lodge. In these experiments the transmission took place only over a short distance; but in the Miles-Ramsden experiments of 1906–8, the percipients were sometimes separated by many miles.

Case Histories on Ghosts

Soon after the foundation of the S P R, various members initiated a systematic and successful attempt to collect firsthand testimonies from persons who had seen apparitions. A considerable amount of testimony was obtained, and examples were found of 'haunting' apparitions, of collectively perceived apparitions, and of apparitions of the dead. By far the largest body of testimony, however, concerned 'crisis' cases, that is, apparitions that coincided in time with some crisis in the affairs of the persons they resembled, and in 1886 a two-volume survey of crisis cases and related material was published by Gurney, Myers, and Podmore under the title of *Phantasms of the Living*.

Gurney was the principal author, and he took the view that crisis apparitions are telepathically initiated hallucinations. In many instances the figures seen contained details which, Gurney felt, must have come from the mind of the percipient, strongly suggesting that the figures were in some sense 'constructed' by the percipients, that is, were hallucinations. The coincidences between the hallucinations and the deaths of the persons whom they represent may be accounted for by supposing that at some level of their personalities the percipients become aware of the crisis telepathically, and 'externalize' this knowledge in the form of a hallucination. Gurney held that this possibility was supported by the evidence for telepathy which had already been obtained both from actual experiments and from accounts of its spontaneous occurrence in everyday life.

The Common Hallucination

Edmund Gurney died in 1888, but his work on crisis apparitions was continued in the so-called 'Census of Hallucinations,' the Report on which was published in the *Proceedings* of the SPR for 1894. One of the principal aims of the census was to determine whether or not the coincidences between apparitions and deaths which marked the numerous recorded crisis cases could be set down to chance; whether, in other words, it might be that people who had hallucinations tended to forget or remain silent about their experiences except in those very rare cases where the hallucination chanced to coincide with the death of the person it resembled. Answers to a questionnaire on hallucinations put to 17,000 persons revealed that hallucinations are commoner among sane persons than might have been supposed (about one person in ten is likely to have had one), but also strongly suggested that the number of reported death coincidences could not be ascribed to chance.

The most interesting single case that was investigated in the early days of psychical research was undoubtedly that of the US trance medium, Mrs. Leonora Piper (1857–1950). Mrs. Piper came to the notice of psychical researchers in the year 1885 through the agency of William James, and she was intensively investigated for a good part of the next thirty years. Most of those who seriously investigated her mediumship became convinced that she possessed paranormal powers, and some (including Richard Hodgson, who had studied the case in great detail) that the 'communicators' who purported to speak or write through her organism were indeed the spirits of deceased human beings.

The most curious development in this, or perhaps any, period of the history of psychical research, however, was not the Piper case (though Mrs. Piper played a part in it) but the series of automatic writings known as the 'cross-correspondences.' The early leaders of the SPR all died relatively early—Gurney, aged forty-one in 1888; Sidgwick, aged sixty-one in

1900; and Myers, aged fifty-seven in 1901. Shortly after the death of Myers there began to emerge through various automatists a series of interlinked communications purportedly coming from Myers and various of his deceased friends. These, known as cross-correspondences, had ostensibly been constructed by these deceased persons as a means of proving their own survival.

Before he died, F. W. H. Myers had almost completed a large-scale survey of the whole field of psychical research. It was published in 1903 under the title *Human Personality and its Survival of Bodily Death*. In addition to presenting a mass of factual evidence, Myers developed a unifying theoretical framework that has had a good deal of influence. He suggested that a man's everyday stream of consciousness is only one of perhaps several streams of consciousness that may be connected with his organism. Many of the phenomena of ordinary life and of psychopathology—for instance, dreams, hypnosis, and hysterical tics and anesthesias—are to be understood as manifestations of these submerged or 'subliminal' streams of consciousness. Telepathy and other supernormal faculties are commonly to be found exhibited in dreams and hypnosis and even in certain hysterical states; and in Myers's view this suggests that the subliminal consciousness possesses powers which the ordinary waking consciousness does not.

Such phenomena as crisis apparitions or automatic writing embodying supernormal knowledge may then be understood as the means by which the subliminal consciousness may pass information in its possession to the

ordinary, waking consciousness, when the latter would otherwise remain ignorant of it.

Myers's studies in psychopathology brought him into contact with many leading psychologists, English, US, and European; and by the first decade of the twentieth century a number of

The contemptuous hostility with which a large part of the academic and scientific worlds had greeted the inception of psychical research had . . . been blunted . . .

them were seriously interested in psychical research. In the United States there was William James; in Austria, Freud (1856–1939); in France, Janet (1859–1947) and Bernheim (1840–1919); in Switzerland, Jung (1875–1961); in England, G. F. Stout (1860–1944), and William McDougall (1871–1938). The contemptuous hostility with which a large part of the academic and scientific worlds had greeted the inception of psychical research had to some extent been blunted by the persistence and the care and candour with which the early psychical researchers had set about their task. It seemed not altogether impossible that before long psychical research would become an accepted branch of scientific endeavour.

Between the Wars
World War I did not bring about any sudden break or change of direction in psychical research. The most influential figure on the English scene remained Mrs. E. M. Sidgwick, widow of Professor Henry Sidgwick. Together with her brother, G. W. Balfour (1853–1945), and her S P R colleagues J. G. Piddington and Miss Alice Johnson, she devoted much of her time to

supervising the collection and analysis of a growing mass of cross-correspondence scripts. She also studied certain aspects of the mediumship of Mrs. Gladys Osborne Leonard (1882–1968), perhaps the most remarkable mental medium of all time.

Mrs. Leonard's mediumship possessed a number of unusual features, in addition to the sheer quantity of impressive material that it provided. There were the celebrated 'book tests,' in which her 'control' Feda showed an apparent ability to read designated pages and lines in books not ordinarily accessible to the medium; there were also her successful 'proxy' sittings, in which the sitter obtained messages on behalf of an absent third party of whose concerns he was himself largely ignorant; and there was her 'direct voice'—a voice apparently not emanating from her own vocal apparatus, which sometimes joined briefly in the conversation under circumstances which made imposture highly unlikely.

In the United States the central figure of the 1920s was Margery Crandon (1888–1941), wife of a Boston surgeon. Around the physical phenomena of her mediumship there grew up controversies that deeply divided the US SPR, and led to the establishment of a separate organization, the Boston SPR, under the leadership of Dr. Walter Franklin Prince (1863–1934). Prince's own studies of the Doris Fischer case of multiple personality and of the automatic writings of Mrs. J. H. Curran (*The Case of Patience Worth*, 1923) remain among the classics of psi research.

A Telepathic Rationalist
Many of the investigations and controversies of the 1920s and the

1930s centered around alleged cases of physical mediumship. Serious investigations of these phenomena were more numerous then than at any other period before or since. Besides Margery Crandon, there was 'Eva C.,' who had been investigated before the war by Charles Richet (1850–1935, the French physiologist, and was studied again by Dr. Gustave Geley (1868–1924), by members of the SPR, and by a committee of the Sorbonne. Franek Kluski, a Polish professional man, was studied by Geley, who claimed startling results. None of these mediums won anything like universal confidence from those who investigated them. Perhaps the most interesting physical mediums of the period were two Austrians, Willi (1903–1971) and Rudi Schneider (1908–57), and especially the latter. Rudi was studied in England by Harry Price (1881–1948), who ran his own National Laboratory for Psychical Research in London, and by various members of the S P R, including Lord Rayleigh (1842–1919), the famous physicist. He was able to produce a variety of minor physical effects under seemingly stringent conditions of control—manual, electrical, and infrared.

Harry Price was from a different mould from the intellectual members of the SPR. He was a part-time salesman who wanted to engage with the realities of ghost hunting by examining the places thought to be haunted. He conducted the first live broadcast from a haunted house in southern England in 1936 and was the author of two books on Borley Rectory, Essex, deemed to be the most haunted house in England. In 1937 he was manager of an experiment lasting for a year to determine whether or not the Rectory was troubled by ghosts. The most reliable finding was that it was difficult to protect the site from curious outsiders. Eventually the house was sold on by the Church Commissioners and afterward burned down in a house fire.

In the study of apparitions, the two outstanding studies being Mrs. Sidgwick's *Phantasms of the Living*, published in the *Proceedings* of the SPR for 1923, and G. N. M. Tyrrell's *Apparitions* (1943), a theoretical discussion. Experiments on telepathy and clairvoyance were at first not numerous; the most interesting of them were perhaps those in which Gilbert Murray (1866 –1957), the noted Hellenist, acted as percipient, reports of which were published in the *Proceedings* of the S P R for 1918 and 1924 and in the *Journal* for 1941. Although a lifelong rationalist,

Professor Murray showed a very curious ability to pick up impressions of scenes . . . which groups of his friends concentrated on; it was these experiments that finally convinced Freud of the reality of telepathy.

Professor Murray showed a very curious ability to pick up impressions of scenes, drawn either from fiction or from real life, which groups of his friends concentrated on; it was these experiments that finally convinced Freud of the reality of telepathy.

Of note in a somewhat different way are the observations made by E. Osty (1887–1991) on a number of 'sensitives' or clairvoyants and published in his *Supernormal Faculties in Man* (1923). Osty's clairvoyants were able to give their sitters correct information not merely about matters known to those sitters, but about matters which, although relevant, were quite unknown to them. Some writers have suggested that the existence of powers of extra-sensory perception so extraordinary as these would, if confirmed, make it plausible to ascribe even the most 'evidential' mediumistic communications to telepathy and clairvoyance on the part of the medium, rather than to the influence of the spirits of deceased human beings.

Experiments at Duke

Later in the period, work on the problem of extra-sensory perception increased and assumed a form which has remained largely characteristic of it ever since. In 1927 William Mc-Dougall, went from Harvard to Duke University at Durham, North Carolina, to establish a department of psychology there. McDougall had been interested in psychical research for many years (he was a member of the SPR Council), and to his laboratory there came a young Harvard biologist, J. B. Rhine (1895–1980), and his wife, Louisa. Rhine set out to apply the ordinary methods of statistical analysis and experimental design to the problems of extra-sensory perception (ESP). He and his collaborators devised the pack of cards commonly called Zener cards. The order of these cards would be randomized, and an 'agent' would then turn them over one by one while a 'percipient' recorded guesses. Most of Rhine's subjects were students or members of the university staff, and a number of them succeeded in scoring well above the level of chance even under strictly controlled conditions. Occasionally—as in the famous Pearce-Pratt experiments of 1933 in which agent and percipient were in separate buildings 100 yards apart—the odds against chance reached an astronomical level. Rhine's early results were summarized in his book *Extrasensory Perception* (1934).

As a result of these findings, the Parapsychology Laboratory of Duke University was formally constituted. The adoption of the term 'parapsychology' instead of the older 'psychical research' marked the shift to a distinctively laboratory-orientated approach. Rhine and his associates weathered criticism from statisticians and academic psychologists, and continued to obtain striking results. They also attempted the first statistical investigations of 'physical phenomena.' Here again they made no use of professed mediums; yet above chance results were obtained. Ordinary persons were required to attempt to influence the fall of dice thrown at first by hand and later by mechanical means. To this effect the name of psycho-kinesis (PK) was given. The insistence on laboratory techniques in psychical research between the wars may be seen as a reaction to the fact that academic psychology had become steadily more behaviouristic and more 'scientific,' and therefore more hostile to the kind of psychical research that had been predominant during the first quarter of the century. Orthodox psychologists showed themselves less tolerant of psychical researchers than scientists from other fields; no doubt they found it hard enough to win recognition of the scientific status of their own subject, without its being joined to so dubious a yoke-fellow.

Recent Developments

In the period since World War II, the centre of activity has shifted away from Great Britain and Europe to the United States, where several important parapsychological institutions have been founded—the Parapsychology Foundation of New York (1952), the Parapsychological Association (1956) and the Foundation for Research on the Nature of Man (1964), successor to the Duke University Laboratories. In 1969, the Parapsychological Society was recognized as a science by the American Association for the Advancement of Science. Parapsychology units were established in various

US universities and research institutions, but these have enjoyed somewhat mixed fortunes, and several have been dissolved through lack of funds. In Europe a chair of parapsychology established at the University of Utrecht in 1974 was lost in 1988 during university cut-backs. Outside Europe and the US there has been academic interest in parapsychology in countries such as Brazil, Russia, and China, although in the two last-named the terms 'parapsychology' and 'psychical research' are avoided.

In recent laboratory-oriented parapsychology (say from the late 1960s onward), two broad tendencies may be discerned, even though much else has gone on outside them. The first, which is shared with psychology in general, is the widespread adoption of electronic technology. Targets are usually presented and guesses recorded by computerized systems, and the randomization of target orders is secured by the use of sub-atomic sources of randomness—'random event generators' or REGs.

The use of REGs has come into its own in PK experimentation. Automated PK experiments incorporating REGS were first pioneered by Dr. Helmut Schmidt (b. 1918) in the 1960s, and have since been extensively conducted by Robert Jahn (b. 1930) and his associates at Princeton University. Jahn's automated machinery generates ones or zeros at a very rapid rate. The (unselected) subjects aim to increase the frequency of targets of a given category, or to decrease it, or not to interfere with the output of the reg at all, and are given continuous feedback of results. A large number of subjects have carried out a very large number of trials, and, though the deviations from chance have been numerically small, very high levels of significance have been attained.

Not all recent PK experiments have used REGs. In some the targets have

been living systems or biological materials—for instance, mice, seedlings, enzymes, yeasts, and bacteria. Some significant results have been obtained, and throw light on the apparent successes of certain healers.

The second general tendency has been an increasing reversion to free response ESP experiments, that is to say experiments in which the range of target material, and hence the range of possible guesses, is not restricted to a small number of predetermined categories. Such experiments are perhaps more interesting to take part in than the dry routines of card guessing. For example, a number of investigators have carried out apparently successful experiments on 'remote viewing.' These are experiments in which subjects (usually 'psychically gifted' individuals) try to pick up images of a locality to which members of the experimental team have gone. Transcripts of the subjects' descriptions are sent to independent judges who rate them for correspondence to a series of sites, one of which was the actual target.

The Ganzfeld

The most celebrated and apparently most successful of modern free-response experiments are those involving the 'ganzfeld' technique. Ganzfeld experiments, which evolved out of the 'dream telepathy' experiments of M. Ullman and his collaborators, are a facet of a revived interest in the subject's state of consciousness as a possible determinant of success in ESP experiments. It is a very old idea that 'inner-directed' states of consciousness may be more conducive to success than 'outer-directed' ones. Ganzfeld situations—situations in which stimulation in all sensory modalities is kept as comfortably even and as undifferentiated as possible—are specially structured to promote a tranquil mental state in subjects, with a copious flow of imagery; then a 'sender' in a separate room tries to influence the flow of imagery in a direction suggested by a target picture, transparency, or video clip randomly selected from four possible targets. Afterward the subject is shown the four possible targets, and asked, by an individual who does not know the answer, to guess which was the actual target; or his description of his imagery may be rated by independent judges for correspondences to the targets. Highly significant results have been obtained in such experiments in a number of laboratories, and experiments (modified in the light of criticisms) are still in progress.

The leading exponent of the ganzfeld technique was Charles Honorton (1946–1992), whose final experimental setup had fully automated randomization and presentation of targets and recording of results.

Turning away from laboratory experiments to the investigation of examples of 'spontaneous' psychical phenomena, there can be no doubt that the most remarkable and most innovative work has been that of Professor Ian Stevenson (1918–2007) of the University of Virginia on children who exhibit verified ostensible memories of previous lives. Stevenson's *Twenty Cases Suggestive of Reincarnation* (1966; revised edition 1974) opened up what was (to Western parapsychologists at least) virtually an unknown field of inquiry, and set new standards in the careful investigation and recording of such cases.

Extensive studies by Stevenson and his collaborators have produced a large body of published case reports from which certain overall patterns have emerged and been confirmed—for instance that the memories are usually exhibited as soon as the child can speak, that the 'reincarnated' individu-

als often met violent deaths in the ostensible previous incarnation, and that the person concerned may exhibit skills and interests, as well as memories, related to the ostensible previous incarnation. The interpretation of this body of material remains controversial; but the material is impressive.

Cases of apparitions and poltergeists continue to be reported from time to time. No momentous discoveries have been made in connection with them, but several new lines of approach are being attempted. One is the detailed statistical analysis (made

Most of these healings are not expressly in the name of religion, although the practitioner may personally believe that it is God's work he is doing.

possible only by the use of computers) of large collections of cases in the hope of uncovering recurrent characteristics and relationships. Another is the application, particularly to cases of poltergeists, of the latest surveillance and recording technology, with the aim both of excluding fraud and of learning more about the physical nature of the phenomena. It remains to be seen what light, if any, these new approaches will throw on the peculiar happenings concerned.

ALAN GAULD

FURTHER READING: A. Gauld. The Founders of Psychical Research. *(Berlin: Schocken, 1968); B. Inglis.* Natural and Supernatural. *(London, UK: Hodder and Stoughton, 1977); J. Beloff.* Parapsychology: A Concise History. *(London, UK: Athlone Press, 1994).*

Psychokinesis

Psychokinesis or PK is what the layman calls 'mind over matter.' It is the ability to influence the objective environment without the use of the motor system of the body (the muscles and glands). PK is the counterpart of extra-sensory perception (ESP), which is the acquisition of knowledge without sensory aid. These two abilities make up the communication or exchange a person may have with his surroundings in the form of experiences that are familiarly called 'psychic.' Such communication is better known as parapsychical or psi behaviour, and its study is called parapsycholoty (or psychical research). PK ability is closely interrelated with ESP but it can well be handled as a separate topic—one that is only beginning to command as much human and scientific interest as the ESP phase of psi behaviour.

Reports of PK happenings appear in the records of the past as far back as records go. Today of course it is impossible to check on the reliability of such older reports as are available, but at least men believed they were witnessing miraculous physical events that seemed to have their origin in superhuman agency.

Whether the production of these mysterious physical effects was associated with the prevailing religious doctrine or attributed to one of the many systems of magic, the individual who was believed to exercise control over them was likely to become an influential member of the community, whether priest or magician. He might be the tribal rainmaker, healer, or the practitioner of some strange power to save or destroy. Belief in this ability to control the physical environment may still be found even today, and not only in less sophisticated cultures. There are

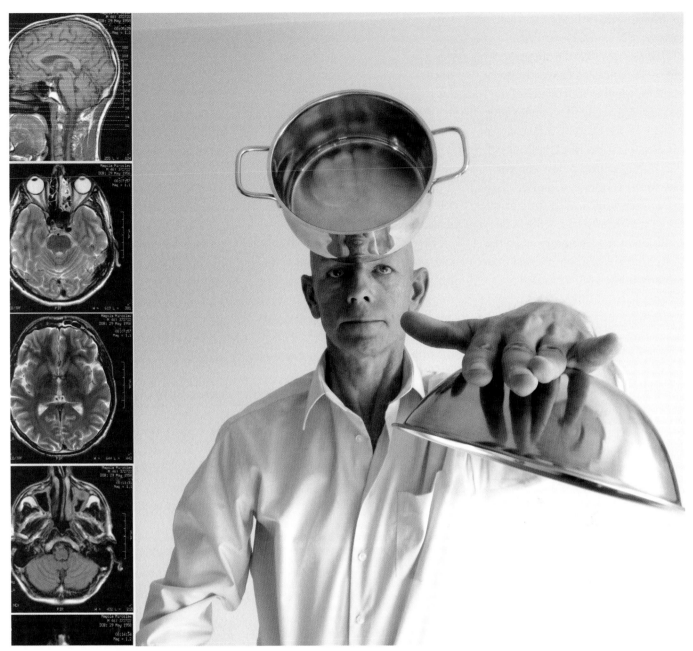

Stan Lee's Superhumans-Mind Force is a television series that follows contortionist Daniel Browning Smith, as he searches the globe for people with extraordinary physical or mental abilities.

actually many unorthodox practices of healing that suggest PK still going on 'within sight of some of the modern medical centres. For example, warts are reported to be removed from men and animals, at least without known physical intermediation. Other 'magical' therapies are practiced as well, such as the control of bleeding or the counteraction of injury from burns. Most of these healings are not expressly in the name of religion, although the practitioner may personally believe that it is God's work he is doing.

How valid these claims are no one can say. No practically dependable application of the alleged powers has emerged and persisted over the centuries as evidence of a reliable principle. Belief in supernatural physical effects has declined with the advancement of sciences, but this does not prove that no PK function ever operated to produce the effects men believed were unexplainable by physics. At most it indicates that the evidence for the PK interpretation has not been good enough for modern intellect.

Heritage from the Casino

The one magical practice that has persisted and even flourished right on down to the present day is gambling. In games of chance, the belief in luck, good and bad, is an intuitive acceptance of the traditional magical interpretation. Consistent winning (or for that matter consistent losing) in an honest game of pure chance would seem to require an element of psi ability. While in some of the games the most likely type of ability that could bring luck would be ESP, in others, such as the dice and roulette systems, PK would be needed.

The point is that the fair game of chance is basically a contest of psi abilities, whether it depends on the successful guessing of an opponent's card or on the effective influencing of his dice. However, the conditions of play do not permit a clear-cut measure of the psi element, and to a large extent they work against the consistent use of it. What was needed was the seclusion of the laboratory and a test design instead of a complicated game.

Early in the 1880s Professor Charles Richet (1850–1935) adapted a gamelike card-guessing technique to the testing of his hypnotized subject Leonie for clairvoyant ability. He also applied the new probability mathematics to the results. Leonie was 'lucky' enough to guess many more cards correctly than mean chance expectation, and when the extra-chance odds of these results were calculated they were (in today's terms) highly significant. It was an important step, but it was little noticed at the time.

The Duke PK Experiments

A half-century later, and in quite a parallel way, the technique of dice throwing was introduced at a climactic point in the ESP experiments that were going on in the department of psychology at Duke University. The idea spouted by many a gambler, Duke undertook to test what some people have long maintained, that in certain states of mind, which they call 'hot,' they can will dice to fall with desired faces turned up. The many volunteer student subjects who took part in these tests were stimulated to high motivation by the gamelike contest with the challenge to beat chance, and a large body of results accumulated, which for the most part favoured the PK hypothesis.

It was easy to apply the mathematics of probability, which furnished us

with the chance expectation for each test. The overall number of hits (as the dice were thrown for a designated face or combination of faces) was found in most of the series conducted to be statistically significant (that is, to exceed the chance rate of scoring by so large a deviation as could not reasonably be ascribed to chance alone). This success continued from experiment to experiment and from one research worker to another.

There had already been a strong case made for the clairvoyant ESP hypothesis, and it seemed logical to think that if the subject could communicate with a deck of cards completely cut off from sensory contact, the principle might be reversible—for every action in Nature there is an equal and opposite reaction. In other words, something might be happening to the deck of cards that was under the influence of the mind of the subject. If so, then it should be more effective on the rolling dice, where a subtle influence could be delicately registered.

Some Unknown Mental Agency

There was also the background of strange physical effects reported in the past, not only miracles and magical practices but spontaneous psychic experiences. Many of these last were purely physical effects, like the unaccountable stopping of a clock at the time of a death, or the falling of a picture at the time of a crisis happening to the person represented.

While these were not as numerous as the ESP type of spontaneous experiences, a substantial collection of cases of unusual physical phenomena had been accumulated, especially by the psychical research societies. Then too there had been a vast amount of reporting of the phenomena of physical mediumship, describing strange happenings that if correctly reported and honestly produced (large questions), would suggest that they had been produced by some kind of unknown mental agency. Even though little credence was given to any of the claims of nonexperimental physical

Gamblers in a casino may will the dice to land with certain faces showing.

happenings that suggested PK, they were puzzling enough to justify attention to the possibility.

It takes more than an open mind, of course, to set off on such a new project. There was the argument that since the ESP experiments had confirmed one type of spontaneous experiences, why should we not look at the others? Only a few months before the start of work on PK, in fact, a beginning had been made on precognition. Then too, coming as it did on top of the first major discoveries about the ESP types, the PK work seemed almost to follow those successes in logical relation. Clairvoyance was apparently a subject-object interaction in one direction. Why not expect a reaction in the other, as the spontaneous cases had suggested? Besides, the sensorimotor parallel suggested ESP and PK as an extra-sensorimotor analogue. So PK fitted into a niche in the developing rational picture.

Yet the work with the dice did not immediately receive full attention from the group at the Duke Laboratory, and for a time was a little overwhelmed. At that stage, with the first report on the ESP work about to appear, the new discovery was just too much to handle with sufficient reflection and comprehension for immediate publication. Even the reporting of the precognition results was delayed for nearly five years and, as it turned out, the findings on PK were held back for almost ten.

An important new consideration arose that nevertheless required that PK be taken quite seriously, even before publication, in connection with some of the ESP experiments. There came a point in the research in precognition at which PK became an important competing hypothesis. Some workers in parapsychology found precognition so hard to take seriously as a hypothesis that even PK was preferable if it could possibly explain the results of the precognition tests.

One of these critics in the laboratory challenged the adequacy of the mechanical card shuffler used for a time in randomizing the order of target cards for precognition tests. He thought PK was a possible factor in favourably influencing the shuffling process so as to make the cards match the predictions made by the subject. This and other methods for preparing targets for precognition (for example, the rolling of dice) had therefore to be discontinued. (Later on, as will be seen, the tables were turned, and precognition gave PK experimenters a difficult time as a counter-hypothesis in their own research.)

Progress Retarded

The PK studies continued throughout the period of delayed publication, so that by 1943, when it was decided to release the first report, there were twenty-four completed projects, most of which would normally have been published over the waiting interval. Even so, the long lead given the ESP side of the field represents a comparative disadvantage to the PK branch, and accounts for the appearance of retarded progress in this important section of the field since the first PK report appeared. More recently there have been signs, however, that this imbalance may soon be corrected.

The problems that needed handling in adapting dice throwing to PK testing were recognized from the start; they are much the same as those that have to be watched if an honest game is to be played in games with dice. Precautions have to be taken against skills in handling the cubes that might influence their fall, as well as in correcting for possible inequalities in the faces.

In the laboratory it was possible to take the necessary steps, which the game situation would not always permit. The 'game' could be modified to suit the experimenter's needs. For instance, correction for imperfections in the dice was best achieved by equalizing the number of throws for all the faces as targets. If all the faces are equally well represented in numbers of trials, any imperfections in one will be balanced off by the others. Similarly, the ways of throwing the dice progressed, from hand and cup throwing to stages of completely mechanized gravity release or rotation in baffled cages, in which no human factor entered.

The Diagonal Decline

The most clinching evidence of PK was a psychological by-product of the research itself, the diagonal decline effect resulting from the quarter distribution (QD) analysis of the records. First of all, it is an independent valuation, and it is one that at a single stroke effectively answers all the major questions that the researcher attempts to cope with in a well-designed and well-controlled PK experiment.

The QD analysis developed as a result of examining, in 1942, the earlier PK records to see whether declines in scoring rates, such as had occurred frequently in ESP experiments, were also to be found in the PK data. It was immediately evident that there was not only a decline from the top to the bottom of the record page but also from the left to the right half, so that on dividing the page into quarters the upper left showed the greatest number of hits and the lower right the fewest. This is the typical diagonal decline. The difference between those two quarters was statistically significant and it made a formidable and independent case in itself, whatever else the experiment showed or failed to show.

All that was necessary to meet the conditions for the analysis was that the page be made up of records of trials made under uniform conditions—as, indeed, most of them were. All the considerations that normally had to be watched, such as dice bias, non-random throwing or recording errors, could not be supposed to decline as the QD analyses had shown the actual results did. One major point was that neither subjects nor experimenter could have had any anticipation that years later these analyses would be made. They were thus as objective as fingerprints.

It turned out that eighteen out of the twenty-four series were recorded in such a way that the QD analysis could be applied. Of these, sixteen showed the diagonal decline from upper left to lower right, and when the entire eighteen were combined the significance of the difference between the upper left and lower right quarters gave astronomically high odds against a chance theory for the results.

This was not all of the QD evidence; there were still smaller blocks of data in the records that could be quartered and treated in the same way to see how general these position effects were. The same effect was found to be widely distributed in a similarly highly significant way. One virtue of these position effects is that they can be examined over and over again and thus have much the same firmness as rock strata to the geologist. It has been especially advantageous to have had this strong foundation laid under the PK work that has not been so well represented in the amount of research done as have the various types of ESP.

The Electronic Era

The conclusive QD evidence for PK came to a head in 1945. By a quarter-century later psi research had entered upon a new period, marked especially by the greater sophistication of testing devices that was possible. It could

be called the electronic era, since much of the apparatus in use in facilitating psi testing is of that character. Dr. Helmut Schmidt (b. 1918), director of the Utrecht Institute for Parapsychology, designed a number of test devices adaptable to specific types of psi, all based upon the same essential mechanical principles.

The randomization of events on which the tests are based was dependent upon the emission of electrons in radioactive decay. This basic process can determine the order of targets for ESP tests or provide a random order of events for the subject to try to influence in PK tests. In these latter, the subject mentally concentrated on trying to make a designated one of two (or more) lamps light up, by influencing the selective action of the random generator. The subject had nothing

One virtue of these position effects is that they can be examined over and over again and thus have much the same firmness as rock strata to the geologist.

to do but concentrate on the lamp assigned to him as target for a given run of trials. The experimenter was not necessary at all except to give the instructions to the subject. Mechanical recording and provision for mechanical analyses of the data were features of the system.

One wonders, of course, in this new stage and style of testing, just as in the ESP testing with the same types of machine, whether the central factor in the equipment—the electron—has any importance in itself. It is still too early to say whether the size of particle has anything to do with the rate of success or whether other systems of generating random targets.

The Nature of PK

Enough is already known about PK, however, to allow some illuminating generalizations about its nature. Of these, first consideration should be given to the relation of PK to the physical world. Almost immediately in the early testing at Duke, it was noticed that none of the physical properties of the dice seemed to be important in relation to the scoring rate—that is, unless they led to psychological preferences. For example, the subjects found that they could achieve a better scoring rate (a better rate per dice) while throwing two dice at a time instead of one. Yet two dice certainly made the task more difficult from a purely physical viewpoint.

Again, when two dice per throw were compared with six, the larger number gave the better rate of success per dice. But the subjects recognized in all these comparisons that they liked to throw two dice better than one, and preferred six to two. The larger number made a faster-moving and more efficient procedure than the smaller.

Essentially the same type of effect was observed with respect to two different sizes of dice used in the test. Very small dice did not do well and exceptionally large ones were not as high in yield as medium sizes (around 0.75 inch cube). Again the rate of success seemed to be largely a matter of the size that could most easily be picked up, observed quickly and handled nicely. The actual size as a factor appeared to have nothing to do with the amount of success.

The actual mass of the material from which dice were constructed seemed to make no difference either, so far as comparisons could be accurately determined. Dice of medium weight were the best-liked by most subjects; for example, those made of plastic or lighter metals such as alu-

A male patient undergoes ESP testing.

minum were popular and gave good results. Dice made of lead and those made of balsa wood were respectively too heavy or too light to be favoured by the subjects, and under the conditions of the early tests, neither yielded scores comparable to the better-liked materials. A number of other comparative tests involving physical features supported the point that the physical characteristics of the target objects in PK were not the determinative ones. The mental factor of preference was usually clearly the dominant one.

Avoiding Physical Preferences
What was most needed was a type of test that would allow the physical differences to be tested without the subject's preference being allowed to

influence him, at least consciously. Such an experiment was carried out at the Institute for Parapsychology by William E. Cox. Lead and celluloid dice were painted alike and compared in PK tests without the subjects being aware that two different weights of dice were being used. They were also handled mechanically in the same apparatus and were made to roll at the same speed so as not to show differences indicating weight.

Not even the observer who did the recording knew there were two different weights of dice; yet the amount of evidence of PK effect was almost identically the same for the light and the heavy ones. The ratio of mass was about one to seven, and such a difference would of course be expected to have an effect upon the energy

required to alter the fall of the cubes. Almost certainly this experiment, if conducted in the manner of the earlier ones mentioned, should have introduced a preferential difference in the amount of PK effect registered. As it is, the effect of density on psi capacity seems to be ruled out again.

In the Schmidt experiment with PK on the electron level of target magnitude, the selection of the lamp to be lighted depended on a single quantum of energy, yet the result did not show a different order of magnitude of scoring success over that of the various dice throwing tests, some of which involved incomparably larger target objects. This would appear to be evidence that physical differences in the targets as such do not affect the comparative magnitude of PK scores.

In the tests on ESP, results on that side of the psi field did not shown any physical relation either. Space-time conditions, which are so limiting in sensorimotor exchange, have not been found to show any well confirmed relation to the results of comparative ESP tests. Thus no purely physical theory of psi gets much of a leg to stand on from the evidence of either ESP or PK.

While this draws a major distinction around psi it does not necessarily imply any discontinuity in Nature. To say that psi is super physical is not to call it supernatural. Rather it is to indicate that some other natural basis of exchange will have to be inferred, and eventually found and confirmed if it is there. Since effective communication is involved (even though not often highly reliable) there should by definition have to be an energetic interaction, and this again raises interesting new questions, not for speculation but for exploration.

At this point the concept of a psi energy is not much more than a working hypothesis. It is true that mental energy has at times been suggested by psychologists, but until the work in experimental parapsychology began they had no way of testing the hypothesis of an energy that is different from the recognized physical systems.

PK research experiments with dice, conducted by Haakon Forwald, were found to produce effects that were measurable in terms of standard units of energy; yet under the test conditions no known physical energy could conceivably have been responsible for these effects. It is true that the only measurement possible was the physical differences in the results produced. These were the mean distances between dice released from the same point and allowed to roll by gravity, with one side of the table the designated target in one set of trials and the opposite side in another. Thus the cubes of known weight

were caused by PK to roll to the side intended to a measurable average distance.

Forwald, of course, was not directly measuring the energy that influenced the dice, but rather the resultant lateral displacement. However, at this point it is a question as to whether concepts such as quantity (associated primarily with the physical order) are indeed applicable to this psi function or for that matter to any process that is distinctly mental.

Targets in PK Tests

What kinds and states of matter can PK influence? First approaches have usually to be made at the easiest point of attack. Clairvoyance was the simplest starting point for assault on the ESP side. In PK it had to be something with moving targets (PK-MT) since matter in motion offers advantages; much of the PK work done since its beginning in 1934 has been with targets in motion, mostly dice.

A certain amount of testing of PK with moving targets has involved the use of electrical equipment adapted to the tests. The attempt has been made also to use the flow of liquids or sand

as target matter. Tests have likewise been made on micro-physical targets, as in the emanation of electrons from radioactive substances.

On the whole, nothing in the PK testing has thus far consistently exceeded the rate of success with the dice-throwing methods. It still remains to be seen how the work with electronic targets will compare with dice tests. So far there is no indication of a new level of magnitude of PK performance to correspond to the microscopic size of the targets.

As stated, all these materials have been inanimate objects in motion. What about PK on living targets, or PK-LT? The idea has long prevailed in folklore that some individuals have the power to influence plant growth and others to affect animals, including man, physically in a variety of ways. The plant specialists are said to possess what is known as a 'green thumb,' and others are believed to be able to induce healing of the sick by unknown powers that suggest PK.

In recent years efforts have been made to test these healing and growth-promoting powers in the laboratory. The PK tests most often tried were

Dice of medium weight were preferred by most subjects in the Duke research

based on the attempt to influence the growth rate of seedlings and the best-known of these efforts is the work of Dr. Bernard Grad (1920–2010) of McGill University Medical School. But there have been a few efforts to influence animal healing and other effects on the animal organism. It would be fair to say that a good beginning has been made on PK tests with living targets; but a hard and fast valuation need not be forced at this stage. The research continues, but it should not be confused with fantastic and prematurely popularized claims of emotional reactions of plants and so-called plant perception.

The stiffest challenge facing the PK researcher today is the question, now being investigated, of whether static inanimate objects can demonstrably be influenced psychokinetically. This is a point at which to reflect on the fact that, one by one, the types of psi effect suggested by the spontaneous cases of psychic experience have been verified by experiment or, as in the sector of the PK of living targets, there is at least a fairly satisfactory case. One cannot of course argue that we may now therefore conclude that PK on static targets (PK-ST) will have to follow, but it does appear much more plausible as one thinks back over the progress in the past on the other target areas of psi.

The more favourable climate of today has led to increased attention being given to some of the claims for the PK-ST type of effect. There has been some attention to the claims for darkroom séances, for example, the reports of tables levitated by PK. Increased attention is also being given to reports of poltergeist and haunting cases in the attempt to verify claims of unexplainable movements of objects that support PK.

On the US scene, the best-known effort to achieve PK-ST has been

in the attempts to project thought impressions onto a photographic film. While some psi workers such as Dr. Jule Eisenbud (1908–99) were led to the conclusion that a genuine psi effect had been involved in these productions, such firm acceptance at this stage would abandon the criteria followed in the other sectors of psi investigation. If the results reported were indeed due to genuine PK the capacity involved should be expected

The stiffest challenge facing the PK researcher today is the question, now being investigated, of whether static inanimate objects can demonstrably be influenced psychokinetically.

to respond, as efforts continue to devise better conditions and make conclusive demonstrations possible in due course.

The relation of PK to the ESP types of psi phenomena has become clearer as the different types have been studied in more detail. During the early investigations it seemed necessary to treat each phenomenon as though it was the result of a separate function, and difficulties resulted from these distinctions, especially in attempting to distinguish clairvoyance and telepathy from each other in the experimental situation.

Another problem arose in trying to perform a PK experiment that completely ruled out the possibility of precognition and conversely (as mentioned above) in trying to investigate precognition with the hypothesis of PK experimentally eliminated. Eventually, however, these conflicts were resolved and each type of psi was satisfactorily established as phenomenologically distinct.

Even though much time was expended in separating PK and ESP by independent demonstration, there

was frank recognition of the fact that PK required ESP for any intelligent hypothesis of its operation. In most of the experiments it was impossible for the subject to give intelligent guidance to PK without using ESP at the same time (for example, to know where, how, and when to apply the effort).

Accordingly, even while the separation experiments were going on, it was recognized that the distinction between types was a superficial one and that PK and ESP were essentially aspects of the same function. Moreover, the similarity of conditions that affected both of them confirmed the hypothesis of the unity of psi. Gradually workers in the field came to regard psi as fundamentally a single process of which the different types of phenomena were surface manifestations.

Some of the experimental studies came in due course to take this unitary character of psi for granted, especially those in which PK tests were carried out with the targets unknown to the subject at the time. In some of these the targets were enclosed in opaque envelopes until the end of the series for which they were intended. In others, as in the distance experiments by the English workers G. W. Fisk and D. J. West, the target was set up at a distance of 170 miles from the subject while she, a medical woman, threw the dice with significant success, depending upon ESP guidance as to the target face. Distance has been found to be no impediment to ESP.

Whether distance between the subject and target would have any effect upon success in an adequately controlled PK test would be difficult to say at present on the basis of the limited evidence. The distances in tests have been relatively short (30 feet) and subjective factors could easily enter in the way of preferences; but the results, such as they are, harmonize well with the other findings regarding the absence of any physical influence.

It is just at this point that the view of PK as being an aspect of the psi function is very important. Since psi is a unitary ability and the ESP tests have shown no limitation thus far due to space-time, it seems to follow logically that PK would not be limited either; it is the same ability with another form of expression. So there should not be any need to do PK experiments at longer distances.

One of the most important findings about PK, and one that was already known about the ESP types, is that it seems to be reversible in its effect. The easiest way to describe this is to go back to the example of luck in games of chance; this form of psi (as it seems likely to be) can be both good and bad, and thus, as everyone knows, lead to winning or losing. The discovery in parapsychology of this tendency to psi-missing, as the opposite of psi-hitting, has been probably the greatest single contribution thus far made to the understanding of the psi process. For some unknown reason psi-missing is much more prevalent in the ESP researches than in those of PK.

It happens, however, that the Cox experiment involving the comparison of lead and celluloid dice offers an instructive example of psi-missing. It will be recalled that the dice were indistinguishable to the subjects and that they gave equally significant results in spite of their large difference in weight. However, there was an important difference: while the celluloid gave the normally expected psi-hitting, the lead dice gave psi-missing results—that is, negative deviations. Both kinds of dice were activated together, and for the same

target face, yet the heavy ones deviated as far below the chance mean as the light ones did above.

The results were fairly uniform too among the different subjects and sessions, indicating that the participants were in some way cognizing the kinds of dice and reacted to both with equal measure but in opposite directions, even while they were unconscious of any difference. Some sort of discrimination was evidently involved in this 'psi differential effect'

> *The discovery in parapsychology . . . psi-missing . . . has been probably the greatest single contribution thus far made to the understanding of the psi process.*

as it has been called, which shows up almost regularly when an experiment is conducted with two different kinds of method or target, or other circumstances. (Such a subtle unconscious differential in the operation of the mind could be an important principle of wider scope.)

Frontiers of PK Research
In his book, *Homo Faber—The Story of Man's Mental Evolution*, G. N. M. Tyrrell put forward an idea about what he termed 'the adapted mind.' His theory was that human evolution has taken place over a very long time period both in terms of body as well as the mind. The physical evolutionary changes are far more apparent that the mental ones, which effectively remain concealed, and yet the mental states have an impact on active thought processes, and this may be the reason why the results of psychical research are not accepted.

The years ahead may be expected to see the expansion of PK investigations into much territory still unexplored.

Interest is growing in meeting the challenge of applying PK to static targets, but it is even more active at present in the use of living targets, with a wide range of plant and animal species and their functions being put to the test. New work with animals has independently confirmed and amplified the discovery of precognition in mice. With the promise this gives of providing parapsychology with a 'guinea pig' there should be accelerated interest in the animal branch of the field.

Is there a foreseeable limit to this PK power of the mind and its other aspect, ESP? Nothing has yet been found that is beyond the range of the extra-sensory ability to apprehend knowledge, and the progress of PK research is approaching a similar generalization on its side. This is to say that man's range of communication has, in principle, no limitation. On the side of modesty, however, let it be recalled that the exercise of these psi abilities is still too slight and uncertain for them to be of serious practical use. When they become reliable, the consequences will be fantastic; but the work to be done is enormous, too. Fortunately it is now possible to do it, and it will get done in time.

J. B. RHINE

Since the preceding article, by one of the most distinguished experimenters in ESP and PK, was written, investigations into the phenomena have continued, although with varied success. In 1972, Uri Geller (b. 1946) came into public awareness with his feats of metal bending. Geller had only to appear on television for reports of forks and spoons being bent out of shape in thousands of homes to flood in. His abilities led to psychokinetic metal bending becoming a field of study in itself.

In 1974, Matthew Manning (b. 1955) gave a demonstration to a group of twenty-one scientists; however, the first scientist to study the metal-bending phenomenon rigorously was Professor J. B. Hasted of Birkbeck College, London, who published his findings in a co-authored article in *Nature*, in April 1975. He took the view that it was in some way the product of the unconscious mind.

Another PK subject was the New York artist Ingo Swann (1933–2003), who apparently could change the temperature of nearby objects and affect magnetic fields.

Recently, research has been directed toward the investigation of PK effects upon biological growth, with all the implications that this might have in the subject of healing. Finding that the control and replication of experiments with standard laboratory subjects was dauntingly complex, researchers turned their attention to more easily handled targets such as live microorganisms, enzymes, and single cells in test-tube cultures.

Some impressive preliminary results have been claimed from these experiments, while other researchers have taken their investigations even closer to the boundary between the organic and the physical world, and experimented with PK effects upon the growth of crystals. In Australia, Bevan L. Reid has claimed to demonstrate influences upon crystals over distances up to hundreds of feet. Mathematical calculations of the thermodynamics of crystal growth suggest that the system is not a closed one, but continuously interacts with its ambient space, and some successful parallels have been drawn with quantum mechanics. There are implications, too, for the theory of morphogenetic fields. Research programs continue all over the world.

Remote viewing—the possibility of an individual 'seeing' an object at a remote distance has been sufficiently intriguing to attract the attention of official agencies. In 2001–02 the British government conducted an experiment to ascertain whether or not there might be some evidence to support this idea. The attempt to collect data was abandoned as there was no indication under the experimental conditions that remote viewing was used by any of the subjects.

FURTHER READING: Hoyt L. Edge, et al. Foundations of Parapsychology. (London, UK: Routledge & Kegan Paul, 1986); J. B. Rhine ed. Progress in Parapsychology. (Durham, NC: Parapsychology Press, 1971); J. B. Rhine and J. G. Pratt. Para-psychology, Frontier Science of the Mind. (Springfield, IL: C. C. Thomas, 1974); L. E. Rhine. Mind Over Matter: Psycho kinesis. (West Conshohocken, PA: Collier, 1970); D. Robinson. To Stretch a Plank: a Survey of Psycho kinesis. (Nelson-Hall, 1980); L. L. Vasiliev. Experiments in Distant Influence. (London, UK: Wildwood House, 1976).

Psychotronics

Originally proposed by researchers in Czechoslovakia in the 1960s as a term to replace 'parapsychology,' and described as 'the bionics of man,' psychotronics has developed as an interdisciplinary study of the interaction of matter, energy, and consciousness. It predicates the existence of psychotronic energy, a vital force that could be the source of all psychic phenomena.

Contemporary with the coining of the term, Robert Pavlita, a Czech inventor and design director for a textile works, made public a range of small devices that he claimed to have spent more than thirty years developing, and which he called psychotronic generators. Made in metal or wood, and frequently resembling the 'ritual objects' exhibited in museums, they were said to accumulate energy from any suitable biological—particularly human—source, which could then be used for a variety of purposes, such as enhancing plant growth or purifying polluted water.

On film, the generators were shown attracting nonmagnetic materials, even under water, causing a rotor blade to turn at a distance, and exhibiting other effects comparable to psychokinesis. Scientists declared that 'experiments have excluded any conceivable physical agent—even heat.'

In the US, a psychotronic generator was developed in 1970 by Woodrow W. Ward. He gave it the name 'psionic generator,' and claimed that it was activated directly when it was stared at; he said that it was more sensitive to children, and that it was more quickly activated during certain planetary aspects or phases of the moon.

Science Fiction and Fantasy

The realm of the fantastic in literature is vast. It is, in fact, altogether too enormous. If we defined as 'fantastic' any phenomenon deemed unreal or impossible or unverifiable through currently accepted scientific means, and if we defined as 'literature' any manifestation of the profound human impulse to tell stories, then we could almost certainly discover some tale of fantasy relevant to every topic discussed in this entire book. In the present context it is not germane to regard all of myth, legend, and folklore as fantasy, nor to treat examples from classical literature as conscious premonitions of the genre of science fiction.

The key term is consciousness. Fantasy proper begins at that historical point in the eighteenth century when writers began to become conscious that realism was a doctrine, and that the dominance of the mimetic novel might have cast a strong new light upon human nature and upon the world, but that it had also crippled the human imagination. Certain dreams could no longer be dreamed or spoken of in public, for anything that touched on the fabulous was relegated to the nursery: unheard-of creatures, unplumbed depths of human possibility, landscapes as yet unseen by mortals, other worlds, other realms, other beings, all were despised as being essentially childish.

William Shakespeare's *The Tempest* (c. 1610) would almost certainly not have been written 150 years later, and certainly would not have reached the stage as a new creation. To the eighteenth-century mind, Prospero was a fraud, Ariel and Caliban were chimaeras, and the profound Shakespearian magic—through which every creature on the island strays into a dreamlike wood and emerges transfigured—was nothing more than a confidence-game.

For eighteenth-century scholars, what seemed most significant about *The Tempest* was Prospero's giving up of his pretence to being a magus; for us (and perhaps for Shakespeare as well) what is important is not only Prospero's retirement, but also that world from which he retires. The first conscious attempts at fantasy could almost be defined as attempts to recapture the empowerment, the vision, and mastery of the thresholds of perception, that Prospero casts down at the very end of his—and his maker's—career.

Fantasy is *The Tempest* reborn. It is a subversive response to the 'real' world defined by writers such as Henry Fielding (1707–54) or Samuel Richardson (1689–1761), an attempt to recapture a fuller spectrum of response

to the mysteriousness of being, and to introject an element of chaos into the Enlightenment vision of an orderly, mechanical universe. A writer such as Horace Walpole (1717–97), whose *The Castle of Otranto* (1765) is one of the first Gothic novels, lived much of his life in a state of dreamlike nostalgia for a time of shadows, romance, hauntings, disarray. His vision of the

With The Castle of Otranto, *'enlightened' Western humanity begins to reinhabit, and once again to explore, some of the dark depths of the human psyche.*

miraculous chiaroscuro of the medieval world was not, perhaps, very accurate in an historical sense; but it served as a clear signal—and releaser—to his many readers and imitators that chaos and old night were legitimate subjects. The self-consciousness of his assault upon the time in which he lived is nowhere more explicit than in the subtitle he affixed to the second edition of his novel: he called it *A Gothic Story*. The gauntlet was cast down.

The Castle of Otranto itself is full of marvels, containing deeply hidden secrets whose revelation has an explosive effect on the tame daylit perspectives of 1765, and an obsessed superman who reminds one of Milton's Satan, and of course the Castle itself, a labyrinthine edifice so complex and fraught with psychological symbolism that it has more than once been likened to an analogue of the human brain. As a novel it is comparatively slight, for Walpole was not a creative mind of the highest intensity; but as a depository of themes and symbols of the most vital interest to twentieth-century humanity, it is far more evocative than any of the novels

of the Great Tradition to which so much attention has been paid over the centuries. With *The Castle of Otranto*, 'enlightened' Western humanity begins to reinhabit, and once again to explore, some of the dark depths of the human psyche.

Horace Walpole wrote another book as well, very much less well known but also of interest in its pushing back yet another of the shrunken boundaries. *The Castle of Otranto* is a tale of the interior of the mind, and pays relatively little heed to exteriors, either mental or physical; but *Hieroglyphic Tales* (1785) begins an exploration of fantasy landscapes that led, a century later, to the creation of entire High Fantasy worlds where the human drama might play itself out in unfettered surroundings. These *Tales* are simpler, and very slender indeed; but they open the way back to the magical territories occupied by *The Thousand and One Nights*, opening once again to the Western world a chance to inscribe its dreams upon the terrains of the marvelous.

The remaining years of the eighteenth century, and the first decades of the nineteenth, saw an explosion of Gothic novels in England, and of literary dream fantasies in Europe, which explored some of the same subterranean chambers of the mind. Many of these tales were routine, but the best of them exemplified what may be the most significant contribution fantasy has made to the human race's long campaign to gain understanding of self. The most daring and most profound artists seem always, at some level, to be aware of the profound dan-

ger inherent in succumbing to convention or fixity, in surrendering to the ineradicable human habit of normalizing the world. When the world is normalized, much is lost, and dreams have little purchase.

Secret Sharer of the Psyche

Great artists always threaten to dislodge our perceptions from the habitual; they always push us toward the edge of perception. For a century, the best fantasy written in the Western world performed a similar function. By subverting the mimetic novel, fantasy also tended to question our very perceptions of the world.

To the secure assertions of the 'normal' novel, fantasy tales responded with a contrary 'yes, but.' Time and space became insecure—protagonists of fantasy tales frequently fell through abysses of time, or stumbled into labyrinths without egress. Identity became problematical—one of the great central themes of the fantasy tale, from almost the beginning of its history, was the doppelgänger, the secret sharer of the psyche who haunted one's dreams. Robert Louis Stevenson's *Strange Case of Dr. Jekyll and Mr. Hyde* (1886) was the culmination of a century of malign doubles in the literature of fantasy, and remains an absolutely central icon of our search to understand our dreams, our fears, the depths of the unconscious self that wells up in fantasy (but shrivels in the daylight of the mimetic novel).

An essential element of the subversive in classic fantasy lies in its capacity precisely to liberate the unconscious, to open the world of story to the heart-rending complexities of the sleeping self; but at the same time to warn us that there are sometimes very good reasons for remaining on the surface of events, that to explore the interior of the labyrinth may well be extremely costly.

The Modern Prometheus

Long before Stevenson's culminating fable, however, fantasy had generated a counterstatement, one that would come, through its own progeny, to dominate the literature of the fantastic for over a century. Mary Shelley's *Frankenstein* (1818) is a novel of horror, a dark fantasy whose effect on readers can be genuinely disruptive; but it is also perhaps the first full-fledged science fiction novel. Even though it is easy enough to read the book's message as a warning against trying to know too much of the mysteries of God's universe, its subtitle should also be kept in mind.

Mary Shelley subtitled her book *The Modern Prometheus*. It was Prometheus who stole the secrets of the Gods and brought them down to humanity; her reference to him can be understood, just as much fantasy can so be understood, as an act of defiance against a fixed world, but with a difference. Where true fantasy casts its net backward into the depths of the psyche, and into the Edens of the ideal landscape, science fiction casts its net forward and futureward into an exterior world that can be understood by the tools of thought and technology. The gift of Prometheus is the ability to understand and manipulate the physical world. Frankenstein is a Promethean Man, and the Monster he creates is an outcome of science. In the book that tells their tale, a new literature is born.

Both fantasy and science fiction, therefore, were born as acts of subversion, and for a considerable time it was well understood that both genres were intrinsically threatening. The one threatened to remind us who we were, and the other threatened to liberate us so that we could become what we wished to be.

Because they acted so close to the dream-work and substructure of the human story, both fantasy and science

fiction, from the first, embodied fundamental mythic patterns. In fantasy, we find echoes of the myths that tell of Eden, of the double under the skin and in the mirror, of metamorphosis as punishment and aspiration, of the Hero with a Thousand Faces, of the sacrifice of the year-king so that the

Clothed in Air

And among the descendants of this Mr. Morris was one almost as sensible and clear-headed as his ancestor. He had just the same stout, short frame as that ancient man of the nineteenth century, from whom his name of Morris—he spelled it Mwres—came; he had the same half-contemptuous expression of face. He was a prosperous person, too, as times went, and he disliked the 'new-fangled,' and bothers about the future and the lower classes, just as much as the ancestral Morris had done . . .

Of course his toilet differed very much from that of his ancestor. It is doubtful which would have been the more shocked and pained to find himself in the clothing of the other. Mwres would certainly have sooner gone forth to the world stark naked than in the silk hat, frock coat, grey trousers and watch-chain that had filled Mr. Morris with sombre self-respect in the past. For Mwres there was no shaving to do: a skilful operator had long ago removed every hair-root from his face. His legs he encased in pleasant pink and amber garments of an air-tight material, which with the help of an ingenious little pump he distended so as to suggest enormous muscles. Above this he also wore pneumatic garments beneath an amber silk tunic, so that he was clothed in air and admirably protected against sudden extremes of heat or cold. Over this he flung a scarlet cloak with its edge fantastically curved. On his head, which had been skillfully deprived of every scrap of hair, he adjusted a pleasant little cap of bright scarlet, held on by suction and inflated with hydrogen, and curiously like the comb of a cock. So his toilet was complete; and, conscious of being soberly and becomingly attired, he was ready to face his fellow beings with a tranquil eye.

H. G. Wells
A Story of the Days to Come

seasons may continue to turn, of all the cycles that bring back the spring, or the green man, or the lost monarch, or the forgotten childhood.

In science fiction, some of the same myths recur: the hero becomes a Competent Man who penetrates the new frontier; the double becomes the android or the robot, and serves humanity (or rebels against us); the metamorphosis of human into beast becomes the story of the human race in confrontation with alien species; Eden becomes the galaxy; but cyclical time—except in the vastest of cosmogonic tales, in which the universe ends and starts again—is transformed into linear time, because science fiction has always, until recent years, focused forward, into the future.

These myth-evoking patterns were clearest at the start of things, with Horace Walpole and Mary Shelley. As the nineteenth century passed, both fantasy and science fiction tended to become somewhat more respectable. The Victorian literary establishment successfully managed to ensure that tales of the impossible were published and consumed by children, although novels such as George MacDonald's *Phantastes* (1858) were explicitly written for grown men and women.

The effect of this sequestration was perhaps damaging—it is fair to wonder what Charles Dickens (1812–70) might have written had he not clearly restricted his impulse to fantasticate either to Christmas whimsy or to the surface rhetoric of his full-scale novels—but it offered writers of fantasy a local habitation. On its part, science fiction evolved very slowly during the nineteenth century, perhaps through the lack of any identifiable market, and until the advent of H. G. Wells (1866–1946), who did not begin to publish until the 1890s, very rarely did a science fiction story grasp what might be called the nettle of transformation.

A Literature of Change

Science fiction, after all, was a literature of change, sometimes of profound change; but for eighty years precious little cognitive risk-taking could be detected in the texts that slowly came together to make up a primitive canon. There were some new inventions, but they had little pile-on effect; there were innumerable lost worlds, most of them deeply tedious and lacking in marvels; there were future-war novels, but most of these were bankrupt of any thought about the effects technology would have on warfare or society; and there were many Utopias, most of them deeply conservative, deeply suspicious of the new, deeply antipathetic to the concept of breaking through into the future.

So it is not surprising that H. G. Wells has been called the father of science fiction, along with Jules Verne (1828–1905). Of the two, it is probably Wells who deserves the description, as Verne wrote something rather different. His 'Extraordinary Voyages' were almost always set in the present day, and featured inventions or speculations that were seldom

Science Fiction Quarterly magazine features a woman-eating plant on the February, 1954 issue, published in New York City

SCIENCE FICTION *Quarterly*

FEB. 1954   25¢

THE CHILDREN OF THON
by Irving E. Cox Jr.

ALL NEW STORIES

technically impossible, according to contemporary science; what remains most striking about these many texts is the sense that geography itself is full of miracles, that just over the horizon one may find marvelous countries, strange doings and rites, new kinds of human enterprise. Our own world, for Verne, contains an infinity of marvels.

Our luck has been greater with Wells. Even more than Robert Louis Stevenson (1850–94) or Arthur Conan Doyle (1859–1930), his books read as though they could have been written yesterday, and the visions and fears they project come across to we twenty-first-century readers with perfect clarity.

At university Wells had been taught by Professor T. H. Huxley (1825–95), the most prominent nineteenth-century advocate of Darwin's theory of evolution, and he embodied an evolutionary perspective in all his significant work. He believed in change, he believed change was constant and inevitable; and he knew how to put his beliefs into convincing fictional form. All previous writers had treated human beings as essentially unchange-able, or had subjected them to apocalyptic transformations that read as *faits accomplis* of God; Wells is the first writer of fiction to subject humans species to a process of change.

Wells's first novel, *The Time Machine* (1895), has in fact become a contemporary myth about the future of our species. The time traveler constructs a time machine that looks rather like a bicycle, and travels into the future. Several hundred thousand years hence, he comes across

a society of beautiful folk, the Eloi, whose elfin fragility fails to disguise an essential stupidity. He is entranced, but troubled, and his premonitions of something awry are confirmed by his discovery of the Morlocks, a brute underground society that preys upon the ethereal Eloi. On reflection he comes to understand that the Eloi and the Morlocks are a kind of parable of evolution at work: that the one had been the leisured classes or homo sapiens, that the other had been the oppressed workers, and that their current

In other terms, science fiction constitued, in the absence of any super-ego, a series of libidinous explosions of the imagination.

shape reflected the inevitable outcome of a process of natural selection.

What *The Time Machine* ultimately explores is the myth of entropy. It has haunted the high technological parade of science fiction for over a century; and for many who do not read science fiction at all it has supplanted the Biblical extravaganza of the Book of Revelations with a harsher doom.

For the next five years or so, Wells continued to generate stories that established paradigms for much of the genre science fiction to come. With his novels *The Island of Doctor Mreau*, *The Invisible Man*, and *When the Sleeper Wakes*, Wells found extreme success and has been canonized in the halls of literature.

The Platform of the Future

What must be remembered are two things, the first, that much of science fiction is set in the future. Verne never moved conspicuously beyond the present day and, with the exceptions of *The Time Machine* and *When the Sleeper Wakes*, neither did

Wells. But the science fiction that began in US pulp magazines around 1925 very soon discovered the platform of the future, and very soon some point in the future became the point at which any science fiction story began. Both of the novels by Wells that have future scenes begin with scenes placed in contemporary settings, and feature protagonists who travel into the future.

The effect was stunning. Tales that might previously be tied to the detail-work of history or mundane probabilities were now freed to explore visions of the universe and of human destiny without apologizing to the present. In other terms, science fiction constituted, in the absence of any super-ego, a series of libidinous explosions of the imagination. It is perhaps for this reason that so much science fiction, featuring childish protagonists one would not want to invite home for dinner, does have the power to evoke mythic longings in its readership. Science fiction gave a platform—the libidinous future—for the telling of twentieth-century myth.

The heart of the US dream in 1925 was almost precisely that. Technological advancements fueled the belief the future could be reached through an application of spunk and will and inventiveness. And there would be no side-effects worth measuring, no costs to drag the adventurers back to Earth. If to lovers of mythological analogues this sounds like a return to Eden, then they are almost certainly right. The Christian myth might move the faithful from the walled garden of Eden at the beginning of the world to the walled city of Jerusalem at the world's end, but for the US dreamer of 1925 there was no reason why the platform of the future should not be a Garden in the Wilderness. Eden was a promised land whose location was easy to pin down: it

Opposite page:
A still from *The Lord of the Rings* film trilogy, based on J. R. R. Tolkien's books

A scene from George Lucas's epic space opera *Star Wars* (1977), one of the few science-fiction classics to be set in the past

was just beyond the Last Frontier that marked the farthest edge of the Territory. When Huck Finn, in Twain's *The Adventures of Huckleberry Finn* (1884), 'lights out for the Territory,' he is taking the first step to Eden. And when Richard Seaton, the inventor-genius who explores the galaxy in E. E. Smith's *The Skylark of Space* (1928), finds a new planet to conquer, he is repeating Huck's triumphant leap into freedom.

So the US dream was of a future that could be reached by an act of gumption. And US science fiction, for half a century, recorded versions of that dream by recounting 1,000—10,000—brilliant exploits in the vast playground of the universe. Even the best writers in the genre shared in the dream, though with reservations; their lesser coworkers had fewer scruples, and constructed innumerable cartoons of easy triumph, effortless (and significantly sexless) heroism.

It was (it could be suggested) heroism without any need to bring home the bacon; as though the Hero with the Thousand Faces had taken up the challenge and made the long journey and defeated the dark foe—and never come back. As a consequence, much science fiction never significantly addressed itself to the long hard task of constructing worlds in which human beings could live, once the heroic era had passed. It was myth without the shadow of death.

Despite the pulp fiction and B movies of aliens and astronauts, there was a distinct dark side of the gloss of progress that inspired a more dystopian view of the future. Orwell and Huxley's dark views of the future of London seem more and more a reality with the advent of CCTV and the invasion of privacy by surveillance cameras. The futuristic totalitarian state was far from an

exclusively British nightmare, however. Ray Bradbury's *Fahrenheit 451* envisioned a world where text itself was contraband, and firefighters light fires to prevent the spread of knowledge. Misuse of technology and the hubris of humanity lead to destruction in Vonnegut's cult favourite *Cat's Cradle*. And the repressive puritanical society created in Margaret Atwood's *The Handmaid's Tale* is set in a post-nuclear world, stoked by fears of the Cold War. Clearly, the press to grasp future today was not uniformly viewed as a ticket to paradise.

A Fantastic Escape

The positive view of the future permeated the popular pulp shelves, and soon science fiction was synonymous with escapism. A thinning of the mythic texture had also been afflicting the larger field of fantasy, within which science fiction floated. The threatening and problematical nature of earlier fantasy, with its interrogation of the boundaries of perception and knowledge, did not long survive the invention—or perhaps recollection—of what might be called Faerie, or perhaps more accurately the Marvelous Landscape. The romances of William Morris, such as *The Wood Beyond the World* (1894) and *The Well at the World's End* (1896), paved the way with their depiction of twilit but eternal lands, where high deeds and magic interwove poetic spells, and time could stop.

Lord Dunsany's early stories, and his later novel, *The King of Elfland's Daughter* (1924), strengthened the sense that it was possible to conceive of kingdoms ungoverned by time and science; and the astonishing Zimiamvian novels of E. R. Eddison (1882–1945, most notably *The Worm Ouroboros* (1922), added an erotic intensity to the mix. (Sexual material was avoided in most English-language fantasy before the twentieth century,

The 2006 novel *Gifts* by Ursula K. Le Guin

except through subtexts, sometimes quite violently eroticized; and in US science fiction sex tended to be seen, with astonishing naiveté, as a domesticating influence to be avoided by the valiant young hero).

The Rebirth of Fantasy

Most fantasy writing in the first half of the twentieth century was caught in whimsy, featuring (for instance) coy tales of gods and goddesses who visit the contemporary world incognito. Fantasy slowly began to creep into the public conscious, particularly in the realm of children's literature, from the beginning of the twentieth century with books such as *The Wizard of Oz, Alice in Wonderland*, and *Peter Pan*. However, it was not until the publication of J. R. R. Tolkien's *The Hobbit* and *The Lord of the Rings* (three volumes, 1954–55)—that fantasy began to establish for itself an identifiable profile in the public mind as enjoyable for adults.

This was not all to the good. Tolkien's *Rings* espoused a conservative, hieratic, moral vision of the universe, and terminated in a return to something like Eden, all these features being consistent with the author's own Catholicism, and his distaste for the twentieth century. Put together with patience and skill, and very cleverly told, *The Lord of the Rings* generated a huge fandom in the 1960s, and inspired a large number of other writers to emulate the form. It resurfaced in popularity in the 2000s with the advent of Peter Jackson's popular film adaptations, and again stoked the fantasy flame.

Innumerable high-fantasy quest tales have seen print since 1965, a huge proportion of them featuring elves and dwarves and ill-tempered but essentially kindly wizards, and hidden kings and dark lords, and ending frequently in the restoration of a monarchy. Myth and magic, legend

and lore, and nostrum and panacea, are mentioned very often in these stories; but very rarely are they successfully evoked.

Working the Deeper Veins

In recent years some fantasy authors have begun, once again, to work the deeper veins. John Crowley's *Little, Big* (1981) sets a typically English Faerie enclave into a US wilderness, interrogates our mortal longings for eternal escape, and ends in a threnody for the thinning out of magic from the planet. Gene Wolfe's *The Book of the New Sun* (1980–3), which can be just as easily read as science fiction, is set so far into the future that the artefacts of the twentieth century have become embedded in the crust of the earth, and can be disinterred only by geologists: we are the deep past of the future, and our lives are the tales they tell over the fire.

And Robert Holdstock's *Mythago Wood* (1984) engages with the Matter of Britain and the perils and allure of the Wild Wood. The Mythagoes themselves—physical creatures, jacks and Robin Hoods and knights and metamorphic monsters, all shaped by the mythopoeic dreams of human beings over aeons—are a deeply evocative concept. These fantasies are all set along the boundaries demarcating the mundane world from the Marvelous, which is perhaps natural enough, as stories and myths tend to cluster along lines of stress.

Myths for the New World

Some of the finest novelists who began in the 1950s or 1960s, such as Philip K. Dick (1928–82), Robert Silverberg (b. 1935), Ursula K. Le Guin (b. 1929), Thomas M. Disch (1940–2008), Samuel R. Delany (b. 1942), Roger Zelazny (1937–95), or Gene Wolfe (b. 1931), created mythic structures for new worlds. It is not yet possible to say whose stories will be retold in a hundred years, but Dick's fables of reality slippage will probably survive, as will Wolfe's fables of transformation and religious revival.

Fantasy and science fiction have grown through literature and beyond, into a counter-culture phenomenon. Pulp fiction and comic books have always complemented one another, the latter gaining a steady audience of loyal superhero fans obsessed with the science fiction worlds their heroes in which their heroes operate. *Dungeons and Dragons*, the role-playing game that initially gained popularity during the 1970s, opened up a whole generation to an interactive relationship with the fantastic. Despite its seemingly under-the-radar cult following, role playing games have resurfaced in the digital era with the popularity of online games such as *World of Warcraft* and *Skyrim*.

Film and television have added a new dimension to the fantastic with everything from the typical exploring adventures of *Star Trek* to time travel, monsters, and even mythical lands. The fascination with shows such as *Doctor Who* and *Game of Thrones* proves that the culture of the fantastic is very much alive, and growing.

JOHN CLUTE

FURTHER READING: K. Amis. New Maps of Hell. *(New York, NY: Arno, 1975); Neil Barron ed.* Anatomy of Wonder. *(New Providence, NJ: Bowker, 1987); John Clute and Peter Nicholls ed.* The Encyclopedia of Science Fiction. *(London, UK: Orbit, 1993); Rosemary Jackson.* Fantasy: The Literature of Subversion. *(London, UK: Methuen, 1981); David Ketterer.* New Worlds for Old. *(New York, NY: Anchor Press, 1974); Alexei and Cory Panshin.* The World Beyond the Hill. *(New York, NY: Tarcher, 1989); Mark*

Rose. Alien Encounters. *(Cambridge, MA: Harvard University Press, 1981); Darko Suvin.* Metamorphoses of Science Fiction. *(New Haven, CT: Yale University Press, 1979).*

Spontaneous Combustion

On the cold morning of Monday January 5, 1835, James Hamilton, professor of mathematics at the University of Nashville, was checking the meteorological instruments on the porch of his house when he felt 'a steady pain like a hornet sting, accompanied by a

> *What can be the cause of such a remarkable fire? The medical profession is understandably skeptical of any supernatural explanation.*

sensation of heat' in his left leg. Looking down, he saw a bright blue flame, 'about the size of a dime in diameter, and somewhat flattened at the top,' flaring several inches out of the leg. He beat at it several times without effect, then cupped his hands over the flame to starve it of oxygen. Eventually it was extinguished, and Hamilton realized that he had experienced—and, unusually, survived—a rare phenomenon that had puzzled and terrified people for many centuries: spontaneous combustion.

It is the relative rarity of the occurrence that has made spontaneous combustion so difficult to document and investigate—that, and the obstinate skepticism of doctors, police, and fire officers. Typically, the body of an elderly person (but sometimes it is a teenager, or even a child) is found indoors, the upper part so totally burned

that it is reduced to ashes, but with one or both legs largely intact. Floorboards or carpet beneath the body will be burned through, but the rest of the room, even combustible materials close by the body, are untouched, except for being stained with soot. Consider the following case.

Dr. J. Irving Bentley, a ninety-three-year-old retired physician, lived on the first floor of an apartment building in Coudersport, northern Pennsylvania. Early in the morning of December 5, 1966, North Penn Gas Company worker Don Gosnell entered the building's basement to read meters, and noticed 'a light blue smoke of unusual odour' and a pile of ashes.

Since he had received no answer to his shouted greeting when he entered the building, Gosnell decided to look in on Dr. Bentley. There was more of the strange smoke in the apartment, but no sign of the old physician. When Gosnell peered into the bathroom he was met with a horrific sight.

A hole about a yard across had burned right through the floor to the basement below, exposing the joists and pipe work. On the edge of the hole Gosnell saw 'a brown leg from the knee down, like that of a mannequin. I didn't look further!' he later said, and he ran from the building.

John Dec, deputy coroner, reported: 'All I found was a knee joint atop a post in the basement, the lower leg from the knee down, and the now-scattered ashes 6 feet below.' Yet the fire, which had burned so fiercely that it had completely consumed the rest of Dr. Bentley's body, left his walking frame untouched beside the hole. Firemen testified that, although they found a few embers around the hole, and a slight scorching on the bathtub about a foot away, there was no other damage.

One of the strangest features about the majority of cases of this sort is the speed with which the fire strikes. The victims seem to have been rendered incapable of movement, either from fear or because they rapidly became unconscious. In 1960, five severely charred bodies were found in a burned-out car near Pikeville, Kentucky. The coroner commented: 'They were sitting there as if they'd just gotten into the car. With all that heat it seems there'd be some kind of a struggle to escape. But there hadn't been.' Charles Fort (1874–1932) collected many newspaper accounts of the occurrence of spontaneous combustion, and drew attention to the fact that the victims seemed often to be unaware of their predicament: 'In their grim submission' he wrote, 'it is almost as if they had been lulled by the wings of a vampire.'

Another remarkable characteristic is the extreme intensity of the heat of the fire. On the night of July 1, 1951, Mrs. Mary Reeser, a widow of sixty-seven, of St. Petersburg, Florida, burned to death in her armchair, leaving nothing but a pile of ashes. The chair itself was burned down to its springs, and a small circle of carpet was charred; but, apart from an area of soot on the ceiling above, the surroundings were untouched, and a pile of papers nearby was not even scorched. Dr. Wilton M. Krogman (1903–87), a forensic scientist from the University of Pennsylvania School of Medicine, with experience of death by fire, reported:

'I cannot conceive of such complete cremation without more burning of the apartment itself. In fact the apartment and everything in it should have been consumed. Never have I seen a human skull shrunk by intense heat. The opposite has always been true: the skulls have been either abnormally swollen, or have virtu-

ally exploded into hundreds of pieces . . . I regard it as the most amazing thing I have ever seen. As I review it, the short hairs on my neck bristle with vague fear. Were I living in the Middle Ages, I'd mutter something about black magic.'

Dr. Krogman said that he had made observations of bodies in crematoria, which burned for over eight hours at 2,000 degrees Fahrenheit without the bones being turned to ashes; and that it required a temperature more than 3,000 degrees Fahrenheit to cause bone to melt. Another reported case is that of Léon Eveille, found burned in his locked car at Arcis-sur-Aube, France, on June 17, 1971. The heat had melted the windows. It has been estimated that a burning car normally attains a temperature of about 1,300 degrees Fahrenheit, but that the temperature must have reached over 1,800 degrees Fahrenheit to melt the glass.

What can be the cause of such a remarkable fire? The medical profession is understandably skeptical of any supernatural explanation. In Victorian times it was believed that heavy drinking resulted in a build-up of inflammable material in the tissues; this was certainly the explanation given by Charles Dickens (1812–70) for the complete destruction of Krook in his novel *Bleak House*. And Mark Twain (1835–1910) wrote, in *Life on the Mississippi* (1883):

'Jimmy Finn was not burned in the calaboose, but died a natural death in a tan vat, of a combination of delirium tremens and spontaneous combustion. When I say natural death, it was a natural death for Jimmy Finn to die.'

The celebrated chemist Justus von Liebig (1803–73), who investigated the phenomenon but refused to believe in it—on the grounds

that he had never observed it—commented on the case of an eighty-year old alcoholic woman, who was reduced to ashes as she sat drinking brandy: 'the chair, which of course had not sinned, did not burn.' He showed conclusively that alcohol-saturated flesh would burn only until the alcohol was consumed.

Other explanations followed. In *Forensic Medicine and Toxicology* (1914), Dixon Mann and W. A. Brend report the case of a very fat man who died two hours after his admission to Guy's Hospital, London, in 1885. The following day the corpse was found bloated with gas, although there were no signs of decomposition. 'When punctures were made in the skin, the gas escaped and burned with a flame like that of carbureted hydrogen

The Death of Krook

Mr. Guppy takes the light. They go down, more dead than alive, and holding one another, push open the door of the back shop. The cat has retreated close to it, and stands snarling—not at them, at something on the ground, before the fire. There is a very little fire left in the grate, but there is a smoldering suffocating vapor in the room, and a dark greasy coating on the walls and ceiling. The chairs and table, and the bottle so rarely absent from the table, all stand as usual. On one chair back hang the old man's hairy cap and coat . . . They advance slowly . . . The cat remains where they found her, still snarling at something on the ground, before the fire and between the two chairs. What is it? Hold up the light.

Here is a small burned patch of flooring; here is the tinder from a little bundle of burned paper, but not so light as usual, seeming to be steeped in something; and here is—is it the cinder of a small charred and broken log of wood sprinkled with white ashes, or is it coal? Oh Horror, he is here! and this from which we run away, striking out the light and overturning one another into the street, is all that represents him.

Charles Dickens
Bleak House

[methane]; as many as a dozen flames were burning at the same time.'

The theory that the fire was fueled by the fatty tissues gained ground, and was generally given as a contributory cause of death in inquests. Recent reports have suggested reasons why the upper part of the body is consumed, but not the legs: 'the cause is a 'candle effect', in which fat from the ignited head of the body saturates clothing, which acts as a wick.'

However, in *Medicine, Science and the Law* (1965), Dr. D. J. Gee. a lecturer in forensic medicine at Leeds University who proposed this effect, described experiments he had performed. He managed to ignite samples of fatty tissue, but the burning could only be sustained in a strong draught, and even this resulted in slow smoldering rather than the fierce blaze characteristic of so many reported cases.

Speculation has also been directed to the build-up of phosphagens—compounds of phosphoric acid with amino acids involved in the complex biochemical reactions that take place in muscle contraction. One such paper in *Applied Trophology* (December 1957) suggested:

> *'Phosphagen is a compound like nitroglycerine . . . It is no doubt so highly developed in certain sedentary persons as to make their bodies actually combustible, subject to ignition, burning like wet gunpowder under some circumstances.'*

The drawback to this explanation is that phosphagens are completely unrelated to nitroglycerine.

And none of these theories explains how the fire begins, nor why it appears to come from within, so that in certain cases the clothing is untouched. An Italian surgeon named Battaglio described the death of a priest, Bertholi, in Filetto in 1789. He was left in his room reading a prayer book,

but only a minute or two later he was heard screaming, and was found lying on the floor surrounded by a pale flame. A devout man, Bertholi wore a sackcloth shirt beneath his clothes; although his outer clothing was burned away, and his charred flesh came off in shreds, the sackcloth was unburned.

Possibly the first explanation of a supernatural (or at least abnormal) cause is to be found in Wu Ch'eng-en's (c. 1500–82) famous classic of the sixteenth century, *Monkey*.

> *'. . . Heaven will send down a fire that will devour you. The fire is of a peculiar kind. It is neither common fire nor celestial fire, but springs up from within and consumes the vitals, reducing the whole frame to ashes . . .'*

Some modern theorists have proposed the (as yet) unexplained phenomenon of ball-lightning as a plausible cause of spontaneous combustion, something which accords closely with Wu Ch'eng-en's text. This would certainly go some way to accounting for the events of April 7, 1938. On this one day, Willem ten Bruik, an eighteen-year-old Dutchman, spontaneously combusted at the wheel of his car near Nijmegen, Holland; George Turner died similarly in his truck at Upton-by-Chester, England; and John Greeley was reduced to a 'human cinder' at the wheel of the S. S. *Ulrich*, some 100 miles of Land's End. In all three cases, there was almost no fire damage to the victim's surroundings.

Support for this theory comes from a report in the magazine *Fate* (April 1961), by Rev. Winogene Savage. An acquaintance was woken one morning by his wife's screams and, running downstairs, found her ablaze on the living-room floor, with a strange 'ball of fire' floating over her burned body. The flames were extinguished, but the

lady subsequently died. Witnesses reported that, although her clothes were badly burned, there were no burns on the rug where she had been found lying.

In 1975, Livingstone Gearhart advanced another (but possibly related) hypothesis in *Pursuit*, a journal devoted to 'Fortean' topics. He reported that he had found a significant correlation between the occurrence of cases of spontaneous combustion and variations in the earth's geomagnetic flux. The strength of the planet's magnetic field varies considerably in relation to the occurrence of solar flares and sunspots, and Gearhart found that a suspicious number of cases had been at times when the flux was at or near a peak. Whether there is any direct connection between observed ball-lightning phenomena and the geomagnetic flux has yet to be established.

The most detailed investigation of cases of spontaneous combustion has been made by the writer Michael Harrison in his book *Fire From Heaven*. He drew attention to the fact that a number of cases had occurred close to a body of water: the sea, a large lake, or an important river. This might be taken as supporting, in some measure, the ball-lightning theory. However, Harrison also pointed out that, in numerous cases, the victims had subsequently been found to have been in a heightened emotional state. He summarized his conclusions as follows:

- Spontaneous combustion is one of a wide range of phenomena associated with poltergeist activity.
- Physical phenomena of any kind ascribed to the poltergeist are due to what he called 'ekenergy,' controlled consciously or subconsciously by the human focus. This ekenergy is part of a cosmic force not normally apparent, because of the balance that usually exists between the corporeal body and the 'parallel' body

evidenced by Kirlian photography.

- Spontaneous combustion and other forms of ekenergetic phenomena are triggered when this balance is disturbed by the will—conscious or subconscious—of the focus. That the force generated is of human rather than external origin is evidenced by the fact that it can be directed—which would explain the remarkable localization, even selectivity, of the consuming fire, as well as most other poltergeist activity.

Harrison finally concluded that 'the nature *and purpose* of the fire from heaven will be discovered through what is already accepted as a fact, especially by those scientists working directly on the various problems of the paranormal: that the fire is merely one manifestation of that wide range of physico-psychic activity that we classify under the general heading of "the unexplained" or "the paranormal."'

FURTHER READING: Charles Fort. Complete Books. *(Mineola, NY: Dover, 1976); Vincent Gaddis.* Mysterious Fires and Lights. *(New York, NY: Dell, 1968); Michael Harrison.* Fire From Heaven. *(London, UK: Sidgwick & Jackson, 1976); Maxwell Cade and Delphine Davis.* Taming of the Thunderbolts. *(New York, NY: Abelard-Schuman, 1969).*

Spontaneous Psi Experiences

Spontaneous psychic experiences include widely diversified kinds of unusual occurrences. They range over unaccountable 'awarenesses,' true dreams, seemingly uncaused movements of physical objects, and unexplainable sights and sounds, sometimes taken to be caused by the

dead. The common element in all is that by them, the persons involved secure information not revealed by their senses, or produce effects not mediated by their muscles. This is the characteristic that divides these experiences from sensor motor ones on the one hand, and instances of fantasy, imagination, or delusion on the other.

Historically, psychic experiences had no rational explanation, since

Spontaneous experiences have played a part in psi research and will continue to do so, even though the individual reports of them cannot produce conclusive reliability.

the phenomena were not caused by the senses or muscles, and therefore seemed mysterious, even supernatural. Research in parapsychology, however, has thrown light on their nature and origin. They turn out to be the result of normal but obscure mental processes, that do not operate like the sensor motor ones but have their own laws and regularities. These processes constitute what is known as psi ability, the subject of parapsychlogical research.

Spontaneous experiences have played a part in psi research and will continue to do so, even though the individual reports of them cannot produce conclusive reliability. Human testimony is fallible and the psi element is difficult to identify with finality. In large numbers of cases, however, the importance of individual or personal variations, even inaccuracies and mistakes, diminishes, while common aspects stand out and make the identification of psi more certain. In fact, the relationship between this mental function as demonstrated in the laboratory and as evidenced in spontaneous experiences is, in a way, a reciprocal one. The experiences came under observation and study first,

and because of their strangeness they were hard to take seriously as actual occurrences. The question of their validity led eventually to experimental tests, and the experiments eventually showed that there could well be something more to many of the manifestations that had been called psychic than a mixture of imagination, exaggeration, and fraud. They showed, in short, that the human mind has two general types of psi ability, that of getting information without the senses through extra-sensory perception (ESP), and that of influencing physical objects without contact through psychokinesis, or PK.

An Unconscious Process

It is easy to see now why psychic manifestations have been baffling and mysterious, because it is now recognized that the psi process is an unconscious one. The person does not know when it operates or that he himself was involved in the operation. It was largely because of this unconscious origin that psi was long unsuspected and its effects generally misunderstood and often misinterpreted. For because the person is unaware of his own role in the production of a psi effect the tendency has been to assume it to be something imposed upon or communicated to him from the outside. This has been particularly true when a dying or dead person seemed to play an active role in the phenomena or when it was possible to suppose that such an influence was involved.

Besides the mystery raised by the unconscious operation of psi, the manifestations themselves took many different forms and no unifying underlying principle was obvious. Only after decades of controlled research has it been established that the phenomena are the result of an underlying mental process (the psi

process), expressed in various ways in different situations.

The concept of the psi process can be simplified by considering it as consisting of two stages. Stage One is that in which an item of information somehow becomes 'accessible,' at an unconscious level. How this can occur is the true unknown of the psychic process.

Also unknown are the factors or influences that permit one specific item to be 'chosen,' picked out from all others, as the topic of a given experience. Stage Two is a psychological rather than a parapsychological one, for in it the selected item is transferred to consciousness in a psychological form or as a physical effect. Nearly all of the facts about the psi process that have now been established concern this second, psychological stage.

Classifying Psi Events
Even though psi effects occur in what superficially appear to be a great many different ways, the seeming confusion they represent is largely dispelled once the basic underlying processes are understood. First of all, although the two main types of psi are very different in their obvious effects, ESP being cognitive and PK physical, still they can now be recognized as two different aspects of the same basic psi process. Consequently, the phenomena produced by each are related. Then the phenomena of these two basic types, particularly those of ESP, can be even further classified into sub-types.

ESP experiences have been distinguished on the basis of the kind of subject matter involved. It may be an object or event, it may involve the thought of another person, or it may

concern an event still in the future, and be clairvoyant, telepathic, or precognitive accordingly. ESP experiences are not limited by time or space, but may involve events at any distance. All three ESP types thus are in sharp contrast to sense perception, which is limited to events happening in the present and within a relatively short distance. Psi thus denotes an extra physical aspect to human nature.

The following is an example of the clairvoyant type of experience, for in it the person's mind somehow 'made contact' directly with the object. A man in Ontario operated a sawmill in the woods, and occasionally stayed at the logging camp with the workmen. One day he found his wallet missing. After searching for it in vain, he gave up hope of finding it. About two weeks later he dreamed it was at the bottom of the well at the camp. The dream was so vivid that the next morning he drove the 13 miles to the camp. He baled out the water from the well and found the wallet, though he never knew how it got there.

Precognition cases can be illustrated by the experience of an Ohio woman. She reported that her mother's new Oldsmobile was stolen from the church parking lot. The police held out little hope of finding it. Two nights later the daughter dreamed that the car was at a certain location in downtown Cleveland. Telling her husband of her dream the next day, she drove to the place and found the car. However, the bystanders testified that it had only been parked there minutes before she came. The dream showed where it would be, not where it was. The case is typical, except that the time interval may cover years as well as minutes.

An instance of the telepathic type of case is the experience reported by a teacher in New Jersey. She was teaching spelling to her class by giving out

a list of words for the children to spell. As she pronounced the words, slowly walking up and down the aisles, she saw that one little boy, Ralph, had misspelled the word 'grief.' But when she asked how many of the children had all the words correct, he raised his hand. She said, 'You missed one, Ralph.' He looked puzzled and she said, 'You misspelled grief.' They examined his paper and the word was not on it. Then a light broke over his face, 'Oh, now I remember. I wasn't sure how to spell it and as I was thinking you gave out the next word and I wrote it and forgot the other.' She asked him how he thought it should be spelled and he misspelled it just as she thought he had, though he had never written it.

Who is the Initiator?
In all three types of experience, it is as if the experiencing person's mind 'reaches out' and makes contact with the item of information. However, in some telepathy cases, because of the second person involved, the superficial impression is given that the action is initiated by him rather than by the experiencing person. An example was given by a woman in New Brunswick. She had gone downtown with a friend to do some shopping. Suddenly she knew she had to go home. She rushed off, regardless of her friend's remonstrance's, and found her husband unconscious in his car in the garage. She was in time to get help and save him. She found that he had closed the garage door, thinking there would be ample air, but carbon monoxide fumes overcame him. The last thought he remembered was an urgent call to his wife to come home.

Apparently the wife was not thinking of her husband when she got the urge to go home, and presumably it was at the time that her husband in his extremity was calling to her. Thus the obvious suggestion would be that

Opposite page:
Photograph of the Welsh medium, Will Thomas. A man's face appears in a haze of drapery on the right of the photograph

his mind, not hers, 'reached out,' and that her impulse to go home was a response to his message. Because of cases like this one, the experiencing person was called the receiver or percipient, and the second person, the agent. These terms, however, are misnomers, for the sending is not the crucial part of the process, as was illustrated by the case of the teacher in New Jersey. The telepathic reception, just like that of the clairvoyant and precognitive types, can occur without it; although, possibly, it adds to the likelihood that the thought will be 'noticed' or picked up by the experiencing person.

Of course, to describe the psi process as one in which the experiencing person's mind 'reaches out' is only to employ a figure of speech based on sense experience, in which distance intervenes between the person and his environment. In ESP, distance as such is not a factor. The language, however, lacks a word for mental contact without distance.

Cases cannot always be exactly classified as to type. For instance, experiences are often reported in which both a thought and an objective event are involved, so that it is not clear whether the situation was one involving telepathy or clairvoyance. The type of such a case cannot be determined exactly and consequently it can only be classified as general ESP (GESP). Today, in the attempt to understand the psi process, it makes little difference just how an individual case is classified. The important point is simply that the types of ESP show its potentially great reach.

The PK type of psi is still in a comparatively early stage of investigation. The meaning or content of spontaneous PK experiences usually concerns the crisis of another person, and usually is one of strong emotional quality for the experiencing person.

The situations thus tend to be similar to those of telepathy, and in any event their associated meaning falls within those of the types of ESP. Potentially, the phenomena of PK fall into three subtypes, which are based on the state of the object affected. It may be moving, or at rest, or it may be a complex combination of the two in living tissue or organisms.

As she reported: 'I honestly did not know I was going to say it. It was as if someone else had said it for me . . .'

Research on falling objects has now well demonstrated the PK effect, and more recently experiments have been reported on living organisms, in which positive results have been secured. As yet no laboratory tests have been reported in which static objects have been caused to move under adequately controlled conditions—though, of course, many spontaneous cases that seem to involve PK deal with the movement of static objects.

Intuitions and Hallucinations
Psi experiences vary not only in the type of information they bring but also in the way or form of manifestation. This is the product of the psychological process of Stage Two by which the information secured by ESP in Stage One is manifested.

ESP experiences may take any of four different forms, but PK only one. They follow closely but not exactly the distinction between waking and dreaming mental states. Two of the ESP forms, the intuitive and the hallucinatory, occur when the person is awake, and two occur as dreams. The PK form is not known to be limited by the mental state of the

person. Each form represents a different process and therefore they must be presented separately.

Certain psi experiences are just like the intuitions of ordinary life except that their subject matter was apparently received (in Stage One) by ESP. The characteristic of intuitive experience, both when ESP is involved and when it is not, is the sudden 'awareness' of the given item of information without any recognizable reason for knowing it and without mental imagery, as in the case reported by a woman in Michigan. During World War II, when she was in hospital, a letter came saying that her husband in France had died of a heart attack. She said, 'It wasn't a heart attack. He was poisoned.'

As she reported: 'I honestly did not know I was going to say it. It was as if someone else had said it for me. I insisted that they check with Washington. They did and I was right. He had been poisoned. I never knew why they first said it was a heart attack.'

The experience brought a complete item of information without a reason and imagery. The case given earlier of the woman who rushed home when her husband was in danger also was apparently based on an intuition. But the information in that instance was not complete. She knew she must go home, but she did not know why. Instances of incomplete information in the intuitive form are frequent. The degree of incompleteness varies, many of the cases consisting only of a strong emotion, or a compulsion to action. It is as if the information is entirely suppressed, unable to cross the threshold of consciousness. However, the accompanying emotion or tendency to act breaks through.

Probably over half of the intuitive experiences reported are incomplete to some degree. This, along with the absence of detail in complete cases, means that the transfer of an idea from unconscious levels to the conscious one of the waking state is accomplished with some difficulty.

Hallucinations are pseudo-perceptual impressions; they occur when no external objective stimulus is present to cause them. Usually they do not involve ESP, but when they do, the experience brings information about a real situation. In these, any sense modality may be involved but the auditory is reported most frequently. The human voice is perhaps the sound most often 'heard.'

Probably better known, even if actually reported more rarely than the auditory, are visual hallucinations. Many of them coincide with the death of the individual 'seen,' the experience thus seeming to serve as a communication to report it. A typical case comes from a woman in Kansas, who said: 'At an early hour one morning my father sat up suddenly in bed. My mother asked: "What is the matter, Bob?" he replied, "Mother is dead." She tried to convince him it was a nightmare, but he said: "No, I was never wider awake. Mother was standing by the bed just looking at me. She was pale, her hair was down, she was dressed in a white gown. There was a large red spot on the right side of her neck. I know she's dead." Word came that she died from an aneurism at about the same time on the same date.'

A couple head-to-head. In ESP, subjects need not be close to each other as distance as such is not a factor.

Rembrandt's *Belshazzar's Feast*. According to Daniel, chapter 5, 1-31, the disembodied fingers of a human hand appear and write on the wall of the royal palace. This vision is similar to a psi experience.

Since the message in such hallucinatory experiences is not expressed directly as an idea but by sensory imagery, its meaning must be inferred. The result is that only about one-third of them transmit a reasonably complete item of information. In fact, when the information is reasonably complete, it usually means that more than one sense modality was involved, as for instance in the case reported by a woman in Illinois. During World War II her family received a telegram from the War Department saying that her brother, a Marine, had been killed

coming up the stairs in his Marine uniform. He said: "Shirley, don't cry. I'm all right." and then when he got to the head of the stairs, he vanished.'

The next evening the family received a second telegram from the War Department, saying that a mistake had been made and her brother was alive and well. When he finally got home he did not know that he had been reported killed in action, but at the time he had been lost from his unit and knew his family would be so worried about him that in his mind he kept telling them he was all right. The experience thus may have been telepathic, although the vehicle of expression was hallucinatory, and used both the visual and auditory modalities.

A Spirit from the Dead

In an occasional report of hallucinatory experience, a concomitant intuition brings added information and thereby gives a hint of the origin of the hallucinatory effect. An example was reported by a woman in California. She had been divorced from her husband for some time when, as she says, one night 'I awakened around midnight in a cold sweat. I sensed I was not alone in the room. I felt a horrible suspense and I shivered as I stared straight ahead. Suddenly about 6 or 8 feet directly in front of my bed I saw the darndest thing I'd ever seen and I was scared out of my wits. It was a greenish grey whitish foamy substance—and then I knew somehow it was the spirit of my husband.' The next morning she read a report in the paper that her ex-husband had drowned in the East River the night before. It happened about the time of her experience.

The point in this case is that she knew 'somehow;' in other words, she intuitively identified her ex-husband in connection with what she saw, although it was not in the shape of a human being. The intuition and the

hallucinatory image together expressed the idea of her ex-husband's death, or were the vehicles by which the fact, accessible by ESP, was brought to consciousness.

Cases like this suggest that the intuition and the hallucinatory effect develop together at the start of Stage Two. For instance, a message in Stage One about the crisis of a family member might create, in Stage Two, an incipient intuitive idea, and along with it, in those individuals for whom a sensory pathway is easily stimulated, an auditory or visual impression of him. Then if the intuitive idea was repressed and did not cross the threshold of consciousness, the result would be a typical visual or auditory hallucination, and this would become the 'figment in consciousness,' the only sign that an ESP impression was received in Stage One. Thus the hallucinatory form may be an adjunct of the intuitive, and limited to those individuals for whom the internal activation of sensory centres is possible.

ESP Dreams

At least half of the spontaneous cases reported are dreams. On the basis of the kind of imagery used, two dream forms can be distinguished—the realistic and the unrealistic. The imagery of realistic psi dreams is detailed and true to the actuality on which presumably it is based. Details may be so profuse as to suggest that the imagery must have been made by a kind of photographic copying process. An example was given earlier in the case of the woman who dreamed of the location of the car. However, occasionally a dream of this kind is defective and does not completely disclose the item on which it is ostensibly centered. In such cases the nature of the defect shows that the mental process involved is not one of automatic copying after all, for it was possible to alter the meaning that presumably lay back

in action. With the family distressed, she had gone into a separate room, when she heard the front door open, and went to see who had come in. She writes: 'I "saw" my brother

of the imagery. The defects in different cases seem to have originated in different stages of the process. Some of them apparently came in the construction of the imagery, in others even before it, and in still others after the imagery had been made.

An instance in which the imagery was defective and did not reveal correctly the identity of the person involved was reported by a California woman. She dreamed that she was attending a funeral. In it she was impressed especially by the rays of the afternoon sun coming through the stained glass windows of the funeral parlour. She also noted floral wreaths, not only banked around the casket but hung on the walls. (She had never actually seen this done before.) She went up to the casket and saw her mother in it. She was awakened then by a phone call telling her of a friend's accidental death. Later she attended his funeral, which was held in the late afternoon. The sun and the wreaths were the same as in the dream. Only the corpse was different, and this fact shows that the copying was not automatic, but that changes could indeed be made in it.

Cases of the second kind, those in which the defect seems to have occurred even before the imagery was made, involve the scene 'selected' to convey the information. It may not be the proper one, as in the experience of a woman in Washington. She dreamed she answered the doorbell and a brother she had not seen for years was there. She saw the details of his clothing, a camelhair coat on his arm, the

peculiar kind of suitcase he carried, and an especially serious look on his face as he walked in the door. Upon waking she wondered if it might have meant that her brother was intending to pay her a visit. Several days later her father passed away quite suddenly. Her brother came to her house and the dream scene was enacted, down to details of the suitcase and the camelhair coat. Now she knew the reason for the serious look on her brother's face, but the scene of the dream had given no

Even though the person himself has constructed it, in some deep unconscious level, that does not mean that he knows it on a higher (conscious) level.

hint of the real reason for the visit. It obviously had not been 'selected' to inform her of her father's death.

The third kind of defect, the one that occurs late in the process, involves the interpretation of the imagery. Even though the person himself has constructed it, in some deep unconscious level, that does not mean that he knows it on a higher (conscious) level. This is shown by instances in which this higher level interpretation is wrong. Such a dream was reported by a woman in California. It was in the early stages of World War I, when a married man still needed his wife's consent to enlist in the army. This woman's husband wanted to enlist, but she had not consented because of their small children and the need for her husband's support. Very worried one night, she fell asleep, to dream that she saw her husband in a field crushed by a big, heavy machine. She told him of it and said she thought it was a warning that if he went to war he would be killed. The next day, a neighbour found her husband dead under his big tractor. He had gotten

off it to take some trash from behind it. The gear slipped into reverse and the tractor ran over him. Although she had constructed the imagery of her dream, she did not interpret it correctly.

While incomplete realistic dreams do not occur very frequently (probably not more than one in ten of those reported is incomplete), the fact that they do occur shows that the person does not have to copy the reality, but can influence the message by changing the imagery, selecting the wrong scene, or misinterpreting the situation. In each instance the influence that leads to the defect seems to be personal. Even though the reasons vary from case to case, they appear in the main to be emotional. While they cannot be pinpointed exactly in material like this, they appear to include factors such as hopes, fears, anxieties, memories, and desires. In view of these possibilities, and since presumably all individuals who have dreams of this kind could so distort the pictured reality, it is rather surprising that a large percentage of these dreams present an essentially true and complete item of information, and so make this form a comparatively effective message-bearer.

Hail and Farewell

Unrealistic dreams, as well as realistic ones, carry their meaning by detailed imagery but in these the details are not true, as can be illustrated by the dream of a woman in New York. She lived away from her parents' home at the time. Though her father was seventy-nine, he was in good health and she was not worried about him. But in this dream she thought she was at home and with the family sitting around the dining table. She, but none of the others, looked at her father. He rose from the table, smiled at her,

Opposite page:
Several visions occur in the Bible. In this *Jacob's Vision* (1754), Jacob sees the gates to heaven open.

pointed to his heart, turned, left the table still smiling and waved his hand at her as if in farewell. He said nothing, but she thought he meant that he was going to die because of a heart ailment. The dream troubled her. A few weeks later her father had a heart attack, his first, and died.

In this form, obviously the imagery is not a copying process based on the item of information secured in Stage One by ESP. Instead, at the beginning of Stage Two a process of suggestion goes on first, and the result of it becomes the basis of the dream scene, as when the woman dreamed that her father waved goodbye to her from the family dinner table. Even though the elements of this fantasy were realistic in that they were true to memory, the scene itself was a dramatization. If the reality was the father's approaching death, it suggested the fictitious scene, which then was embodied in the dream imagery. However, the meaning in this instance was fairly clear.

Incomplete cases are frequent, and again the defect may occur in a number of different ways. One fairly common one is that personalities are substituted in the imagery. A frequent substitution is that of the dreamer himself for the one actually involved. Such was the case of a woman who dreamed she was driving along a lonely stretch of road when suddenly a black car loomed up ahead in the early morning light. A woman and child were in the front seat. The woman lost control of the car, swerved into the other lane and a head-on collision resulted. All three persons were thrown against a lone tree, and she 'saw' all of them, including herself, hanging as if dead from its limbs. The reality was that her brother Bill and his wife set out on an early morning trip. They were on a lonely highway

with few trees when suddenly a black car loomed up with a woman and child in the front seat. The woman lost control of her car and headed for Bill's. Just before he saw it, his wife grabbed the wheel and jerked the car to one side where it came to a stop beside a lone tree. Although the woman's car swerved into Bill's lane, she got control of it in time and no one was hurt. The tendency toward fantasy introduced by the initial substitution of identity was plainly illustrated here

> *In other cases the fantasy may be so remote from the actual situation that the latter may not be shown at all.*

by the striking embroidery that went on in the dream beyond the reality, although that had been reproduced fairly realistically.

In other cases the fantasy may be so remote from the actual situation that the latter may not be shown at all. The suggestion made by the actual situation takes off from it without embodying any recognizable detail of it. In 1948 a man in Los Angeles dreamed one night that a salesman was trying to sell him a two-toned grey Hudson. He tried to explain to the salesman that he could not buy it, but the latter was insistent and the contract was eventually signed. The next morning the man's sister called to say that the night before at a charity ball she had drawn the lucky ticket and won a two-toned grey Hudson. She said her first thought was to call her brother.

Sometimes a dream is repeated under circumstances that make it appear to be symbolic. For instance, if a dream fantasy is recognized as being connected with a given situation, then a similar dream may precede a

comparable situation if one occurs. A man in Minnesota had been convicted as an accessory to a serious crime. As the result of much pressure he pleaded guilty and was held for years without a hearing. His family worked for his parole, but each time when their efforts seemed about to succeed he would dream he saw his dead parents sadly turning their heads from side to side as if saying no, and each time the parole effort was unsuccessful. Finally he did secure a hearing. A few days before it he again saw his parents in a dream and they were smiling and giving evidence of joy. Believing he was going to be successful, he went to the hearing and succeeded in being freed.

One feature of dreams like the preceding two is that the fantasy is obviously suggested by the person's own individual situation. It is not really symbolic, as it was in the case of a woman who dreamed for three nights of swirling muddy water. When ten days later her sister died of peritonitis after an appendectomy, the dreams were taken to have been 'signs' of it. This woman's grandmother, who died before she was born, was said also to have dreamed of muddy water as a sign of death, so that muddy water taken to mean a death had no doubt been mentioned in the family. It therefore could have been a natural association from which an apparently 'stylized' and impersonal symbol had developed.

However, when the fantasy has no personal connection the likelihood that it was based on ESP is questionable. Take for instance the kind of

Opposite page:
Scene from Shakespeare's *A Midsummer Night's Dream:* 'Titania Sleeps'. Dreams are often a gateway to psi experiences.

Beliefs, Rituals, and Symbols of the Modern World

dream imagery reported by a man in Michigan, who said: 'When I dream of ice or snow I always have trouble on the job or am laid off. It has happened so many times that I can't ignore it.

In such cases, if no time or other limit was set, the next 'trouble on the job' could be taken as a fulfillment of the dream without any necessary ESP impression at all. As a matter of fact, the unrealistic ESP dreams most frequently reported scarcely support the commonly held belief that dream imagery tends to be symbolic. In the first place, the majority of unrealistic dreams that are reported do not show the impersonal imagery involved in symbolism, and many dreams that appear to be symbolic do not involve ESP.

Not all of the ESP experiences that feature imagery occur in sleep. Occasionally a person, while awake, may have an experience involving imagery (day-dream) which also brings information by ESP. Since the form is the same as that of a dream such experiences, whether realistic or unrealistic, can be classed as dreams even though the person was not sleeping.

All ESP experiences come in one or other of these forms—intuitive, hallucinatory, or realistic or unrealistic dreams—and bring items of information in varying degrees of completeness. The forms usually are fairly distinct from one another, although in occasional instances a tendency to change from one to another in the same dream may occur.

The Falling Picture

PK, the second main type of psi, is manifested by effects on objects without physical contact. They usually appear to bring messages, much as do the forms of ESP experience; as if the physical manifestation was a method of signaling a message without using the ESP channels. In them, instead

of a hallucinated effect, a real objective one occurs. Such occurrences can thus be considered a fifth form of psi. While theoretically the information might concern a thing, a thought or a future event, just as in ESP experiences, it generally concerns another person, often one at a distance, and usually one who is undergoing a crisis at the time. The other person, the target person, almost invariably is one with whom the experiencing individual is emotionally involved. The physical effect then appears to the experiencing person to be a message or 'sign' of the crisis.

The crisis very frequently is that of dying, but sometimes the person is already dead, sometimes still living. There seems to be no connection between his or her state or condition and the specific kind of effect that marks the crisis. It may be different or the same from case to case, regardless of whether he or she is dying, dead, or still living.

Regardless of the actual kind of effect observed, an occurrence such as a portrait falling off a wall until recently was usually taken as a message from the target person, particularly in cases in which the target person was dying or dead. Instances in which he was still living were seldom taken into consideration, and probably, if noticed at all, were put down to 'coincidence.' The natural assumption when the dying or dead were involved was that an unusual ability to affect objects at a distance must have been activated, an ability that living persons were not known to have.

The Experimenter Effect

However, since PK has been demonstrated in the laboratory to be a capacity that does belong to the living, the interpretation now is different. It now hinges on the question whether the messages came from the target person, or were instead spontaneous PK effects

Marc Franz's *The Dream* painted in 1912

produced by the persons in whose presence or vicinity they occurred. The question is whether the effects were produced by the target persons or by the experiencing persons. This question of who is responsible for a PK effect comes up in the laboratory as well

as in life-situations. If an individual subject produces evidence of PK when alone, he himself of course can be assumed to have caused it. However, the exercise of PK, like that of ESP, is an unconscious process and can only be recognized by its end product.

Therefore if a subject and an experimenter are both present in a PK test, both aware of the target and both eager to succeed, and do then succeed, it is not possible to decide with certainty which one is responsible.

The experimental results thus may not show which of two individuals involved in PK is the effective one. But they do show that living persons can exercise the PK effect. Whether or not the deceased can do so, or even whether they 'survive' death at all, are still unsettled questions. In occasional

Photograph taken of President Kennedy as he drove through Dallas, Texas, in an open-top car shortly before he was shot on November 22, 1963.

cases the likelihood that the target person created the effect is ruled out entirely by the fact that he did not know (or perhaps, even know of) the experiencing person. These are mostly instances in which the target person is a public figure. Such a case was reported by a man who said that a clock in his home stopped on November 22, 1963, at the very time that President Kennedy was assassinated. It had run perfectly for years and he did not feel that it stopped at that precise time just by coincidence. The

effect could not be ascribed to an influence from the target person. Instead some of those in the home who were shocked, must be supposed to have exercised PK, if indeed something other than coincidence was involved. But in all cases the experiencing person could have caused the effect. He could have done so regardless of the nature of the crisis of the target person or whether he was dying, dead, or still living.

The experiencing person thus appears to be the one who causes the

physical effect. It would be, in a way, a sign to himself of the unconscious reception at Stage One of the item of information. There is reason to think that in Stage Two, the PK effect may occur in a way quite analogous to that of a hallucinatory effect; that is, in conjunction with an incipient intuition which is then usually blocked. The reason for thinking this is that here, too, in an occasional report, an intuitive component is recognizable. For instance the daughter of a coal miner, asleep in her home miles from that of her parents, was awakened by her light suddenly coming on. She says: 'I knew something was wrong down home,' an intuitive idea, of course. It was correct, for at that time a motor down in the mine fell and crushed her father.

The physical effect in such cases thus appears to have originated with the intuition at the start of Stage Two. The origin of the PK form thus appears to be quite parallel with that of hallucinatory experiences.

The PK form never produces a complete item of information, and is also the form least frequently reported. This may mean that few personalities can produce cases of spontaneous PK. It also may be partly because this is the most difficult form of all to identify with certainty. For not only must the effect be timed with the crisis but the absence of ordinary causes, too, must be established. These points often are difficult to make, for usually it is only some time afterward that the details are noted. Consequently they are often unconvincing.

The general observation that follows from this catalog of the forms of psychic experiences is that psi ability has no form that is exclusively its own, except that of PK. All of the other forms, and especially the intuitive and the dream forms, are common mental experiences that usually have nothing to do with psi. Hallucinations, while not so common, also occur in situations that have nothing to do with psi. They have been associated mostly with abnormal mental states; psi hallucinations, however, are not commonly associated with abnormality.

Since ESP does not have a characteristic form of its own, and the PK form occurs so obscurely that it is seldom recognized, psi is difficult to identify as such, and can be only

tentatively recognized in everyday life by considering the meaning of the information transmitted. It must be such that it could not have been supplied by sense experience. Also it must be beyond reasonable explanation as a case of chance coincidence. Reliable identification of psi has therefore depended on experiments, in which sensory cues were ruled out by the conditions and in which the unlikelihood of coincidence could be estimated.

Who Chooses the Message?

Even though psi experiences may bring information about an unlimited range of topics, the message in any case concerns only one specific topic. It is selected from all other thoughts, things or future events that might have

Even telepathy . . . is not dependant on outside initiative, but is a function of the experiencing person just as are the other types.

concerned the person. But is it a topic that impresses itself upon the person from the outside, something like a telegram bringing an item of news? Or does he himself 'reach out' and pick this particular item from all the others, because of his interest in it? Indirectly, if not directly, it is possible now to get something of an answer to this question, both logically and by studying the range of topics involved in a large number of experiences.

Logically, the choice between the two alternatives is different now from in the past. Before the occurrence of precognition had been recognized, it seemed more likely that the person was the receiver of a message impressed upon or communicated to

him from the outside, for all experiences under consideration then were contemporaneous with the time of the event. However, now no such necessary temporal connection exists. Presumably an experience involving a future event could occur at any time beforehand, and besides that it would be difficult to think of a future event as being 'sent' to a person.

Earlier, another impression was also current, which was that psychic experiences nearly always concern crises of great importance to the person, and that they frequently involve communications from the dead. Both ideas implied that the psi message was at least urgent, if not that it actually induced a sensitive person to have an experience about it.

The impression of the usually critical nature of the topics of spontaneous psi was based in part on nineteenth-century studies in psychical research, in which emphasis was put on crisis cases and those involving the deceased. In the background of this work was interest in finding evidence that had a bearing on the survival question, and so there was naturally an emphasis on experiences involving crises.

But in addition to establishing the occurrence of precognition, research in parapsychology has shown that the psi process is essentially unitary; not only do ESP and PK seem to be aspects of the same process, but the types of ESP too are the result of a single process acting on different kinds of subject matter. Even telepathy, as shown above, is not dependent on outside initiative, but is a function of the experiencing person just as are the other types. This changes the likelihood that the event triggers the experience, rather than the experiencing person's interest in it.

Psi Experiences and the Dead

Psi experiences in which someone dead appears to play an active part are infrequent in comparison to those in which no such personality is involved. They occur, but since all types of spontaneous ESP, and especially the precognitive, are now recognized, those that involve the deceased make up a very small part of the total number.

Reported cases that seem to involve the deceased are of two general kinds that are different superficially, though not in the basic psi process. One of these is the simple isolated kind, like those mentioned above; the other is more complicated and the phenomena tend to recur in much the same way for an indefinite time. The second category includes haunting and poltergeist phenomena.

Dreams involving the deceased are usually realistic in details, but the appearance of someone dead in an active role in a dream cannot be considered to be realistic. Such dreams are therefore classified as unrealistic in form. An example was reported by a woman in Detroit. She said that, after her mother died, her father said she should have her mother's jewels; they lived in the same apartment and he kept them in his possession. Later he moved to another city and she supposed he took the jewels with him. After his death, she did not find them among his belongings and she began to worry about them. One night in a dream her father appeared and told her she had worried enough, and she would find the jewels in the dresser in his old room. She should pull out a certain drawer and at the back she would find a small box built into the dresser, so that it could not be seen unless one knew where to look. She did as he said and found the jewels.

Even better known than dreams of the deceased are hallucinatory experiences involving them. (Hallucinatory, it should be recalled, is a term to denote that the person thought a sense, or senses, was involved when no objective reason was present.) A visual hallucinatory experience was reported by a woman in Connecticut. Her father had died some years before. She was awakened very early one morning and saw her father standing at the foot

> *Dreams involving the deceased are usually realistic in details, but the appearance of someone dead in an active role in a dream cannot be considered to be realistic.*

of her bed. Somehow, though he did not speak, she got the command to go to her mother's home at once. She felt it was so urgent that she got up and within the hour had started on the trip home, a distance of more than 400 miles. She found her mother very ill and alone, and almost certain to have died without her daughter.

Even more frequent than visual hallucinations are auditory ones involving someone deceased. An example comes from a woman in South Dakota. Her father, on whom she had depended a great deal, had recently died, and she felt very much alone and helpless in the midst of many troubles. She was behind in car payments, and a man came one day to repossess the car. As she reports: 'While I was talking to the man at the front door, just as clear as my own voice, I heard my father say: "Tell him to wait till Friday." Without hesitation I told him to wait till Friday and I would pay him. He agreed and went on. Then I began to wonder how I could raise the $280 due. Thursday afternoon my father's lawyer called me and told me to come to his office and pick up a check for

$417. The court had collected an old account owed to my father.'

PK effects that seem to relate to the deceased also occur. Such an experience was reported by a woman in New York. The occasion was a dinner party that she gave for five couples, all of whom had known a man who had suddenly died of a heart attack two days before, while on a trip to South America. When the wine was passed, the closest friend of the deceased rose and proposed the toast. She was holding her glass by the bowl, the stem broke off and fell to the floor. Her glass had not touched anything; she was just holding it. They all felt that their deceased friend was present.

No Evidence of Survival

These are the main forms of spontaneous cases in which the dead seem to play an active part—dreams, hallucinatory experiences, and instances of PK. Of course, the question in all of them is whether the communications do actually come from discarnate personalities. Before the establishment of ESP and PK as abilities of living persons, it was necessary in the interpretation of such cases as evidence of survival to suppose that the deceased somehow had powers beyond those of living persons. And it was by these unusual powers that they could return and communicate with the living as they purported to do. It is now known that, since living persons could themselves secure the needed information in ESP cases like the three cited above, any person or persons present could have been responsible for effects such as the breaking of the wine glass during a moment of intensified emotion.

The imagery of dreams carries information secured by psi to levels of consciousness where memory of the dream can take over, and it is clear that the imagery itself is unconsciously constructed to fit the case. The hallucinatory forms and PK are also vehicles for the expression of information below the conscious level, and are forms in which information may be expressed when no deceased person is involved. Presumably, therefore, when a spirit agent appears as a character in the drama he could be another imaginary creation. The forms of the experiences in themselves can thus have no definitive significance for survival.

If spirit personalities exist after death and are in any way actually involved in these experiences, then detection of the fact would have to depend on evidence other than that the dead person appeared to play an active role in the drama of a psi experience. It would have to distinguish between influences ascribable to the deceased and those exerted by the living person.

Possibly such evidence might be found in any differences between the reasons or motives for communicating which the two persons, the living and the dead, might be presumed to have had. If the motive of the dead person in making the specific communication was evidently much stronger than that of the living, then the bearing of the case would at least give some weight to the idea that the deceased had influenced or caused the experience.

In the examples already given no great difference in motives exists, and it is rarely that a situation is such that the deceased person's interest in the communication can be presumed to have been much greater than that of the living person. One such, reported by a woman in Florida, happened when she was a girl in her twenties and travel was still mainly by train. In her Pullman one night she woke up, she said: 'to see the face of a nice man, probably in his late fifties, brown hair and eyes, and a Van Dyke beard. He apologized, said his family was on the train and he was looking for them, and that I looked so much like

his daughter that he thought he had found them. I went back to sleep resolved to waken early and try to get a look at the girl who looked like me. I did not find her until I was in the station. Then I saw her and with her were her mother and brother. The brother looked just like his father. Just then from the baggage car a coffin was taken off the train, and the girl, her mother and brother, in deep mourning and weeping followed with sad eyes the transfer of the coffin. I did not have the presence of mind to tell them of my experience, but I realized then that the buttons of my berth had not been opened and it was dark in it, yet that face and head had certainly been very visible.'

More Complicated Levels

In this instance, as in many of the cases when the emotional situation is strongly weighted toward the deceased, he was a stranger to the experiencing one. The latter had no apparent reason for making the contact implied in the psi experience, while the deceased one seemed to have a motive. However, still the evidence is not conclusive.

It can be observed, however, that experiences in which the dead seem to play an active role, if considered as unconscious dramatizations, do involve more complicated levels of it than other unrealistic psi dreams usually do. In these not only do the deceased appear as self-activated characters, but they also deliver the message. This may mean that these appearances of the deceased are not purely dramatizations, but actual influences; or, on the other hand, it may mean that the unconscious dramatizing ability of very few dreamers is sufficient to produce this level of fantasy.

The situation regarding these experiences, therefore, is that they cannot be finally interpreted now that psi is known to be an ability that living

persons possess. At the same time that psi prevents an interpretation for or against the survival hypothesis, it does permit the question to be raised. If survival does occur, psi would be the necessary form by which communications from the deceased to the living would take place. If it does occur, the methods of research by which the fact could be established have not yet been developed.

LOUISA E. RHINE

FURTHER READING: L. E. Rhine. Hidden Channels of the Mind. *(New York, NY: Sloane, Duell and Pearce, 1961); L. E. Rhine.* Mind Over Matter. *(London, UK: Macmillan, 1970); C. Greene & C. McCreery.* Apparitions. *(New York, NY: State Mutual Books, 1977).*

Subud

When Gurdjieff died in 1949, his work was carried on by several groups throughout the world, but there was no acknowledged inspirational leader. His successor was finally announced, however, in a curiously tangential manner: when John Bennett, who ran the Gurdjieffian school just outside London, visited Damascus in 1955, he had a meeting with a local holy man who told him: 'A Messenger is already on Earth . . . before long he will come to the West . . . you are one of those chosen to prepare the way.'

That Messenger was Subuh, a humble bookkeeper from Semarang in Indonesia. Born in 1901, sickly and puny, he seemed destined for an early grave. A stranger passing the child's home, and hearing the distress over his condition, said this would change if he was renamed 'Muhammad.' As they had little to lose, his parents did this—and the child flourished.

He soon showed signs of psychic ability, announcing that a newly-mar-

1950s actress, Hungarian-born Eva Bartok (1929–1998) was a faithful follower of Subud.

ried couple would separate within a year. When this prophecy was fulfilled, he was (not unnaturally) kept away from other wedding ceremonies. As he grew older, several fortunetellers told him that he would die by the age of thirty-two, so he began to seek out spiritual teachers who would enlighten him about the meaning of this fate. Finally one Sheikh Abdurrahman, a dervish, informed him that the enlightenment he sought would not come from any holy man, but from a source outside the human race.

It came in 1925 in the form of a blinding light 'resembling the sun' which blotted out the moonless night sky. When this ball of light came down and touched Muhammad Subuh on the head he was immediately convulsed. For the next '1,000 nights' he was visited by psychic experiences, including visions and moments of inner illumination, although he was able to carry on a normal life in all other respects. When he was thirty-one an inner voice told him to retire from all material concerns, and a year

later, when he had reached the age at which it had been prophesied he would die, he was told that 'the wealth of power and illumination which had been given to him . . . must be freely handed on to all who asked for aid.' From then on, Subuh initiated many others into receiving, and in turn passing on, the 'spiritual current' he had been given.

Gurdjieff had taught his followers to achieve mastery over themselves through a system of physical and spiritual exercises, and Subud follows in this tradition. It is not a religion, nor a philosophy, but a complete and practical system for awakening one's inherent godlike abilities. The word 'subud' is derived from the Sanskrit words *sushila*, 'right living according to the will of God,' *budhi*, 'inner force,' and *dharma*, 'submission to God.' Subud teaches that one's inner life can be dramatically changed by the discovery of, and adherence to, the dictates of one's higher self. In one who has achieved an awareness of this soul power the outer, everyday life will also change dramatically: they will be capable of 'miracles' such as healing, and the barriers between the seen and unseen worlds will be removed.

Muhammad Subuh initiated others with what he called the 'opening,' which is often described as an 'electrical current' or 'vibration'—a blissful sense of open-ended consciousness and the cessation of restless mental striving. In this it resembles other systems, such as transcendental meditation, although few disciplines promise such a dramatic shift of consciousness. Those on the path of Subud undergo a form of spiritual training called the 'latihan,' which brings a balance between conscious and unconscious power and a means of developing that potential with immediate effect.

One of the more famous followers of Subud was the actress Eva Bartok, who was cured of severe abdominal pain in 1957 by the techniques taught in the latihan. She said later 'I felt as if my old self had died, being replaced by something new and alive.'

Edward van Hien (1916–78), in his *What is Subud?*, says there is no strict teaching in Subud, but 'a fact which works and grows and goes on by itself . . . our hearts change, our characters change, our physical health changes, and what was wrong in us is put right—all this is the working of a powerful force of life, which cannot be known by our ordinary instruments and organs of perception.'

Never intended to be a mass cult, Subud continues to thrive quietly, content to pass on its secrets to those whose motives are pure and who are ready to receive them.

Synchronicity

On the morning of April Fool's Day in 1949, C. G. Jung (1875–1961) made a note about an inscription that contained a figure that was half-man and half-fish. There was fish for lunch and someone mentioned the custom of making an 'April fish' (in French, *poisson d'avril*) of a victim. In the afternoon he was unexpectedly shown some pictures of fish by a former patient and in the evening he saw a piece of embroidery with fishes and sea monsters in it. Next morning, a patient told him how she had dreamed the previous night of a large fish, which swam across a lake to her and landed at her feet. That was all for the moment, but later he had occasion to write about this series of coincidences. After finishing writing, he strolled to a nearby lake—and what should he find lying on the bank? A fish a foot long!

'When coincidences pile up in this way,' Jung wrote in an essay, 'On Synchronicity,' which he published in 1951, 'one cannot help being impressed by them—for the greater the number of terms in such a series, or the more unusual its character, the more improbable it becomes.'

He took it that the curious accumulation of fishes had occurred by chance, but all the same it seemed improbable.

A Dream Comes True

Another experience of a similar kind that impressed him occurred when a woman patient was telling him about a dream in which she was given a piece of jewelry—a golden scarab. While she was talking, Jung heard a tapping at the window behind him. He looked round and found that a flying insect was bumping against the glass. It flew into the room when he opened the window and he caught it. It was a scarabaeid beetle, of a golden-green colour. He handed it to his patient and said, 'Here is your scarab.'

Jung also cited the splendid story of a Monsieur Deschamps who, as a boy in Orléans, was given a piece of plum pudding—a rarity in France—by a Monsieur de Fortgibu. It made an impression on him and ten years later,

Photograph of Austrian biologist Paul Kammerer in about 1925

in a Paris restaurant, he saw a plum pudding and asked for a piece, but it turned out that the pudding had been specially made for Monsieur de Fortgibu. Many years after this Deschamps was with friends for the evening and was given a piece of plum pudding. Delightedly eating it, he remarked that the only thing missing was Monsieur de Fortgibu. At that moment the door opened and in walked an elderly, sadly disorientated gentleman. It was Monsieur de Fortgibu, who turned out to have muddled the address and come to the wrong house.

Jung coined the term 'synchronicity' for what he suggested might be an 'a-causal connecting principle' behind the occurrence of two or more events which are apparently linked together in some significant way, but are not connected by cause and effect.

When you are thinking of someone you know and the telephone rings, and on the other end of the line is the person you were thinking about, you do not expect to discover any causal relationship between the two events. When a clock stops at the moment when someone in the house dies—an occurrence quite frequently reported—it does not appear that the death causes the clock to stop (or that the clock causes the death, for that matter), and yet it is natural to feel that the two events are linked.

The Cosmic Kaleidoscope

Although it was Jung who coined the word synchronicity itself, he had been preceded in the field by the Austrian biologist Paul Kammerer (1880–1926), a tragic figure who committed suicide. Kammerer suspected that there might be more to coincidences than met the eye and he noted down significant examples for many years.

Most of them were trivial in themselves. For instance, he noted that one day in 1910 his brother-in-law went to a concert where his seat number was nine and his cloakroom ticket was also number nine, and at another concert the following day he sat in seat number twenty-one and his cloakroom ticket was number twenty-one.

Kammerer spent hours in parks and in trams carefully noting down the particulars of passers-by or passengers—by sex, age, type of costume, and whether they carried objects such as parcels or umbrellas. Analyzing these phenomena, he found that they tended to cluster in groups, in the same way that gamblers enjoy runs of good luck, or that we all sometimes experience one of those times when for no apparent reason everything goes right. He concluded that 'the recurrence of identical or similar data in contiguous areas of space or time is a simple empirical fact which has to be accepted and which cannot be explained by coincidence—or rather, which makes coincidence rule to such an extent that the concept of coincidence itself is negated.'

Kammerer published his findings in his book *Das Gesetz der Serie* in 1919. He believed that nonphysical, noncausal factors must be at work and put forward the idea of a force that causes similar events to occur—like the person's death and the clock stopping. He suggested the image of 'a world mosaic or cosmic kaleidoscope which, in spite of constant shuffling and rearrangements, also takes care of bringing like and like together.' This principle of like being connected with like, incidentally, is an extremely old one in magic.

A Fourth Principle

Jung used Kammerer's work in his essay on 'Synchronicity: an Acausal Connecting Principle,' which he issued from his institute in Zurich in 1952. It is included in the eighth volume of the English edition of his *Collected Works*. Like so much that he wrote, it is not at all easy to follow.

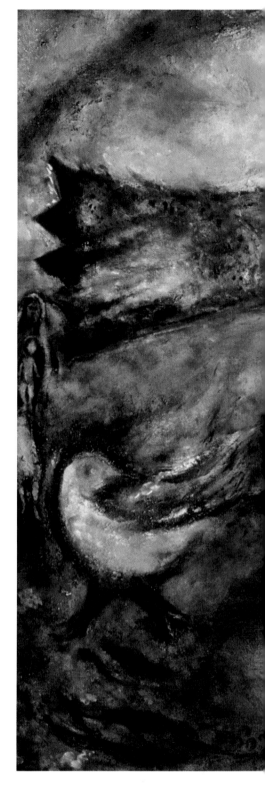

Science, he said, had become obsessed with the need to explain everything in terms of cause and effect, and was consequently closing its eyes to the possibility of noncausal explanations. 'The synchronistic factor merely stipulates the existence of

Flying Fish by Marc Chagall (1887–1985). C. G. Jung seemed to be followed by the image of a fish, leading him to come up with the idea of synchronicity.

an intellectually necessary principle which could be added as a fourth to the recognized triad of space, time, and causality.'

Jung was encouraged to look for such a noncausal factor by the great physicist and Nobel prize-winner

Wolfgang Pauli (1900–58), for in the study of sub-atomic theoretical physics the occurrence of meaningful non-causal events had already been recognized. 'The causality principle,' Jung wrote, 'asserts that the connection between cause and effect is a neces-

sary one. The synchronicity principle asserts that the terms of a meaningful coincidence are connected by simultaneity and meaning.'

He went on to link this new principle with the unconscious mind and to track it to a lair in the collective

BRINGING IN THE PLUM PUDDING

Bringing in the Plum Pudding, twentieth century, English School

this mill. Jung studied a collection of 180 horoscopes of married couples and came to the conclusion that there were positive correlations between the astrological interpretations and the lives of the subjects, too strong to be put down to chance. He could not explain this in terms of cause and effect, and he suggested that his 'a-causal connecting principle' was responsible.

Koestler pointed out that, before the scientific revolution of the seventeenth century, the idea of hidden links and affinities between outwardly unconnected phenomena was part of Western Europe's accepted way of explaining the world. All things were connected together by unseen 'correspondences' and 'sympathies' in a vast, connected whole in which nothing occurred by coincidence. Kammerer's cosmic kaleidoscope and Jung's principle of synchronicity are both ways of returning to an older understanding of reality.

FURTHER READING: C. G. Jung. The Structure and Dynamics of the Psyche. (Collected Works, Vol 8) (London, UK: Routledge, 1960); Arthur Koestler. The Roots of Coincidence. (London, UK: Hutchinson, 1972).

Teilhard de Chardin

Born on May 1, 1881, at Sarcenat near Clermont-Ferrand in the Auvergne, France, Pierre Teilhard de Chardin died of a heart attack in New York on Easter Sunday, April 10, 1955. In 1901 he took his first vows as a Jesuit and remained within the order until his death. Teilhard was not only a priest but also a scientist—a paleontologist—of some distinction. Before his death he enjoyed a considerable

unconscious—the unconscious which all human beings share in Jungian theory. Here lie the archetypal figures and symbols created by the common experiences of the human race. The archetypes sometimes invade the conscious mind and somehow give rise to synchronicity in action—for example, the coincidence of the flying beetle with the patient describing her dream of the golden scarab. How this works, however, is far from clear. Even Arthur

Koestler (1905–83), whose book *The Roots of Coincidence* is the best treatment of the subject, was unable fully to elucidate Jung's meaning.

ESP and Astrology

Jung wanted to explain clairvoyance and telepathy in terms of synchronicity rather than extrasensory perception. The success of J. B. Rhine's card-guessing experiments, the *I Ching,* and astrology were all grist to reputation in his chosen field and in 1948, was offered a chair in Prehistory at the Collège de France. This offer he had to decline because his Jesuit superiors in Rome would not allow him to publish his most famous book, *The Phenomenon of Man*. For Teilhard had ideas of his own, and these did not correspond to the official Roman orthodoxy of the day. Hence his superiors considered it more 'prudent' that he should spend most of his life working 'in the field,' mostly in China, while the last four years of his life were spent in the United States where the impact of his ideas was less likely to be felt than in France where he was already well known. Right up to his death, however, he was not allowed to publish anything except papers of a purely scientific nature within his own specialty, but fortunately he had the prudence to entrust his manuscripts to a friend and not long after his death *The Phenomenon of Man* was published in the original French, the English translation appearing with a warmly sympathetic introduction by Sir Julian Huxley (1887–1975), in 1959.

The Soul of the World

The publication of *The Phenomenon of Man* created a sensation. The worlds of both science and theology were split down the middle in their attitude toward the 'phenomenon' of Teilhard. Some scientists denounced him as insufficiently grounded in biology, while others took up his ideas with enthusiasm. The theologians were also split, the orthodox remaining obdurately antagonistic while the liberals hailed his totally new approach to Christianity as a real breakthrough in that it seemed to make Christianity once again relevant to the modern world. Rome severely discouraged the reading of his works since they had been published without permission under the auspices of a committee that was largely scientific and not by any means entirely Christian. Then came Pope John XXIII and the Second Vatican Council, and the rock of Peter, monolithic and unmoving since the Council of Trent in the fifteenth century, lurched forward with unforeseen and unforeseeable speed.

Teilhard was dead; but at last his ideas received a sympathetic hearing

> *In scientific terms he saw the world as evolving to ever-higher stages of 'complexity-consciousness,' . . . there was no reason to suppose that evolution had suddenly come to a halt . . .*

from the great majority of his fellow churchmen. Posthumously he had his reward, for the contradictions of his life reflected the integrity and completeness of his thought. Within the Church he was the apostle, prophet, and mystic of a purposeful progress, and yet, despite constant setbacks, despite what often seemed petty and timorous persecution, he remained not only a loyal son of the Roman Catholic Church but also faithful to his vows of absolute obedience to the Society of Jesus and the pope. His non-Catholic friends could not understand why he did not break with such pusillanimous lack of understanding. But his own philosophy of life, and vision of the future, made it impossible for him to break away from what he saw as the one 'axis' of cohesion in a world in travail. He had been attacked as a theologian, as a scientist, and as a philosopher, but basically he was none of these things. True, he was a scientist but his science was the prehistoric past of this planet, whereas his real and absorbing interest was the goal toward which evolution was, in his opinion, guiding and pushing not only Earth, but the whole universe. As a theologian and philosopher he was never more than an amateur and he knew it. He was one of those human beings who could not be pigeonholed into any obvious category: he was a mystic, a visionary, and a prophet.

Basically he saw the salvation of the world in terms of a real reconciliation between science and religion, a situation in which religion would be able to reinterpret itself in terms of evolution, and in which science itself would be 'tinged with mysticism and charged with faith,' in terms of a 'synthesis of the (Christian) God "above," with the (Marxist) God "ahead."' In scientific terms he saw the world as evolving to ever-higher stages of 'complexity-consciousness,' for, quite rightly, he saw that there was no reason to suppose that evolution had suddenly come to a halt with the emergence of self-conscious man. The very troubles of our times were a sign that the human race was undergoing a new 'mutation,' a new qualitative change that would result in a new and higher form of consciousness in which the individual consciousness would be transcended in some form of collective consciousness. The precursors of this were the modern totalitarian movements. During World War II, most of which he spent in China where he was out of touch with the ghastly realities of the European situation, he refused to see the conflicting powers as black-and-white alternatives. Nazism, insofar as it was a cohesive and progressive force, he considered as an advance on what had gone before, although he was well aware that ultimately it could only lead to an 'ant-hill' civilization, which would be an evil parody of his own vision of the 'totalization' of humanity as a union of free persons

Pierre Teilhard de Chardin (1881–1955), the Jesuit philosopher and paleontologist divided opinion with the posthumous publication of his work, *The Phenomenon of Man*

animated and propelled forward by what he had once called the 'soul of the world' toward a unique point of convergence. He was later to call this point 'Omega,' that is, God or Christ as the ultimate term of human evolution and history.

The Cosmic Christ

At a time when the Vatican under Pius XII was fulminating against international Communism as the chief enemy, Teilhard saw in it the shape of things to come. In China where he had seen it at firsthand and had witnessed the vast human

energies it had been able to unleash, he was convinced that here was a power working along the very 'axis' of evolution, which no earthly force could stop. Yet he saw that the new 'totalized' society could never be wholly valid unless it were underpinned by love. 'The world cannot endure, advance, or realize itself,' he wrote, 'without the action of a power that is a species of love. This is why, much as I sympathize with the "totalitarian" faith of popular fronts, I am forced to acknowledge that their *impersonal* forms of ideal "Humanity," "society," (*a fortiori* the "Race" or "Empire of fascist doctrines") without soul or "face," are going to nip the Evolution that they want to promote and save in the bud.' What Teilhard had been anticipating actually came to pass for an all too brief period in Czechoslovakia, when 'Communism with a human face' became a living reality.

Despite the divisive tendencies that seemed to be tearing this world to pieces during two world wars and their aftermath, he remained optimistic; for he had an unshakable faith in Christ and the Catholic Church, which he liked to speak of in biological terms as the Christian 'phylum' (in biology a 'phylum' is a main division of the animal or vegetable kingdom). But what kind of Christ did Teilhard worship? His was not Christ as preached by the 'orthodoxy' of the Roman bureaucrats but the cosmic Christ preached by St. Paul in his letter to the Colossians in whom 'were created all things in heaven and Earth,' and who 'holds all things in unity.' As to the Roman Catholic Church (and Teilhard, far from denying his Catholic faith, described himself as 'hyper-Catholic'), according to this same letter of St. Paul 'the Church is his body, and he its head;' and 'in this body lives the fullness of divinity, and in him you too find your own fulfillment, in the one who is the head of every Sovereignty and Power.' All this was vitally real to Teilhard, and this was the 'gospel' of which he felt himself to be the prophet.

'Spirit of the Earth'

In his vision, the Church was not just a divinely appointed organization designated to save individual souls through a more or less mechanical administration of the sacraments. Rather, it was a living organism—a single phylum—which had to be saved in its totality, for he could not conceive of the salvation of the part except in the context of the salvation of the

> He looks forward to the Marxist 'association in which the free development of each will be the condition for the free development of all' . . .

whole. Nor was his God simply 'our Father which art in heaven,' but the God 'ahead,' the point of convergence at which the human race, through the instrumentality of the Church, was to find its consummation and meaning. This vision presented itself to Teilhard with irresistible force when he was serving as a stretcher-bearer in World War I; and it never left him till his dying day.

In his vision there were two ingredients always present. Christ as the point of convergence in the future and his own almost physical awareness of the 'spirit of the earth'—an awareness of the 'holiness' of matter and the 'essence' of the world that had 'hit' him when he was still a child and from which his 'whole internal life had sprung and grown . . . a personal psychological experience: nothing more, but also nothing less.'

A Paroxysm of Love

Teilhard was a pantheist and he knew it; but according to him there were two types of pantheism. These were what he describes as Hindu pantheism—the pantheism of diffusion and dissolution of all individual personality into an indeterminate whole—and a pantheism of 'centration' in which personality, so far from being obliterated, is heightened and clarified through love and centered on to the cosmic Christ who is the point to which all creation (or at least all of it that can be saved) is destined by evolution itself to converge. The 'oriental' pantheism of diffusion, which he had himself experienced time and again, is a blissful experience all right, but it is nonetheless essentially retrograde, a step back into a state of '*co*-consciousness' before *self*-consciousness was born. The new mysticism neither abolishes personality nor sinks back into the beatific peace of undifferentiated oneness, but throws itself in a paroxysm of love into him who is both the source and goal of all personality and the collective fulfillment of all personalities.

Teilhard was both a mystic and a Marxist. He looks forward to the Marxist 'association in which the free development of each will be the condition for the free development of all' and to a state of cosmic awareness which will be suffused by love, and concentrated on and toward that ultimate unity to which evolution is driving us and which is the true goal of Christianity and the Catholic Church—Christ Omega, the cosmic fulfillment of mankind. This is the gospel according to Pierre Teilhard de Chardin, humanist, Marxist, mystic, and 'hyper-Catholic'

R. C. ZAEHNER

FURTHER READING: Pierre Teilhard de Chardin. Hymn of the Universe. *(New York, NY: Harper and Row, 1964); Pierre Teilhard de Chardin.* Le Milieu Divin. *(New York, NY: Harper and Row, 1960); Pierre Teilhard* de Chardin. The Phenomenon of Man. *(New York, NY: Harper and Row, 1959); R. Speaight.* Teilhard de Chardin. *(New York, NY: Harper and Row, 1968).*

Telekinesis

Paranormally caused movement of objects: examples include the fall of a picture at someone's death, the flight of the Communion wafer to the recipient's mouth, and the movement of furniture or flinging of stones or crockery in poltergeist cases; teleportation, or apportation, is the mysterious conveyance of objects into closed rooms.

Telepathy

Communication between one mind and another without the use of speech, gesture, or any of the normal methods of communicating; thought transference; 'the direct experience of another person's mental state;' a type of extra-sensory perception.

Time and the Fourth Dimension

The publication of Einstein's Theory of Relativity in the early years of the twentieth century radically altered the way in which scientists regarded time. The experiments of Michelson (1852–1931) and Morley (1838–1923) had demonstrated that the speed of light remained constant, whether emitted by a body moving at speed (in which case, according to the mechanics of Isaac Newton (1642–1727), the speed of the body should be added to that of the light), or by a body at rest. Einstein's theory, which soon received practical proof,

postulated that the speed of light was always constant.

An unexpected consequence of this argument was that elapsed time can no longer be taken as an absolute measurement: each observer of a physical event will have his own measure of time, and even identical clocks used by different observers will not necessarily agree.

Perhaps the best known part of Einstein's theory is the concept of the 'space-time continuum:' a four-dimensional space made up of three linear dimensions and the 'fourth

> *Passage of time arises because we think of occupying different realities. In fact, we occupy only different givens. There is only one reality.*

dimension' of time. Within this continuum, any three dimensions can be used to define the spatial position of a point—and a concomitant of this is that the remaining dimension, whichever it may be, can define the temporal position. In other words, there is no way, in mathematical calculations, in which the time dimension can be distinguished from the spatial dimensions.

In everyday life, we are very conscious of three-dimensional space: when we take a step forward, we can subsequently take a step back; the same is true for sideways movement, and for movement up and down. However far we move from a point, we can always return to it, in a spatial sense. Why should the same not be true of time, which, in theory, is indistinguishable from the other linear dimensions?

It was the distinguished logician Kurt Gödel (1906–1978) who first showed, in 1949, that traveling backward in time was theoretically possible

according to Einstein's equations. This presented him with a logical absurdity. As he put it:

> '. . . it enables one, e.g., to travel back into the near past of those places where he himself has lived. There he would find a person who would be himself at some earlier period of his life. Now he could do something to this person which, by his memory, he knows has not happened to him.'

Modern physicists have seized on this absurdity as justification for their dismissal of time travel as impossible. They appeal to our common sense (not always a wise thing to do in the light of current developments in theoretical physics), and bolster their argument with recourse to the Second Law of Thermodynamics, which can be briefly summarized as 'disorder always increases.' We have all seen, they say, a cup fall from the table and break in pieces on the floor; we have never seen the pieces rise from the floor and reassemble themselves on the table. The breaking cup results in a dissipation of energy, the energy that held the cup together up on the table, and a resultant decrease in order, from the ordered shape of the cup to a pile of disordered pieces. It is inconceivable, physicists maintain, that energy from an outside source, from the cosmos, should somehow be concentrated on the fragments to reform the cup and lift it back to the table.

The Arrow of Time
From this argument has developed the concept of Time's Arrow, a concept that accords with our everyday experience that time appears to move inexorably in one direction, from the past to the future. Yet there are innumerable people who claim to be able to observe events in the past

A time machine, perhaps not dissimilar to those found in science fiction novels

and the future. Are they deluded, do they physically transport themselves through time, or is it that they have observed an event at another point in time in the same way that they can observe one at another point in three-dimensional space?

Gödel devoted much thought to the possibility that the human awareness of the passage of time is an illusion. In 'A remark on the relationship between relativity theory and idealistic philosophy,' (1959) he wrote:

'The existence of an objective lapse of time . . . means that reality consists of an infinity of layers of "now" which come into existence successively. But, if simultaneity is something relative . . . [it] cannot be split up into such layers in an objectively determined way. Each observer has his own set of "nows," and none of these various systems of layers can claim the prerogative of representing the objective lapse of time.'

In a later conversation with the mathematician (and science fiction writer) Rudy Rucker (b. 1946), Gödel put this argument another way. 'The illusion of the passage of time,' he said, 'arises from confusing the *given* with the *real*. Passage of time arises because we think of occupying different realities. In fact, we occupy only different givens. There is only one reality.'

From this it is possible to argue that the absurdity Gödel observed in 1949

Experiment with Time

The aeronautical engineer (designer of Britain's first military aircraft in 1906–7) and philosopher J. W. Dunne (1875–1949) devoted much of the latter part of his life to considering the problem of time. He began by examining the nature of prophetic dreams, and in his book *An Experiment with Time* (1927) he proposed an interesting theory.

Dunne suggested that each of us travels upon our own 'time-line' through the cosmos, rather like a passenger in a train running along a rail track. This explains our everyday awareness of the passage of time. At intervals these lines converge or intersect, when we experience an event simultaneously with another person. But, much as someone can put his head out of the train window and see something that has already passed, or something up the track ahead, we can (given the right conditions) experience not only an event that has already happened but also an event that is yet to come. Moreover, in the same way that a passenger in one train can observe events taking place in another train running close by on a parallel track, it may be possible to observe events in the life of another whose timeline runs close to ours, but which—because their time-line is separate from ours— are occurring at a different time.

In subsequent books, notably *The Serial universe* (1934), Dunne developed a theory that comes close to Gödel's concept of an infinity of layers of 'now.' Each layer of 'now' had to be observed by an observer, but this observer was himself part of another layer of 'now,' and so, apparently, *ad infinitum*. Dunne did not put it in so many words, but it seems to be implied that the ultimate observer of all these layers, of reality, could be nobody else but God.

Dunne's theories have been largely neglected by later philosophers, but an

can be resolved. The observer who travels back in time and sees himself at an earlier date is *only* an observer: his frame of reference in the space-time continuum is different from that of his earlier self, and the two cannot interact. He *cannot* 'do something to this person which, by his memory, he knows has not happened to him.'

Since the cosmos as we observe it contains all linear measurements as we know them, from the smallest to the largest—there is no measurement *outside* the infinite universe—it is arguable that all time is also contained within it. In other words, all time, past, present, and future, exists simultaneously, and our everyday illusion of the passage of time in one direction is perhaps due to our everyday inability to make observations in this fourth dimension. Physicists who insist upon the inexorability of Time's Arrow are happy to accept the theory that a subatomic particle can exist in two places at the same time—could it not be that the particle is in one place, but at two simultaneous points in time? Extensions of this argument could go some way to account for the phenomenon of pk.

interesting point remains. In experiments with Zener cards, the subject was required to forecast the order in which twenty-five cards were selected, but it was not customary, at the end of each experiment, to inform the subject what the actual order of cards was. At least one critic pointed out that this made it harder for the subject to forecast the correct order, since it did not constitute an event on his timeline but only on that of the experimenter.

Franklin St., looking South from Main St., Johnstown, Pa. Sci-Fi in the Valley Con

Doctor Who's Tardis is seen on Johnstown's Franklin Street. *Doctor Who* is a television program that depicts the adventures of the Doctor, a Time Lord. He explores the universe in his Tardis, the exterior of which appears as a blue British police box.

And, after all this, is physical time-travel a possibility or not? Can the time-traveler change trains? The US theoretical physicist John Wheeler (1911–2008) was the first to show that certain solutions of Einstein's equations allowed for the existence of 'wormholes' that could connect distant parts of a single universe, or even what would otherwise be separate universes. In a development of this theory, a traveler who passed through a suitable

wormhole could fetch up at the same place in his past or future.

The apparent drawback, if classical Newtonian, or even Einsteinian, mechanics apply, is that the wormhole (analogous to a 'black hole') would be pinched so tightly at its middle that the traveler would be crushed to death. However, three cosmologists—Michael Morris, Kip Thorne (b. 1940) and Ulvi Yurtsever—suggested in 1988 that, if allowance is made for

quantum theory, it is possible that this disaster could be averted. The possibility of such a worm-hole was exploited by Carl Sagan (1934–96) in his science-fiction novel *Contact* (1986).

Academics continue to speculate whether the concept of time travel is possible given the laws of physics. Current theories suggest that traveling forward through time, that is, relatively faster than Earth, is possible, yet traveling backward into the past still

Time appears to move in one direction, from the past, through the present, to the future

Martin Gardner. The Ambidextrous Universe. *(New York, NY: Basic Books, 1964); Stephen Hawking.* A Brief History of Time. *(London, UK: Bantam, 1988); C. H. Hinton.* Selected Writings. *(Mineola, NY: Dover, 1980).*

Transcendental Meditation

At the height of its popularity in the 1970s, Transcendental Meditation (TM) was practiced by millions of people worldwide. Developed by the Indian guru Maharishi Mahesh Yogi, it claimed to be a synthesis of ancient philosophy and meditation techniques and offered a drug-free state of self-realization and enlightenment.

Maharishi claimed to have learned everything he knew from Guru Dev, a reclusive holy man who lived in an isolated mountain cave deep in the Himalayas in the early 1950s. After two years of seclusion with him, Maharishi emerged into the world to teach TM in southern India, and published a book, *The Beacon Light of the Himalayas*, which laid great emphasis on the original teachings of the Indian scriptures. In 1958 he established the Spiritual Regeneration Movement in Madras, before setting off to spread his message around the world.

Maharishi set up an ashram in the foothills of the Himalayas, where he taught all who came to learn his techniques, including many Westerners. By 1970 he was teaching several hundred eager students, and by 1975 he had already trained nearly 10,000 seekers as teachers of TM. In other parts of the world—notably in California—TM became something of a craze, and by 1975 there were an estimated 550,000 people who had learned the technique in the US alone. The Maharishi International University (MIU) was set up in Swit-

A Formula for Travel

What form could this projected time travel take? Let us consider the mathematics of wave mechanics in the three spatial dimensions. Seen in the context of Cartesian coordinates, multiplying a linear dimension by -1 will reverse its direction; multiplying it by the square root of -1 (i) will rotate it through 90 degrees, thus converting it to another dimension. Within the four-dimensional continuum, therefore, theoretically it should be possible to apply the same mathematics to the linear dimension of time. From the Greek *tropos*, meaning turn or movement, and the scientific symbol for time, t, De Canular has dubbed this theoretical possibility of travel through time '*ti*-trope.'

Ninian Bres
O Tempora

appears improbable. The idea of time travel is a seductive one but perhaps one that will be realized only in the imagination of writers and filmmakers. One of the UK's most popular programmes ever remains *Doctor Who*, a BBC television series that has been screened for more than fifty years, featuring an alien Time Lord traveling the universe in a space ship, the exterior of which looks exactly like a police box.

FURTHER READING:
S. G. F. Brandon. History, Time and Deity. *(Manchester, UK: Manchester University Press, 1965); P. T. Landsberg ed.* The Enigma of Time. *(Bristol, UK: Adam Hilger, 1984); Peter Coveney and Roger Highfield.* The Arrow of Time. *(London, UK: W. H. Allen, 1990);*

zerland, a focus for thousands hoping to expand their spiritual horizons.

TM, its practitioners stressed, could not—and should not—be learned without the benefit of a trained teacher. Indeed, it is hard to find any details of the actual technique involved in any of the many writings on the subject.

Essentially, it is a method of stilling the conscious mind through a series of mental exercises and breathing techniques so that a stage of complete serenity and mystical awareness is reached by the practitioner.

Central to TM is the use of mantras, special sounds that are not chanted, but vibrated within the student as he meditates. As Peter Russell (b. 1946) says in *The TM Technique* (1976): 'In TM the mantra has no associations and, more importantly, is not chanted—either verbally or mentally. The mantra is not so much an object for the attention to be focused on as a vehicle on which the attention rests and which leads it down to the subtler levels of thinking.'

However, once again it is stressed that a mantra is a personal thing which is not transferable from student to student, and may even cause damage if it is so abused.

Paradoxical Philosophy

The philosophy behind TM is, like many other Eastern spiritual systems, paradoxically complex and simple at the same time. It is based on the idea that the technique can help elevate the student's awareness through at least five 'states of consciousness,' finally reaching 'cosmic consciousness.' As the student progresses through these stages, all stress and inner toxins— both physical and spiritual—will fall away. The Maharishi claimed that a state of stress was an abnormal state, and cosmic consciousness was normality. At the fifth state of consciousness the pure Self is seen as 'becoming a

permanent feature of awareness,' and is known as Self-realization. Maharishi said that the enlightened man gained 'freedom from bondage,' saying: 'It is not the action or its fruits which bind a man; rather it is the inability to maintain freedom which becomes a means of bondage.' He also stressed that one should not give up the material world to become a recluse, but use TM in order to function

more efficiently at all levels. He often quoted the greatest test of his system as being 'the ability to stand in the middle of Manhattan and still maintain the experience of the Self.'

Practitioners of TM have made some dramatic claims for the technique, and a number of scientific tests appear to have backed up at least some of them. In the 1970s it was claimed that TM enabled people to access the

Maharishi Mahesh Yogi during a 1979 visit to the Maharishi University of Management campus in Fairfield Iowa

right hemisphere of the brain, the part that deals in intuition and creativity, as easily as they have access to the logical left brain. Yet, as Peter Russell points out: 'TM is more than just a turn to right hemisphere activity—if it were only that it would be little different from sitting down and listening to good music. TM is a transcending of both types of mental activity.'

Dr. Jean-Paul Banquet, working at Harvard, showed that when the practitioner reached a particularly deep state of meditation, a corresponding burst of faster brain activity and a marked increase in synchronization between the front and rear of the brain centres was recorded. Control groups who merely relaxed quickly showed an increase in left-brain activity, which suggested that they were consciously trying to relax.

Other, more spectacular, side effects of TM have been reported, including a kind of 'remote viewing,' and even physical levitation has been demonstrated. The claims for this latter talent have provoked sceptical comment, for it resembles more a sort of energetic hopping about in the lotus position—even such physical activity, however, appears to be beyond the abilities of critics.

In the 1970s, when many famous people flocked to the Maharishi to learn TM, it achieved something of a cult status, and (as is often the way with such 'high profile' movements) dissension and accusations of commercial impropriety soon spoiled its image. Today TM is practiced by relatively few, having been superseded by the many self-development 'workshops' of the New Age. Yet the Maharishi's teachings are not without relevance, and have helped a great many people to a wider understanding of themselves and their part in the world. One of his strongest points,

perhaps, was his insistence on looking for the positive in every individual and situation. He never spoke of evil, only of good, stressing that Man's true condition is happiness. He said:

'A happy man would be able to see the unhappiness of others much more than an unhappy man. An unhappy man is busy suffering himself, he has no time to see the suffering of others.

Observations of UFOs tend to come in waves, as the news of a sighting spreads, and enthusiasts gather in the hope of sharing the experience.

Compassion is not awake in an unhappy, miserable mind. But compassion and kindness are awake in a man who is happy, who is peaceful.'

LYNN PICKNETT

FURTHER READING: Maharishi Mahesh Yogi. Meditations. *(London, UK: Bantam Books, 1968); Peter Russell.* The TM Technique. *(London, UK: Routledge & Kegan Paul, 1976).*

UFOs

Documentary reports of strange lights and vessels in the sky date back at least to Pliny's *De Natura Rerum* (c. AD 70), in which there are references to heavenly 'burning shields' and 'flying torches.' From medieval times, the account written by Jacques Duclerc of Arras is typical:

'On All Saints' Day, 1 November 1461, appeared in the sky an object as bright as a bar of iron, as long and wide as a half-moon; it hung stationary for about a quarter-hour, clearly visible, then suddenly spiralled, twisted and turned, and rose into the heavens . . .'

A more widespread and dedicated interest in the phenomena arose in the years following World War II. At first dubbed 'flying saucers,' they were later dignified with the title of UFO—unidentified flying object. It had long been believed that they were due to heavenly or Satanic powers, but with the decline in conventional religious credulity in the twentieth century, and a belief in the real possibility of space travel, a more modern form of extra-terrestrial influence was postulated: UFOs, it was said, were spaceships from another world. Observers attribute a range of physical effects to the objects, some even claim to have been abducted.

Observations of UFOs tend to come in waves, as the news of a sighting spreads, and enthusiasts gather in the hope of sharing the experience. Mundane explanations for the sightings include reflection of spots of light between the component lenses of cameras and binoculars, or through the curved windows of aircraft; an unusual type of lenticular cloud, which forms over mountain ranges; and secret tests of experimental military aircraft.

This last would explain the reluctance of air forces around the world to take part in serious discussion of UFOs, but as a result enthusiasts have suspected a 'cover-up,' and even a conspiracy to suppress information.

Opposite page:
UFOs in New York on the cover of *Science Fiction: Fantastic Universe* (c. 1955)

FANTASTIC
UNIVERSE
SCIENCE FICTION
NOW
35c
JULY
A KING-SIZE PUBLICATION
MARGARET ST. CLAIR • LESTER DEL REY • F. L. WALLACE
PHILIP JOSE FARMER • FRANK BELKNAP LONG • ALGIS BUDRYS
SAM CARSON • IDRIS SEABRIGHT • JOHN VICTOR PETERSON
ALL STORIES IN THIS ISSUE BRAND NEW

Glossary

Clairvoyance Ability to perceive beyond the ordinary, associated with ESP.

Crass Lack of sensitivity, often showing stupidity.

Dowsing Technique used to find things underground with a rod.

Dynasty Hereditary passage of power.

Dystopia World considered bad, typically in the future, the opposite of Utopia.

Ebb Moving away slowing but continually, as a tide out to sea.

Egress Leaving, the action of going away.

Envisage Think about or consider the possibility of a desired event.

Eyrie Large nest of a bird of prey, usually an eagle.

Focal point The centre of interest, the point at which all things come into focus.

Germ plasm Germ cells as a collective.

Ionise To covert into an ion by adding or removing electrons.

Latent Dormant or hidden, to appear later.

Manifestation Something that embodies a concept or abstraction.

Mesmeric Causing one to become unaware of their surroundings.

Occult Mystical or supernatural.

Ostensible Appearing to be true.

Percipient To be perceptive or aware.

Phantasmagoria Dreamlike, surreal or imaginary.

Prognosticate To predict or foretell.

Psychotherapy The treatment of a mental disorder through psychological mean.

Puritanical Strict, to be against self-indulgence, usually for religious reasons.

Purulent Dealing with the discharge or consisting of pus.

Radiesthesia Connecting to water dowsing.

Stigmata Body marks, cuts, or bleeding associated with wounds of Jesus.

Stringent Exacting or very precise.

Tenet One of the main principles of a given religion.

Theocracy System of government based on a particular religion.

Totalitarian A Centralized, dictatorial government which restricts personal freedom.

Index

dreams 97, 124
    day-dreams 132
    ESP dreams 21–22, 25, 26, 28, 29,
        47, 127, 129–130, 132
    Freudian analysis 45–46
    of the deceased 136
    unrealistic 129–130
Dreamtime 90
Drummer of Tedworth 49, 50
Dunne, J. W. 148
dystopian fiction 116

E
Eckankar 20
Eckart, Dietrich 81
ectoplasm 31
Edda sagas 81, 86, 87
Eden 112, 113, 115, 116, 117
Eglinton, William 95
ego 46
Egypt 9, 59
Einstein, Albert 44, 146, 149
ekenergetic phenomena 120–121
Ellis, Havelock 44
encounter groups 21
entropy 115
Esalen Institute 21
escapology 56
eugenics 90, 91
evolutionary theory 79–80, 108, 115
The Exorcist (movie) 39
extra-sensory perception (ESP) 21–32,
        47, 98, 100, 101, 102, 108, 121,
        123, 124, 125, 127, 130, 135,
        136
    ESP dreams 21–22, 25, 26, 28, 29,
        47, 127, 129–130, 132
    experimental work 23–32, 99, 103,
        104, 106, 107
    general ESP (GESP) 124
    see also clairvoyance; hallucination;
        intuition; precognition; telepathy
extroverts and introverts 31, 57

F
Fahrenkrog, Ludwig 87, 88
fairy paths 66
Father Divine (George Baker) 76, 77
Fichte, Johann 87
film 32–42, 49, 56, 114, 116, 117
Fischer, Doris 97
flying saucers see UFOs
Fort, Charles 42–44, 119
Fortean Society 44
Fortune, Dion 66
fourth dimension 146
    see also time
France 20, 51, 52, 53, 74, 97
Frankenstein 34, 112
free association 45, 46
Freemasonry 48, 80, 81
Freud, Sigmund 44–47, 57, 58, 97, 98
Fritsch, Theodor 48

G
Gaddis, Vincent 44
Galgani, Gemma 89
games of chance 22–23, 101–102, 108
ganzfeld technique 29–30, 31, 99–100
Gardner, Martin 43
Garvey, Marcus 77
Geller, Uri 48, 71, 108
geomagnetic flux 120
geomancy 66
German Order Walvater of the Holy
    Graal 80
Germanen Order 48–49, 80, 81
Germany 18, 36, 48–49, 53, 65,
    80–89
Gestalt therapy 21
Ghostbusters (movie) 34, 36, 49
ghosts 35, 36, 64, 95
    ghost hunting 49–50, 98
Gilgamesh 51
Glanvill, Joseph 50
Gnosticism 58, 59
God 12, 20, 73, 144, 145

Gödel, Kurt 146, 147
Goebbels, Joseph 83
Gog and Magog 63, 64
Golden Flower meditation 58
Golem 34
Gordon, General George 74
Gothic horror 35, 68, 110
Great Depression 69
Great Isosceles Triangle of England 66
Great Mother 18, 57, 64
Gurdjieff, George Ivanovich 50–53,
    137, 138
Gurney, Edmund 94, 95

H
Haile Selassie, Emperor 76, 77
hallucination 22, 26, 95, 124, 125–
    127, 134, 135, 136, 137
    auditory 22, 125, 127, 136
    crisis apparitions 95, 97
    visual 22, 125, 127, 136
Hare Krishna 54
healing 71, 74, 93, 101, 106, 107,
    138–139
Heaven's Gate 78–79
Heinrich the Fowler 85
Hero 18, 112, 113, 116
Hess, Rudolf 81, 83–84
Higher Self 90, 138
hill-figures 63–64, 65, 66
Himmler, Heinrich 48, 65, 80, 81, 83,
    84, 85, 88, 90, 91
Hinduism 90, 145
Hitler, Adolf 49, 81, 82, 83, 84, 88,
    90, 91
Holland 23, 53, 74
Honorton, Charles 29, 30, 100
Houdini, Harry 54–56
human aura 61, 62
humanistic psychology 21
Hung Hsui-chuan 73–74
hypnosis 29, 45, 51, 54, 93, 97
hysteria 45, 97

18, 45, 48, 49, 80–85, 91, 143
near-death experience 58
neo-pagan German cults 85–88
Neo-Platonism 59
Neumann, Teresa 88–89
New Age 79, 89–90, 152
New Templars 80, 82, 90–92
Newton, Sir Isaac 59, 60, 146
Nietzsche, Friedrich 63, 85
Nosferatu 33, 35, 37
Nostradamus 83
nuclear weapons 35, 116
numerology 47

O
occultism 39, 49, 66, 80, 81, 82–83,
    83, 84, 85, 91
Oedipus complex 46
The Omen (movie) 39
oracles 22
Organization Consul 49

P
Padre Pio 89, 92
Palladino, Eusapia 95
pantheism 145
Paracelsus 58, 59, 87
paranormal phenomena 43, 49, 60
    see also clairvoyance; ghosts; pre-
        cognition; psychical research;
        psychokinesis; telepathy
parapsychical (psi) behaviour 100
psi energy 106
see also extra-sensory perception
    (ESP); parapsychology (psi);
    psychokinesis (PK)
parapsychology (psi) 21, 24–32, 58,
    98–99, 100, 103, 108
spontaneous psi experiences 25, 26,
    28–29, 32, 100, 102, 121–137
    see also extra-sensory perception
        (ESP); psychokinesis (PK)
Pauwels, Louis 79

Peace Missions 76
pendulum dowsing 48, 64, 66, 84
Pendulum Institute 84
People's Temple 77–78
Perls, Fritz 21
Persia (Iran) 9, 11, 12, 14
Persona 18
Peru 9, 20
The Phenomenon of Man (Teilhard de
    Chardin) 143
Philosopher's Stone 59
phrenology 91
pictograms 20
Piper, Leonora 95
plasma-vortex theory 19, 20
Pliny 152
Pohl, Hermann 48, 80
poltergeist activity 43, 44, 58, 71, 95,
    100, 107, 120, 146
Popper, Karl 43
Powys, John Cowper 44
precognition 21, 23, 25, 26, 31, 58,
    80, 88, 103, 108, 123, 135
Price, Harry 98
Prince, Henry James 75
Prince, Walter Franklin 97
Prometheus 112
prophecy 22, 23, 47, 64
    see also precognition
psionic generator 109
psychedelic drugs 29
psychic energy 66
psychical research 92–100
    Society for Psychical Research 23,
        25, 50, 92, 94–95, 97–98
    see also parapsychology
psychoanalysis 44–47, 57
psychokinesis (PK) 21, 22, 23, 44, 58,
    71, 80, 99, 100–109, 121, 123,
    124, 132–135, 136, 148
psychotherapy 58
psychotronic generators 109
psychotronics 109

Puharich, Andrija 48
pyramids of Egypt 9

R
Randi, James 48
random event generators (REGs) 99
Rasputin, Grigori 63
Rastafarian movement 76–77
reincarnation 100
relaxation techniques 29, 31
remote viewing 99, 109, 152
revelation 23
Rhine, J. B. 24, 26, 27, 98, 99, 108,
    137, 142
    see also parapsychology
Rhine, L. E. 24, 25, 26, 28–29, 98
    see also parapsychology
Ridvan Festival 12
Robert-Houdin, Jean Eugène 54
Roman Catholic Church 89, 92,
    143–145
Rosemary's Baby (movie) 39
Rosicrucian Order 56
Roux, Georges 74
rune symbolism 81
Russell, Eric Frank 44
Russia 50–51, 99
Ryan, Leo 78

S
St. Francis of Assisi 89
St. Thomas Aquinas 59
Salvationist schemes 69
Satanism 63
Schneider, Rudi 98
Schopenhauer, Arthur 85
science and religion, reconciliation
    between 143
science fiction and fantasy 32, 36, 44,
    68, 79, 109–118, 149
seances 44, 107
    see also mediumship
Sebotendorff, Rudolf Freiherr von 80

Author List

Contributors to *Man, Myth, and Magic: Beliefs, Rituals, and Symbols of the Modern World*

Sir Cyril Burt is an educationist and psychologist; formerly Professor of Psychology, London; author of *The Young Delinquent; The Subnormal Mind; The Backward Child; The Factors of the Mind* and many other titles.

John Clute is an author and co-editor of *The Encyclopedia of Science Fiction* and *The Encyclopedia of Fantasy,* and editor of *A Visual Companion to Science Fiction.*

Alan Gauld is Lecturer in Psychology, Nottingham; member of the Council of the Society for Psychical Research; author of *The Founders of Psychical Research.*

Ellic Howe is a specialist in the prehistory of German National Socialism; author of *Urania's Children; the Strange World of the Astrologers* and many other titles.

Ann Lloyd was editor of *The Movie* and is a freelance writer on the cinema. Her books include *The Films of Stephen King.* She also teaches colour therapy and the healing art of *tao-yin-fa.*

Lynn Picknett is a consultant to London Capital Radio on occult matters and editor of *The Encyclopedia of the Paranormal.*

John Lofland is Assistant Professor of Sociology, Michigan; author of *Doomsday Cult* and *Deviance and Identity.*

Elizabeth Loving has worked in publishing for many years and is a historian with a special interest in landscape change and development, and environmental psychology.

J. B. Rhine is Executive Director, Foundation for Research on the Nature of Man; previously Director of the Parapsychology Laboratory, Duke University. His numerous books include *Extrasensory Perception; The Reach of the Mind; Parapsychology; Frontier Science of the Mind* (with J. G. Pratt).

Louisa E. Rhine is author of *Hidden Channels of the Mind; ESP in Life and Lab; Mind over Matter.* She is an editor of the *Journal of Parapsychology.*

Robert Rickard is founder and co-editor of *Fortean Times.* His books include *Phenomena* and *Living Wonders* (both with John Michell).

Malcolm Saunders is assistant editor on *Man, Myth, and Magic.*

Lancelot Sheppard is the former general editor of the 'Faith and Fact' series; author of *The Mass in the West; Blue-print for Worship.*

P. Travers is author of *Mary Poppins.*

Dr Caroline Watt is postdoctoral Research Fellow with the Koestler Chair of Parapsychology at Edinburgh University.

Pat Williams is a journalist and co-author of *The Supernatural* (with Douglas Hill).

Bryan Wilson is a Fellow of All Souls and Reader in Sociology, Oxford; author of *Sects and Society; Religion in Secular Society.*

R. C. Zaehner (the late): is a Fellow of All Souls and Spalding Professor of Eastern Religions and Ethics, Oxford; edited *Hindu Scriptures; Concise Encyclopedia of Living Faiths;* books include *The Dawn and Twilight of Zoroastrianism; Mysticism Sacred and Profane.* He is a member of the Editorial Board of *Man, Myth, and Magic.*